OUR FATHERS

OUR FATHERS
Reflections by Sons

Edited by
Steven L. Shepherd

Beacon Press
Boston

Beacon Press
25 Beacon Street
Boston, Massachusetts 02108-2892
www.beacon.org

Beacon Press books
are published under the auspices of
the Unitarian Universalist Association of Congregations.

© 2001 by Steven L. Shepherd
All rights reserved
Printed in the United States of America

05 04 03 02 01   8 7 6 5 4 3 2 1

This book is printed on acid-free paper that meets the uncoated paper ANSI/NISO
specifications for permanence as revised in 1992.

Text design by Preston Thomas
Composition by Wilsted & Taylor Publishing Services

Library of Congress Cataloging-in-Publication Data

Our fathers : reflections by sons / edited by Steven L. Shepherd.
      p. cm.
   ISBN 0-8070-6246-4 (cloth : acid-free paper)
   1. Fathers and sons—United States.   2. Biography—20th century.   3. Authors,
American—Biography.   4. United States—Biography.   I. Shepherd, Steven L.
   CT220 .O97 2001
   920'.009'04—dc21

                                                        00-012324

TO THE SHEPHERD FATHERS—PAST, PRESENT, AND FUTURE

I never knew anyone quite like my father, but then I never really knew my father either. —Daniel J. Boorstin

Contents

INTRODUCTION xi

JAMES BALDWIN **Notes of a Native Son** 1

GEOFFREY WOLFF **Heavy Lifting** 28

TOBIAS WOLFF **Civilian** 51

ROBERT BENSON **Rising to the Light** 73

SAM PICKERING **Son and Father** 92

SCOTT RUSSELL SANDERS **Under the Influence** 115

ROBERT B. STEPTO **Hyde Park** 134

THOMAS LYNCH **Embalming Father** 154

HENRY LOUIS GATES, JR. **Playing Hardball** 167

BERNARD COOPER **Picking Plums** 179

ROLAND MERULLO **What a Father Leaves** 196

GREG JALBERT **In the Kingdom of the Jalberts** 219

DAVID BEERS **Blue Sky, California** 232

TOM JUNOD **My Father's Fashion Tips** 248

ACKNOWLEDGMENTS 272

My wife and I went to see *Field of Dreams* shortly after it came out. Not long before that we had been to visit my father and his wife in Lexington, Kentucky, where they then lived. It was the first time I had visited my father since he had last visited *his* father a year earlier. My grandfather, who lived his whole life in Oklahoma and who supported himself and his family through a series of such varied occupations as teacher, car dealer, truck driver, and dairyman, was then in the latter stages of congestive heart failure. My father had known his father was sick, but still it was a surprise when days after his arrival his father's condition dramatically worsened and he was hospitalized. He remained lucid, however, and in his final days each of his six children and a great many of his twenty-three grandchildren, thirty-plus great-grandchildren, and myriad other relatives came to say good-bye. He was eighty-five when he died.

When my father returned home he brought with him some photographs he had retrieved from his father's house. He placed these on a wall and there they hung when I visited. I couldn't recall having seen them before and I was riveted by what I saw. The pictures were of my father when he was young, before he had met my mother, before he became a scientist, before he was my father.

In the earliest of the pictures, my father is perhaps eight to ten years old. In one there is snow on the ground covering what would have been red dirt and he is standing in a field holding a .22 rifle; he wears high laced boots with the pants tucked inside, gloves, and a strange fur hat. The negative of the picture must have been reversed in the printing, because he is holding the gun as if he were left-handed, which he is not. In another photograph from about the same age it is spring or summer: his shirt sleeves are rolled high and he sits at the wheel of an ancient farm tractor against a background of orchard trees; he is driving, or sitting, either one, intently.

Four pictures show my dad in uniform. He joined the National Guard at the age of eighteen so he could earn a bit of spending money while he went to college, and was no doubt surprised when, two years into the bargain, President Truman federalized the Oklahoma division and sent it to Korea, where my father landed at Inchon and spent the winter of 1951–1952 in subzero weather and mountainous terrain with an ambulance company that "collected" the wounded from the front and transported them to the field hospitals of M.A.S.H. fame. He does not talk about this much.

Another four pictures seem to bracket or are interspersed with the years of the war photos. His age appears roughly the same, but he's in civilian clothes and on his parents' farm. In one there are bare trees—winter again—and in the background a dilapidated chicken coop with a nearby hen pecking at the ground. Another is dated—August 25, 1954—which means that not only is the National Guard behind him, but so are his undergraduate years; he's twenty-four and just about to begin his master's program at Oklahoma State University; this may even be his "going away" picture.

Most interesting is a picture of my father as a teenager. He is sitting at one end of a sofa and wearing a T-shirt, work boots, and rolled-up dungarees. He looks to be about seventeen. Opposite him on the sofa is my grandfather, dressed in khakis and looking unperturbed and relaxed—stogie in his mouth, arm draped casually over the arm of the sofa. My grandfather appears not to be looking at anything in particular, but my father's eyes are locked on his father, and the look he looks is one only a teenager can give—that look of hot, scornful defiance that indicates without mistake that this boy's father must be the world's biggest horse's ass. I know that look, for I have looked it and been looked at by it—for now I am the father of a teenage son. It is a look, I am sure, that came out of the Olduvai Gorge along with the first teenager to follow his father from the depths.

All these photos are black and white. But their greater constant is my father. No matter his age, he appears trim. And in all the pictures he bears an expression of competence and utter seriousness. A stranger seeing my father for the first time in these pictures would know without even thinking to ask that here was a man who meant to get where he was going and to do so by the most direct route possible.

I suppose these pictures were still on my mind when we saw *Field of Dreams.* I'd read the novel—*Shoeless Joe,* by W. P. Kinsella—and found it wonderfully imagined: man hears a voice in a cornfield, builds a baseball field, long-dead ghost players arrive, the author is a fictional character in his own book, the past mingles with the present, and so on. It is a fine book, and when my wife asked what it was about, I told her, "It's about love, and magic, and baseball." To a lesser extent, it is also about a man and his father.

Rarely does a movie add anything worthwhile to a good book. But my wife likes Kevin Costner, who plays Kinsella, and I was curious, so we went. I thought I had a pretty good idea of what to expect, and I was pleased to find the script hewing true to its source. But the movie adds emphasis and a few twists to the father-son part of the story: the father had been a minor league catcher as a young man, but the son had only known his father when he was tired and broken, beaten by life; once close, the two had quarreled, the son left home as a teenager, the father died, the two had never reconciled. This background is doled out in bits, but then, in the last scene, after Shoeless Joe and the other apparitions have finished a game and walked off the field, the son's father appears. He is dressed in an old-time uniform and wears an old-time glove, but he is young—"His whole life before him"—innocent, and remarkably handsome: dark-haired, poised, and graceful, a man at the peak of his potential. The son, concealing his own identity, greets his father, introduces him to his family, and the movie ends as the two begin to play catch.

Occasionally I will grow moist-eyed at a movie, usually at some predictably sappy moment. And so it was that I teared up as the father-to-be first appeared to his future son. But as the scene progressed, I found myself crying in earnest—and then crying harder still, until soon I was sobbing, my body shaking and the tears coursing in rivers. Not since I was a child have I cried like that.

The unexpected intensity of my emotion, I think, had to do with the power of the father's appearance as a contemporary of his son—with the father shorn of his usual advantages of experience, power, and authority, but having gained in return the optimism and assuredness of youth. The father and son on an otherwise impossible equal footing.

As I grow older and move through my own years of fatherhood, I spend an increasing amount of time thinking of what my father was doing in his life when he was my age or ages I have been. It is, I suppose, a way of measuring my progress through life. At forty-five my father was a full professor at the University of California, and had been for three years; he was among the most prominent men in his field, having made possible some of the early critical work in genetic engineering, and he was well on his way to eventual election into the National Academy of Sciences. I, at forty-five, can fancy-up a résumé, but the truth unadorned is that, as a writer, I've spent a fair amount of time without formal employment, and what I'm "on my way to" is hard to say; I've got a tiny little master's degree, earned at the age of thirty-two (he had his Ph.D. by the time he was twenty-nine—with time out for war), and I've thrice abandoned paths that would have led to doctorates or a medical degree. My father is twenty-four years older than me, his oldest of three children, and I am twenty-nine years older than my son and only child, meaning not only that he embarked on the journey of father-hood sooner than me, but that he also shouldered a greater weight while doing so. Viewed in this manner, I have fallen short. I do not intend to suggest that I think myself a failure—I've done things my father hasn't, and there are countless other yardsticks against which I could measure myself—but still it is useful to know that in the main I have borne out the principle of regression to the mean, which simply states that after an unusual or remarkable event the next event is likely to be less unusual or remarkable.

Often while performing these gymnastics I will try also to remember who I was or what I was doing at my son's age or some age he has been, and then to try and recall the impressions I had at that age of my father, of the role he was playing in my life and of his place and actions in the outside world. I do this with a view towards trying better to understand my son and how he must see *his* father. Yet I fail in these efforts, because though it seems to me that I must be as transparent to my son as I am to myself, that he must know as well as I of my dreams, failings, and inadequacies, when I was sixteen I don't recall having ever thought of my father as a man with self-doubts, unvoiced desires, regrets, or knowledge of error. That is, as a man apart from his role as my father. I was at that age just too preoccupied with myself.

But surely my father harbored such inner turmoils. Today I am certain of it, simply because I know now that such are part of the human condition. But this is knowing something at a rational level only, in the abstract, and try as I might I still can't get more than a layer deep in discerning the inner workings of the man in those pictures and in my memories. And my son, I must also conclude, will find it equally difficult to unravel what he will perceive as the mystery of me.

And yet he will try. For sons are compelled to puzzle over the enigma of their fathers. Fathers form an essential piece of the picture sons build of themselves, and as a son struggles throughout life to make that picture ever more accurate—as he tries, that is, to better understand himself (which is the thing growing and maturing is about)—it becomes correspondingly more important for a son to better understand his father. Events from long ago are revisited time after time in memory in the hopes of teasing out that last drop of insight. "I am like this," says the son, "Because he was like that." And this is true whether that father was present or absent, honest or dishonest, cowardly or courageous, a model to emulate or a model to avoid. All those men you see every day in crowds on the street, scrimmaging on the soccer fields, in cars on the freeway, all of them are sons and all have spent a good deal of time trying to figure out one man—their father. All these men have reached conclusions about their fathers ("My father was . . .") and their fathers' effects on their lives, but what is fascinating is how different those conclusions are apt to be from those reached by another observer.

I have a friend whose father's formative experiences (many of them, at least) occurred during World War II. He was in the navy in the South Pacific and his ship was torpedoed; he and some fellow crewmen survived the sinking in a raft and managed to land on a nearby island, where they spent two weeks evading (and sometimes killing) Japanese soldiers until they were rescued by a U.S. submarine. This is dramatic stuff, and understandably did it leave a strong imprint on the young sailor; after the war he remained in the navy until he retired, but he was plagued ever after by an incendiary temper and problems with alcohol, and these in turn badly damaged his relations with his wife and children. These problems have led my friend to all but renounce his father. "I have lived my whole life," he once told me, "trying not to be what he was."

My friend was of military age when the United States began ratcheting up its involvement in the Vietnam War. Trying to be what his father was not, he took what he perceived as the most contrary action possible to that his father had taken a generation earlier—he joined the marines. He served in a combat unit, was in constant battle, and five months into his tour was seriously wounded; since then his life has never been the same.

Perhaps there are significant differences between joining the marines and joining the navy. My friend insists this is so. To me the acts and their outcomes appear uncannily similar. But whether these two paths are seen as parallel or divergent, what is certain is that the son made his choice in response to the father.

I began to think more of my friend and his father, and of other friends and their fathers, as I began also to encounter similar stories in my incidental reading. Without design, and in no particular order, I read over a period of years several books and essays that on reflection seemed to have certain similarities, or else I found myself underlining passages in works on other subjects in which the writer had slipped in a bit of rumination about himself and his father. During this time (in which also came *Field of Dreams*) I read the poet Donald Hall's *Fathers*

Playing Catch with Sons, and his later exquisite memoir, *Life Work,* in which he says of his father, who was trapped by the Depression into working in the family's dairy business, "He hated what he did and I love what I do. Opposites are never accidental. He shook his fist over my cradle, I was always told, saying, 'He'll do what he wants to do'—and he stuck to it years later even when it turned out to be poetry that I wanted to do." I read David Mas Masumoto's *Epitaph for a Peach.* Masumoto, a third-generation Japanese-American, grows peaches in California's central valley. Masumoto grows peaches because his father before him grew peaches—and because Masumoto loves his peaches, his land, and working side by side with his father. Richard Manning, who invokes his father's wisdom often in *Grassland,* his fine ecological musings on the Great Plains, recounted that when he was a teenager, "My father told me several truths that I, like most adolescents, disregarded. . . . Only half flippantly, he said this: 'Remember, I have taught you everything you know, but I haven't taught you everything I know.' Only later I learned that all fathers have been saying this for all of time, but it's true." And, far too late in my life for a person with an interest in words, I read James Baldwin's *Notes of a Native Son,* wherein he chronicles his titanic struggles with his father and their lasting effects: "I had inclined," wrote Baldwin, "to be contemptuous of my father for the conditions of his life, for the conditions of our lives. When his life had ended I began to wonder about that life and also, in a new way, to be apprehensive about my own." Fathers, it seemed, were everywhere. And everywhere they were under scrutiny by their sons.

I began to collect these works in a haphazard way and without larger plan—placing a sticky note in a book or tearing out and saving some magazine pages. But as the wealth of the material began to dawn on me, it began also to seem that a more comprehensive effort was warranted and that the works individually would benefit from a collective presentation—that reading how one son thought of his father would help in better understanding how another thought of *his* father, and ultimately maybe even your own.

There is an excellent and voluminous literature of introspections by daughters about their mothers and themselves, and much of this work is represented in anthologies. Collections of corresponding works by men, however, are far fewer in number; moreover, those that do exist tend primarily to consist of fiction or poetry or uncritical homage, or else their portraits of fathers are rich but reveal little about the sons who wrote them. It is also often the case that genres are mixed and no indications given as to which is which—a particular problem when fiction and nonfiction are presented together. As a reader, I believe it imperative to know whether the work before me is an invention or a presentation of events as experienced and remembered by the writer; both types of works may (and should) contain truths that teach, but the truths of fiction are different from the truths of nonfiction and to give each their due requires that one be recognized and distinguished from the other.

To supplement my original folder of notes and essays I conducted several computerized literature searches. I also added works mentioned by other writers, by friends, and from my own now more focused reading; in all, I reviewed over two hundred candidate pieces. From these I made selections based on several criteria, the most fundamental being that the work was by a son about his father and that the portrayal yielded in its course some insight into the son. Almost as important, I have chosen only works of high literary quality—meaty, well-written prose with a strong narrative and a distinctive voice; in all cases that voice is first-person singular—these are stories rich in "I" and "me" and the first-person possessive pronoun: "*my* father." To avoid injustice to a writer's original work—cutting and pasting together my own string of excerpts—I have included only works that were self-contained to begin with; largely this turned out to mean pieces that were conceived and came to print as personal essays, though many were later incorporated by their writers into books. One selection, however, "Blue Sky, California," by David Beers, was first published as an adaptation prepared by the author from his own book. To keep the anthology focused, I imposed another criterion that is otherwise completely arbitrary: all the works are by American writers, though we can well presume that the dilemmas posed by American dads to their American sons differ little from those posed by fathers to sons elsewhere.

Finally, as suggested by the term "personal essay," all the works presented here are nonfiction. They are stories not just of truth but also of fact. To put it another way, when I told a friend that I was making selections for an anthology—a friend who had spent years suppressing difficulties he had had with his father, until one day they could no longer be suppressed—he said, "Just be sure they are honest."

That they are.

OUR FATHERS

JAMES BALDWIN

One of the most respected American writers of the latter half of the twentieth century, James Baldwin (1924–1987) mastered an astounding range of literary forms. He published three best-selling volumes of essays; his first novel, Go Tell It on the Mountain, *was published in 1953 and has never gone out of print; he wrote two stage plays that were performed on Broadway and have seen frequent revivals, a screenplay that became the basis for Spike Lee's movie* Malcolm X, *short stories, poetry, and a children's book. Recipient of an impressive list of awards and prizes, a 1948 fellowship enabled Baldwin to leave New York and move to France, where he lived for most of the rest of his life.*

The predominant theme in Baldwin's work was racism and the decisions we each must make in its presence. As a child growing up in Harlem in the 1930s, Baldwin was surrounded by the physical manifestations of racism. But it was his father who provided him his most profound example of racism's inner, psychic costs.

Born in Louisiana in the mid-1860s, David Baldwin was the son of slaves. In part, said James, because "lynching had become the national sport," David left New Orleans in 1919 for Harlem, where he eventually found work in a bottling plant. But his true vocation was the ministry, where he preached a searing gospel of retribution in which it was understood that the damned were white and the saved black.

David Baldwin brought his "unrelenting hatred" home with him and he ran a harsh and repressive household. Forty years his junior, his wife called him "Mr. Baldwin," and both she and her nine children were the subject of frequent beatings. Although James eventually learned that his mother had borne him out of wedlock by another man, he noted that David "did not beat me worse than the others because I was not his son." He did, however, tell James he was "the ugliest boy he had ever seen," and in this James felt his attacks were meant to include his "real, and unknown, father."

The young Baldwin feared and despised his father, David, but as he grew older he began to recognize the pressures of his life and "the pride and sorrow and beauty" in his face. "For that man I called my father really was my father in every sense except the biological, or literal one. He formed me, and he raised me, and he did not let me starve: and he gave me something, however harshly, and however little I wanted it, which prepared me for an impending horror which he could not prevent."

David Baldwin also provided his son with his most important early material. Go Tell It on the Mountain tells the story of a black youth and his struggles with a dictatorial stepfather. It was, said Baldwin, "the book I had to write if I was ever going to write anything else." In 1955 he wrote about his father again in the selection presented here, which first appeared in Harper's Magazine and then became the title piece for Baldwin's first collection of essays. It has since become a classic.

Notes of a Native Son

ONE

On the twenty-ninth of July, in 1943, my father died. On the same day, a few hours later, his last child was born. Over a month before this, while all our energies were concentrated in waiting for these events, there had been, in Detroit, one of the bloodiest race riots of the century. A few hours after my father's funeral, while he lay in state in the undertaker's chapel, a race riot broke out in Harlem. On the morning of the third of August, we drove my father to the graveyard through a wilderness of smashed plate glass.

The day of my father's funeral had also been my nineteenth birthday. As we drove him to the graveyard, the spoils of injustice, anarchy, discontent, and hatred were all around us. It seemed to me that God himself had devised, to mark my father's end, the most sustained and brutally dissonant of codas. And it seemed to me, too, that the violence which rose all about us as my father left the world had been devised as a corrective for the pride of his eldest son. I had declined to believe in that apocalypse which had been central to my father's vision; very well, life seemed to be saying, here is something that will certainly pass for an apocalypse until the real thing comes along. I had inclined to be contemptuous of my father for the conditions of his life, for the conditions of our lives. When his life had ended I began to wonder about that life and also, in a new way, to be apprehensive about my own.

I had not known my father very well. We had got on badly, partly because we shared, in our different fashions, the vice of stubborn pride. When he was dead I realized that I had hardly ever spoken to him. When he had been dead a long time I began to wish I had. It seems to be typical of life in America, where opportunities, real and fancied, are thicker than anywhere else on the globe, that the second generation has no time to talk to the first. No one, including my father, seems to have known exactly how old he was, but his mother had been born during slavery. He was of the first generation of free men. He, along with thousands of other Negroes, came North after 1919 and I was part of that generation which had never seen the landscape of what Negroes sometimes call the Old Country.

He had been born in New Orleans and had been a quite young man there during the time that Louis Armstrong, a boy, was running errands for the dives and honky-tonks of what was always presented to me as one of the most wicked of cities—to this day, whenever I think of New Orleans, I also helplessly think of Sodom and Gomorrah. My father never mentioned Louis Armstrong, except to forbid us to play his records; but there was a picture of him on our wall for a long time. One of my father's strong-willed female relatives had placed it there and forbade my father to take it down. He never did, but he eventually maneuvered her out of the house and when, some years later, she was in trouble and near death, he refused to do anything to help her.

He was, I think, very handsome. I gather this from photographs and from my own memories of him, dressed in his Sunday best and on his way to preach a sermon somewhere, when I was little. Handsome, proud, and ingrown, "like a toenail," somebody said. But he looked to me, as I grew older, like pictures I had seen of African tribal chieftains: he really should have been naked, with warpaint on and barbaric mementos, standing among spears. He could be chilling in the pulpit and indescribably cruel in his personal life and he was certainly the most bitter man I have ever met; yet it must be said that there was something else in him, buried in him, which lent him his tremendous power and, even, a rather crushing charm. It had something to do with his blackness, I think—he was very black—with his blackness and his beauty, and with the fact that he knew that he was black but did not know that he was beautiful. He claimed to be proud of his blackness but it had also been the cause of much humiliation and it had fixed bleak boundaries to his life. He was not a young man when we were growing up and he had already suffered many kinds of ruin; in his outrageously demanding and protective way he loved his children, who were black like him and menaced, like him; and all these things sometimes showed in his face when he tried, never to my knowledge with any success, to establish contact with any of us. When he took one of his children on his knee to play, the child always became fretful and began to cry; when he tried to help one of us with our homework the absolutely unabating tension which emanated from him caused our minds and our tongues to become paralyzed, so that he, scarcely knowing why, flew into a rage and the child, not knowing why, was punished. If it ever entered his head to bring a surprise home for his children, it was, almost unfailingly, the wrong surprise and even the big watermelons he often brought home on his back in the summertime led to the most appalling scenes. I do not remember, in all those years, that one of his children was ever glad to see him come home. From what I was able to gather of his early life, it seemed that this inability to establish contact with other people had always marked him and had been one of the things which had driven him out of New Orleans. There was something in him, therefore, groping and tentative, which was never expressed and which was buried with him. One saw it most clearly when he was facing new people and hoping to impress them. But he never did, not for long. We went from church to smaller and more improbable church, he found himself in less and less demand as a minister, and by the time he died none of his friends had come to see him for a long time. He had lived and died in an intolerable bitterness of spirit and it frightened me, as we drove him to the graveyard through those unquiet, ruined streets, to see how powerful and overflowing this bitterness could be and to realize that this bitterness now was mine.

When he died I had been away from home for a little over a year. In that year I had had time to become aware of the meaning of all my father's bitter warnings, had discovered the secret of his proudly pursed lips and rigid carriage: I had discovered the weight of white people in the world. I saw that this had been for my ancestors and now would be for me an awful thing to live with and that the bitterness which had helped to kill my father could also kill me.

He had been ill a long time—in the mind, as we now realized, reliving instances of his fantastic intransigence in the new light of his affliction and endeavoring to feel a sorrow for him which never, quite, came true. We had not known that he was being eaten up by paranoia, and the discovery that his cruelty, to our bodies and our minds, had been one of the symptoms of his illness was not, then, enough to enable us to forgive him. The younger children felt, quite simply, relief that he would not be coming home anymore. My mother's observation that it was he, after all, who had kept them alive all these years meant nothing because the problems of keeping children alive are not real for children. The older children felt, with my father gone, that they could invite their friends to the house without fear that their friends would be insulted or, as had sometimes happened with me, being told that their friends were in league with the devil and intended to rob our family of everything we owned. (I didn't fail to wonder, and it made me hate him, what on earth we owned that anybody else would want.)

His illness was beyond all hope of healing before anyone realized that he was ill. He had always been so strange and had lived, like a prophet, in such unimaginably close communion with the Lord that his long silences which were punctuated by moans and hallelujahs and snatches of old songs while he sat at the living-room window never seemed odd to us. It was not until he refused to eat because, he said, his family was trying to poison him that my mother was forced to accept as a fact what had, until then, been only an unwilling suspicion. When he was committed, it was discovered that he had tuberculosis and, as it turned out, the disease of his mind allowed the disease of his body to destroy him. For the doctors could not force him to eat, either, and, though he was fed intravenously, it was clear from the beginning that there was no hope for him.

In my mind's eye I could see him, sitting at the window, locked up in his terrors; hating and fearing every living soul including his children who had betrayed him, too, by reaching toward the world which had despised him. There were nine of us. I began to wonder what it could have felt like for such a man to have had nine children whom he could barely feed. He used to make little jokes about our poverty, which never, of course, seemed very funny to us; they could not have seemed very funny to him, either, or else our all too feeble response to them would never have caused such rages. He spent great energy and achieved, to our chagrin, no small amount of success in keeping us away from the people who surrounded us, people who had all-night rent parties to which we listened when we should have been sleeping, people who cursed and drank and flashed razor blades on Lenox Avenue. He could not understand why, if they had so much energy to spare, they could not use it to make their lives better. He treated almost everybody on our block with a most uncharitable asperity and neither they, nor, of course, their children were slow to reciprocate.

The only white people who came to our house were welfare workers and bill collectors. It was almost always my mother who dealt with them, for my father's temper, which was at the mercy of his pride, was never to be trusted. It was clear that he felt their very presence in his home to be a violation: this was conveyed by his carriage, almost ludicrously stiff, and by his voice, harsh and vindictively polite. When I was around nine or ten I wrote a play which was directed by a young, white schoolteacher, a woman, who then took an interest in me, and gave me books to read and, in order to corroborate my theatrical bent, decided to take me to see what she somewhat tactlessly referred to as "real" plays. Theater-going was forbidden in our house, but, with the really cruel intuitiveness of a child, I suspected that the color of this woman's skin would carry the day for me. When, at school, she suggested taking me to the theater, I did not, as I might have done if she had been a Negro, find a way of discouraging her, but agreed that she should pick me up at my house one evening. I then, very cleverly, left all the rest to my mother, who suggested to my father, as I knew she would, that it would not be very nice to let such a kind woman make the trip for nothing. Also, since it was a schoolteacher, I imagine that my mother countered the idea of sin with the idea of "education," which word, even with my father, carried a kind of bitter weight.

Before the teacher came my father took me aside to ask *why* she was coming, what *interest* she could possibly have in our house, in a boy like me. I said I didn't know but I, too, suggested that it had something to do with education. And I understood that my father was waiting for me to say something—I didn't quite know what; perhaps that I wanted his protection against this teacher and her "education." I said none of these things and the teacher came and we went out. It was clear, during the brief interview in our living room, that my father was agreeing very much against his will and that he would have refused permission if he had dared. The fact that he did not dare caused me to despise him: I had no way of knowing that he was facing in that living room a wholly unprecedented and frightening situation.

Later, when my father had been laid off from his job, this woman became very important to us. She was really a very sweet and generous woman and went to a great deal of trouble to be of help to us, particularly during one awful winter. My mother called her by the highest name she knew: she said she was a "Christian." My father could scarcely disagree but during the four or five years of our relatively close association he never trusted her and was always trying to surprise in her open, midwestern face the genuine, cunningly hidden, and hideous motivation. In later years, particularly when it began to be clear that this "education" of mine was going to lead me to perdition, he became more explicit and warned me that my white friends in high school were not really my friends and that I would see, when I was older, how white people would do anything to keep a Negro down. Some of them could be nice, he admitted, but none of them were to be trusted and most of them were not even nice. The best thing was to have as little to do with them as possible. I did not feel this way and I was certain, in my innocence, that I never would.

But the year which preceded my father's death had made a great change in my life. I had been living in New Jersey, working in defense plants, working and living among southerners, white and black. I knew about the South, of course, and about how southerners treated Negroes and how they expected them to behave, but it had never entered my mind that anyone would look at me and expect *me* to behave that way. I learned in New Jersey that to be a Negro meant, precisely, that one was never looked at but was simply at the mercy of the reflexes the color of one's skin caused in other people. I acted in New Jersey as I had always acted, that is as though I thought a great deal of myself—I had to *act* that way—with results that were, simply, unbelievable. I had scarcely arrived before I had earned the enmity, which was extraordinarily ingenious, of all my superiors and nearly all my co-workers. In the beginning, to make matters worse, I simply did not know what was happening. I did not know what I had done, and I shortly began to wonder what *anyone* could possibly do, to bring about such unanimous, active, and unbearably vocal hostility. I knew about Jim Crow but I had never experienced it. I went to the same self-service restaurant three times and stood with all the Princeton boys before the counter, waiting for a hamburger and coffee; it was always an extraordinarily long time before anything was set before me; but it was not until the fourth visit that I learned that, in fact, nothing had ever been set before me: I had simply picked something up. Negroes were not served there, I was told, and they had been waiting for me to realize that I was always the only Negro present. Once I was told this, I determined to go there all the time. But now they were ready for me and, though some dreadful scenes were subsequently enacted in that restaurant, I never ate there again.

It was the same story all over New Jersey, in bars, bowling alleys, diners, places to live. I was always being forced to leave, silently, or with mutual imprecations. I very shortly became notorious and children giggled behind me when I passed and their elders whispered or shouted—they really believed that I was mad. And it did begin to work on my mind, of course; I began to be afraid to go anywhere and to compensate for this I went places to which I really should not have gone and where, God knows, I had no desire to be. My reputation in town naturally enhanced my reputation at work and my working day became one long series of acrobatics designed to keep me out of trouble.

I cannot say that these acrobatics succeeded. It began to seem that the machinery of the organization I worked for was turning over, day and night, with but one aim: to eject me. I was fired once, and contrived, with the aid of a friend from New York, to get back on the payroll; was fired again, and bounced back again. It took a while to fire me for the third time, but the third time took. There were no loopholes anywhere. There was not even any way of getting back inside the gates.

That year in New Jersey lives in my mind as though it were the year during which, having an unsuspected predilection for it, I first contracted some dread, chronic disease, the unfailing symptom of which is a kind of blind fever, a pounding in the skull and fire in the bowels. Once this disease is contracted, one can never be really carefree again, for the fever, without an instant's warning, can recur at any moment. It can wreck more important things than race relations. There is not a Negro alive who does not have this rage in his blood—one has the choice, merely, of living with it consciously or surrendering to it. As for me, this fever has recurred in me, and does, and will until the day I die.

My last night in New Jersey, a white friend from New York took me to the nearest big town, Trenton, to go to the movies and have a few drinks. As it turned out, he also saved me from, at the very least, a violent whipping. Almost every detail of that night stands out very clearly in my memory. I even remember the name of the movie we saw because its title impressed me as being so patly ironical. It was a movie about the German occupation of France, starring Maureen O'Hara and Charles Laughton and called *This Land Is Mine*. I remember the name of the diner we walked into when the movie ended: it was the "American Diner." When we walked in the counterman asked what we wanted and I remember answering with the casual sharpness which had become my habit: "We want a hamburger and a cup of coffee, what do you think we want?" I do not know why, after a year of such rebuffs, I so completely failed to anticipate his answer, which was, of course, "We don't serve Negroes here." This reply failed to discompose me, at least for the moment. I made some sardonic comment about the name of the diner and we walked out into the streets.

This was the time of what was called the "brownout," when the lights in all American cities were very dim. When we re-entered the streets something happened to me which had the force of an optical illusion, or a nightmare. The streets were very crowded and I was facing north. People were moving in every direction but it seemed to me, in that instant, that all of the people I could see, and many more than that, were moving toward me, against me, and that everyone was white. I remember how their faces gleamed. And I felt, like a physical sensation, a *click* at the nape of my neck as though some interior string connecting my head to my body had been cut. I began to walk. I heard my friend call after me, but I ignored him. Heaven only knows what was going on in his mind, but he had the good sense not to touch me—I don't know what would have happened if he had—and to keep me in sight. I don't know what was going on in my mind, either; I certainly had no conscious plan. I wanted to do something to crush these white faces, which were crushing me. I walked for perhaps a block or two until I came to an enormous, glittering, and fashionable restaurant in which I knew not even the intercession of the Virgin would cause me to be served. I pushed through the doors and took the first vacant seat I saw, at a table for two, and waited.

I do not know how long I waited and I rather wonder, until today, what I could possibly have looked like. Whatever I looked like, I frightened the waitress who shortly appeared, and the moment she appeared all of my fury flowed toward her. I hated her for her white face, and for her great, astounded, frightened eyes. I felt that if she found a black man so frightening I would make her fright worthwhile.

She did not ask me what I wanted, but repeated, as though she had learned it somewhere, "We don't serve Negroes here." She did not say it with the blunt, derisive hostility to which I had grown so accustomed, but, rather, with a note of apology in her voice, and fear. This made me colder and more murderous than ever. I felt I had to do something with my hands. I wanted her to come close enough for me to get her neck between my hands.

So I pretended not to have understood her, hoping to draw her closer. And she did step a very short step closer, with her pencil poised incongruously over her pad, and repeated the formula: ". . . don't serve Negroes here."

Somehow, with the repetition of that phrase, which was already ringing in my head like a thousand bells of a nightmare, I realized that she would never come any closer and that I would have to strike from a distance. There was nothing on the table but an ordinary watermug half full of water, and I picked this up and hurled it with all my strength at her. She ducked and it missed her and shattered against the mirror behind the bar. And, with that sound, my frozen blood abruptly thawed, I returned from wherever I had been, I *saw*, for the first time, the restaurant, the people with their mouths open, already, as it seemed to me, rising as one man, and I realized what I had done, and where I was, and I was frightened. I rose and began running for the door. A round, potbellied man grabbed me by the nape of the neck just as I reached the doors and began to beat me about the face. I kicked him and got loose and ran into the streets. My friend whispered, "*Run!*" and I ran.

My friend stayed outside the restaurant long enough to misdirect my pursuers and the police, who arrived, he told me, at once. I do not know what I said to him when he came to my room that night. I could not have said much. I felt, in the oddest, most awful way, that I had somehow betrayed him. I lived it over and over and over again, the way one relives an automobile accident after it has happened and one finds oneself alone and safe. I could not get over two facts, both equally difficult for the imagination to grasp, and one was that I could have been murdered. But the other was that I had been ready to commit murder. I saw nothing very clearly but I did see this: that my life, my *real* life, was in danger, and not from anything other people might do but from the hatred I carried in my own heart.

TWO

I had returned home around the second week in June—in great haste because it seemed that my father's death and my mother's confinement were both but a matter of hours. In the case of my mother, it soon became clear that she had simply made a miscalculation. This had always been her tendency and I don't believe that a single one of us arrived in the world, or has since arrived anywhere else, on time. But none of us dawdled so intolerably about the business of being born as did my baby sister. We sometimes amused ourselves, during those endless, stifling weeks, by picturing the baby sitting within in the safe, warm dark, bitterly regretting the necessity of becoming a part of our chaos and stubbornly putting it off as long as possible. I understood her perfectly and congratulated her on showing such good sense so soon. Death, however, sat as purposefully at my father's bedside as life stirred within my mother's womb and it was harder to understand why he so lingered in that long shadow. It seemed that he had bent, and for a long time, too, all of his energies toward dying. Now death was ready for him but my father held back.

All of Harlem, indeed, seemed to be infected by waiting. I had never before known it to be so violently still. Racial tensions throughout this country were exacerbated during the early years of the war, partly because the labor market brought together hundreds of thousands of ill-prepared people and partly because Negro soldiers, regardless of where they were born, received their military training in the South. What happened in defense plants and army camps had repercussions, naturally, in every Negro ghetto. The situation in Harlem had grown bad enough for clergymen, policemen, educators, politicians, and social workers to assert in one breath that there was no "crime wave" and to offer, in the very next breath, suggestions as to how to combat it. These suggestions always seemed to involve playgrounds, despite the fact that racial skirmishes were occurring in the playgrounds, too. Playground or not, crime wave or not, the Harlem police force had been augmented in March, and the unrest grew—perhaps, in fact, partly as a result of the ghetto's instinctive hatred of policemen. Perhaps the most revealing news item, out of the steady parade of reports of muggings, stabbings, shootings, assaults, gang wars, and accusations of police brutality, is the item concerning six Negro girls who set upon a white girl in the subway because, as they all too accurately put it, she was stepping on their toes. Indeed she was, all over the nation.

I had never before been so aware of policemen, on foot, on horseback, on corners, everywhere, always two by two. Nor had I ever been so aware of small knots of people. They were on stoops and on corners and in doorways, and what was striking about them, I think, was that they did not seem to be talking. Never, when I passed these groups, did the usual sound of a curse or a laugh ring out and neither did there seem to be any hum of gossip. There was certainly, on the other hand, occurring between them communication extraordinarily intense. Another thing that was striking was the unexpected diversity of the people who made up these groups. Usually, for example, one would see a group of sharpies standing on the street corner, jiving the passing chicks; or a group of older men, usually, for some reason, in the vicinity of a barber shop, discussing baseball scores, or the numbers, or making rather chilling observations about women they had known. Women, in a general way, tended to be seen less often together—unless they were church women, or very young girls, or prostitutes met together for an unprofessional instant. But that summer I saw the strangest combinations: large, respectable, churchly matrons standing on the stoops or the corners with their hair tied up, together with a girl in sleazy satin whose face bore the marks of gin and the razor, or heavy-set, abrupt, no-nonsense older men, in company with the most disreputable and fanatical "race" men, or these same "race" men with the sharpies, or these sharpies with the churchly women. Seventh Day Adventists and Methodists and Spiritualists seemed to be hobnobbing with Holy-rollers and they were all, alike, entangled with the most flagrant disbelievers; something heavy in their stance seemed to indicate that they had all, incredibly, seen a common vision, and on each face there seemed to be the same strange, bitter shadow.

The churchly women and the matter-of-fact, no-nonsense men had children in the army. The sleazy girls they talked to had lovers there, the sharpies and the "race" men had friends and brothers there. It would have demanded an unquestioning patriotism, happily as uncommon in this country as it is undesirable, for these people not to have been disturbed by the bitter letters they received, by the newspaper stories they read, not to have been enraged by the posters, then to be found all over New York, which described the Japanese as "yellow-bellied Japs." It was only the "race" men, to be sure, who spoke ceaselessly of being revenged—how this vengeance was to be exacted was not clear—for the indignities and dangers suffered by Negro boys in uniform; but everybody felt a directionless, hopeless bitterness, as well as that panic which can scarcely be suppressed when one knows that a human being one loves is beyond one's reach, and in danger. This helplessness and this gnawing uneasiness does something, at length, to even the toughest mind. Perhaps the best way to sum all this up is to say that the people I knew felt, mainly, a peculiar kind of relief when they knew that their boys were being shipped out of the south, to do battle overseas. It was, perhaps, like feeling that the most dangerous part of a dangerous journey had been passed and that now, even if death should come, it would come with honor and without the complicity of their countrymen. Such a death would be, in short, a fact with which one could hope to live.

It was on the twenty-eighth of July, which I believe was a Wednesday, that I visited my father for the first time during his illness and for the last time in his life. The moment I saw him I knew why I had put off this visit so long. I had told my mother that I did not want to see him because I hated him. But this was not true. It was only that I *had* hated him and I wanted to hold on to this hatred. I did not want to look on him as a ruin: it was not a ruin I had hated. I imagine that one of the reasons people cling to their hates so stubbornly is because they sense, once hate is gone, that they will be forced to deal with pain.

We traveled out to him, his older sister and myself, to what seemed to be the very end of a very Long Island. It was hot and dusty and we wrangled, my aunt and I, all the way out, over the fact that I had recently begun to smoke and, as she said, to give myself airs. But I knew that she wrangled with me because she could not bear to face the fact of her brother's dying. Neither could I endure the reality of her despair, her unstated bafflement as to what had happened to her brother's life, and her own. So we wrangled and I smoked and from time to time she fell into a heavy reverie. Covertly, I watched her face, which was the face of an old woman; it had fallen in, the eyes were sunken and lightless; soon she would be dying, too.

In my childhood—it had not been so long ago—I had thought her beautiful. She had been quick-witted and quick-moving and very generous with all the children and each of her visits had been an event. At one time one of my brothers and myself had thought of running away to live with her. Now she could no longer produce out of her handbag some unexpected and yet familiar delight. She made me feel pity and revulsion and fear. It was awful to realize that she no longer caused me to feel affection. The closer we came to the hospital the more querulous she became and at the same time, naturally, grew more dependent on me. Between pity and guilt and fear I began to feel that there was another me trapped in my skull like a jack-in-the-box who might escape my control at any moment and fill the air with screaming.

She began to cry the moment we entered the room and she saw him lying there, all shriveled and still, like a little black monkey. The great, gleaming apparatus which fed him and would have compelled him to be still even if he had been able to move brought to mind, not beneficence, but torture; the tubes entering his arm made me think of pictures I had seen when a child, of Gulliver, tied down by the pygmies on that island. My aunt wept and wept, there was a whistling sound in my father's throat; nothing was said; he could not speak. I wanted to take his hand, to say something. But I do not know what I could have said, even if he could have heard me. He was not really in that room with us, he had at last really embarked on his journey; and though my aunt told me that he said he was going to meet Jesus, I did not hear anything except that whistling in his throat. The doctor came back and we left, into that unbearable train again, and home. In the morning came the telegram saying that he was dead. Then the house was suddenly full of relatives, friends, hysteria, and confusion and I quickly left my mother and the children to the care of those impressive women, who, in Negro communities at least, automatically appear at times of bereavement armed with lotions, proverbs, and patience, and an ability to cook. I went downtown. By the time I returned, later the same day, my mother had been carried to the hospital and the baby had been born.

THREE

For my father's funeral I had nothing black to wear and this posed a nagging problem all day long. It was one of those problems, simple, or impossible of solution, to which the mind insanely clings in order to avoid the mind's real trouble. I spent most of that day at the downtown apartment of a girl I knew, celebrating my birthday with whiskey and wondering what to wear that night. When planning a birthday celebration one naturally does not expect that it will be up against competition from a funeral and this girl had anticipated taking me out that night, for a big dinner and a night club afterwards. Sometime during the course of that long day we decided that we would go out anyway, when my father's funeral service was over. I imagine *I* decided it, since, as the funeral hour approached, it became clearer and clearer to me that I would not know what to do with myself when it was over. The girl, stifling her very lively concern as to the possible effects of the whiskey on one of my father's chief mourners, concentrated on being conciliatory and practically helpful. She found a black shirt for me somewhere and ironed it and, dressed in the darkest pants and jacket I owned, and slightly drunk, I made my way to my father's funeral.

The chapel was full, but not packed, and very quiet. There were, mainly, my father's relatives, and his children, and here and there I saw faces I had not seen since childhood, the faces of my father's one-time friends. They were very dark and solemn now, seeming somehow to suggest that they had known all along that something like this would happen. Chief among the mourners was my aunt, who had quarreled with my father all his life; by which I do not mean to suggest that her mourning was insincere or that she had not loved him. I suppose that she was one of the few people in the world who had, and their incessant quarreling proved precisely the strength of the tie that bound them. The only other person in the world, as far as I knew, whose relationship to my father rivaled my aunt's in depth was my mother, who was not there.

It seemed to me, of course, that it was a very long funeral. But it was, if anything, a rather shorter funeral than most, nor, since there were no overwhelming, uncontrollable expressions of grief, could it be called—if I dare to use the word—successful. The minister who preached my father's funeral sermon was one of the few my father had still been seeing as he neared his end. He presented to us in his sermon a man whom none of us had ever seen—a man thoughtful, patient, and forbearing, a Christian inspiration to all who knew him, and a model for his children. And no doubt the children, in their disturbed and guilty state, were almost ready to believe this; he had been remote enough to be anything and, anyway, the shock of the incontrovertible, that it was really our father lying up there in that casket, prepared the mind for anything. His sister moaned and this grief-stricken moaning was taken as corroboration. The other faces held a dark, noncommittal thoughtfulness. This was not the man they had known, but they had scarcely expected to be confronted with *him;* this was, in a sense deeper than questions of fact, the man they had not known, and the man they had not known may have been the real one. The real man, whoever he had been, had suffered and now he was dead: this was all that was sure and all that mattered now. Every man in the chapel hoped that when his hour came he, too, would be eulogized, which is to say forgiven, and that all of his lapses, greeds, errors, and strayings from the truth would be invested with coherence and looked upon with charity. This was perhaps the last thing human beings could give each other and it was what they demanded, after all, of the Lord. Only the Lord saw the midnight tears, only He was present when one of His children, moaning and wringing hands, paced up and down the room. When one slapped one's child in anger the recoil in the heart reverberated through heaven and became part of the pain of the universe. And when the children were hungry and sullen and distrustful and one watched them, daily, growing wilder, and further away, and running headlong into danger, it was the Lord who knew what the charged heart endured as the strap was laid to the backside; the Lord alone who knew what one *would* have said if one had had, like the Lord, the gift of the living word. It was the Lord who knew of the impossibility every parent in that room faced: how to prepare the child for the day when the child would be despised and how to *create* in the child—by what means?—a stronger antidote to this poison than one had found for oneself. The avenues, side streets, bars, billiard halls, hospitals, police stations, and even the playgrounds of Harlem—not to mention the houses of correction, the jails, and the morgue—testified to the potency of the poison while remaining silent as to the efficacy of whatever antidote, irresistibly raising the question of whether or not such an antidote existed; raising, which was worse, the question of whether or not an antidote was desirable; perhaps poison should be fought with poison. With these several schisms in the mind and with more terrors in the heart than could be named, it was better not to judge the man who had gone down under an impossible burden. It was better to remember: *Thou knowest this man's fall; but thou knowest not his wrassling.*

While the preacher talked and I watched the children—years of changing their diapers, scrubbing them, slapping them, taking them to school, and scolding them had had the perhaps inevitable result of making me love them, though I am not sure I knew this then—my mind was busily breaking out with a rash of disconnected impressions. Snatches of popular songs, indecent jokes, bits of books I had read, movie sequences, faces, voices, political issues—I thought I was going mad; all these impressions suspended, as it were, in the solution of the faint nausea produced in me by the heat and liquor. For a moment I had the impression that my alcoholic breath, inefficiently disguised with chewing gum, filled the entire chapel. Then some-one began singing one of my father's favorite songs and, abruptly, I was with him, sitting on his knee, in the hot, enor-mous, crowded church which was the first church we attended. It was the Abyssinian Baptist Church on 138th Street. We had not gone there long. With this image, a host of others came. I had forgotten, in the rage of my growing up, how proud my fa-ther had been of me when I was little. Apparently, I had had a voice and my father had liked to show me off before the mem-bers of the church. I had forgotten what he had looked like when he was pleased but now I remembered that he had always been grinning with pleasure when my solos ended. I even re-membered certain expressions on his face when he teased my mother—had he loved her? I would never know. And when had it all begun to change? For now it seemed that he had not always been cruel. I remembered being taken for a haircut and scrap-ing my knee on the footrest of the barber's chair and I remem-bered my father's face as he soothed my crying and applied the stinging iodine. Then I remembered our fights, fights which had been of the worst possible kind because my technique had been silence.

I remembered the one time in all our life together when we had really spoken to each other.

It was on a Sunday and it must have been shortly before I left home. We were walking, just the two of us, in our usual silence, to or from church. I was in high school and had been doing a lot of writing and I was, at about this time, the editor of the high school magazine. But I had also been a Young Minister and had been preaching from the pulpit. Lately, I had been taking fewer engagements and preached as rarely as possible. It was said in the church, quite truthfully, that I was "cooling off."

My father asked me abruptly, "You'd rather write than preach, wouldn't you?"

I was astonished at his question—because it was a real question. I answered, "Yes."

That was all we said. It was awful to remember that that was all we had *ever* said.

The casket now was opened and the mourners were being led up the aisle to look for the last time on the deceased. The assumption was that the family was too overcome with grief to be allowed to make this journey alone and I watched while my aunt was led to the casket and, muffled in black, and shaking, led back to her seat. I disapproved of forcing the children to look on their dead father, considering that the shock of his death, or, more truthfully, the shock of death as a reality, was already a little more than a child could bear, but my judgment in this matter had been overruled and there they were, bewildered and frightened and very small, being led, one by one, to the casket. But there is also something very gallant about children at such moments. It has something to do with their silence and gravity and with the fact that one cannot help them. Their legs, somehow, seem *exposed,* so that it is at once incredible and terribly clear that their legs are all they have to hold them up.

I had not wanted to go to the casket myself and I certainly had not wished to be led there, but there was no way of avoiding either of these forms. One of the deacons led me up and I looked on my father's face. I cannot say that it looked like him at all. His blackness had been equivocated by powder and there was no suggestion in that casket of what his power had or could have been. He was simply an old man dead, and it was hard to believe that he had ever given anyone either joy or pain. Yet, his life filled that room. Further up the avenue his wife was holding his newborn child. Life and death so close together, and love and hatred, and right and wrong, said something to me which I did not want to hear concerning man, concerning the life of man.

After the funeral, while I was downtown desperately celebrating my birthday, a Negro soldier, in the lobby of the Hotel
Braddock, got into a fight with a white policeman over a Negro
girl. Negro girls, white policemen, in or out of uniform, and
Negro males—in or out of uniform—were part of the furniture
of the lobby of the Hotel Braddock and this was certainly not
the first time such an incident had occurred. It was destined,
however, to receive an unprecedented publicity, for the fight between the policeman and the soldier ended with the shooting of
the soldier. Rumor, flowing immediately to the streets outside,
stated that the soldier had been shot in the back, an instanta-
neous and revealing invention, and that the soldier had died
protecting a Negro woman. The facts were somewhat different—for example, the soldier had not been shot in the back,
and was not dead, and the girl seems to have been as dubious a
symbol of womanhood as her white counterpart in Georgia
usually is, but no one was interested in the facts. They preferred
the invention because this invention expressed and corrobo-
rated their hates and fears so perfectly. It is just as well to remember that people are always doing this. Perhaps many of
those legends, including Christianity, to which the world clings
began their conquest of the world with just some such con-
certed surrender to distortion. The effect, in Harlem, of this
particular legend was like the effect of a lit match in a tin of gasoline. The mob gathered before the doors of the Hotel Braddock simply began to swell and to spread in every direction, and
Harlem exploded.

The mob did not cross the ghetto lines. It would have been
easy, for example, to have gone over to Morningside Park on the
West Side or to have crossed the Grand Central railroad tracks
at 125th Street on the East Side, to wreak havoc in white neighborhoods. The mob seems to have been mainly interested in
something more potent and real than the white face, that is, in
white power, and the principal damage done during the riot of

the summer of 1943 was to white business establishments in Harlem. It might have been a far bloodier story, of course, if, at the hour the riot began, these establishments had still been open. From the Hotel Braddock the mob fanned out, east and west along 125th Street, and for the entire length of Lenox, Seventh, and Eighth avenues. Along each of these avenues, and along each major side street—116th, 125th, 135th, and so on— bars, stores, pawnshops, restaurants, even little luncheonettes had been smashed open and entered and looted—looted, it might be added, with more haste than efficiency. The shelves really looked as though a bomb had struck them. Cans of beans and soup and dog food, along with toilet paper, corn flakes, sardines and milk tumbled every which way, and abandoned cash registers and cases of beer leaned crazily out of the splintered windows and were strewn along the avenues. Sheets, blankets, and clothing of every description formed a kind of path, as though people had dropped them while running. I truly had not realized that Harlem *had* so many stores until I saw them all smashed open; the first time the word *wealth* ever entered my mind in relation to Harlem was when I saw it scattered in the streets. But one's first, incongruous impression of plenty was countered immediately by an impression of waste. None of this was doing anybody any good. It would have been better to have left the plate glass as it had been and the goods lying in the stores.

It would have been better, but it would also have been intolerable, for Harlem had needed something to smash. To smash something is the ghetto's chronic need. Most of the time it is the members of the ghetto who smash each other, and themselves. But as long as the ghetto walls are standing there will always come a moment when these outlets do not work. That summer, for example, it was not enough to get into a fight on Lenox Avenue, or curse out one's cronies in the barber shops. If ever, indeed, the violence which fills Harlem's churches, pool halls, and bars erupts outward in a more direct fashion, Harlem and its citizens are likely to vanish in an apocalyptic flood. That this is not likely to happen is due to a great many reasons, most hidden and powerful among them the Negro's real relation to the white American. This relation prohibits, simply, anything as uncomplicated and satisfactory as pure hatred. In order really to hate white people, one has to blot so much out of the mind—and the heart—that this hatred itself becomes an exhausting and self-destructive pose. But this does not mean, on the other hand, that love comes easily: the white world is too powerful, too complacent, too ready with gratuitous humiliation, and, above all, too ignorant and too innocent for that. One is absolutely forced to make perpetual qualifications and one's own reactions are always canceling each other out. It is this, really, which has driven so many people mad, both white and black. One is always in the position of having to decide between amputation and gangrene. Amputation is swift but time may prove that the amputation was not necessary—or one may delay the amputation too long. Gangrene is slow, but it is impossible to be sure that one is reading one's symptoms right. The idea of going through life as a cripple is more than one can bear, and equally unbearable is the risk of swelling up slowly, in agony, with poison. And the trouble, finally, is that the risks are real even if the choices do not exist.

"But as for me and my house," my father had said, "we will serve the Lord." I wondered, as we drove him to his resting place, what this line had meant for him. I had heard him preach it many times. I had preached it once myself, proudly giving it an interpretation different from my father's. Now the whole thing came back to me, as though my father and I were on our way to Sunday school and I were memorizing the golden text: *And if it seem evil unto you to serve the Lord, choose you this day whom you will serve; whether the gods which your fathers served that were on the other side of the flood, or the gods of the Amorites, in whose land ye dwell: but as for me and my house, we will serve the Lord.* I suspected in these familiar lines a meaning which had never been there for me before. All of my father's texts and songs, which I had decided were meaningless, were arranged before me at his death like empty bottles, waiting to hold the meaning which life would give them for me. This was his legacy: nothing is ever escaped. That bleakly memorable morning I hated the unbelievable streets and the Negroes and whites who had, equally, made them that way. But I knew that it was folly, as my father would have said, this bitterness was folly. It was necessary to hold on to the things that mattered. The dead man mattered, the new life mattered; blackness and whiteness did not matter; to believe that they did was to acquiesce in one's own destruction. Hatred, which could destroy so much, never failed to destroy the man who hated and this was an immutable law.

It began to seem that one would have to hold in the mind forever two ideas which seemed to be in opposition. The first idea was acceptance, the acceptance, totally without rancor, of life as it is, and men as they are: in the light of this idea, it goes without saying that injustice is a commonplace. But this did not mean that one could be complacent, for the second idea was of equal power: that one must never, in one's own life, accept these injustices as commonplace but must fight them with all one's strength. This fight begins, however, in the heart and it now had been laid to my charge to keep my own heart free of hatred and despair. This intimation made my heart heavy and, now that my father was irrecoverable, I wished that he had been beside me so that I could have searched his face for the answers which only the future would give me now.

GEOFFREY WOLFF

Novelist, biographer, and essayist Geoffrey Wolff (1937–) has been a Fulbright scholar, Guggenheim fellow, and book editor of the Washington Post; *in 1995 he became Professor of English and Creative Writing at the University of California, Irvine.*

In 1979 Wolff published his hugely successful memoir, The Duke of Deception: Memories of My Father. *A fascinating mixture of autobiography and biography,* The Duke of Deception *interleaves a recounting of Geoffrey's early years with the larger tale of his father, Arthur S. Wolff III—known to his friends as Duke.*

Arthur Wolff, writes Geoffrey, was a chameleon and "a bullshit artist"—a man who gave other people what they wanted and created his own history as the need arose. Throughout his life he claimed (falsely) to have graduated from Yale, to have a master's in aeronautical engineering from the Sorbonne, to have flown with the RAF during the Battle of Britain, to have served with the OSS, to have parachuted into France to help with the Resistance.

His very name was an exaggeration. He was indeed the son of an Arthur, but he shunned the diminutive Junior and as a teenager elected first to follow his name with a pair of Roman numer-

als and then, for greater effect, to add a third. Later, he transmogrified the name again in a variety of bad check and credit schemes. "He was a lie, through and through," writes Geoffrey. "There was nothing to him but lies, and love."

Not surprisingly, a man so multifaceted inspired intense and conflicting emotions, the untangling of which has been no simple or one-time matter. Long before he wrote The Duke of Deception, Wolff's first novel featured a larger-than-life confidence man and pretender whose actions rain fallout on a young adult son with aspirations to legitimate respectability. In 1996 he returned again to the subject of his father in the piece selected here, originally published in the San Diego Reader.

"Heavy Lifting" describes a grand reunion in the summer of 1961 between Geoffrey Wolff, his younger brother and only sibling, Tobias, and their father—an event occasioned by the boys' parents' divorce ten years earlier, after which Geoffrey stayed with their father and Tobias left with their mother. At the outset of "Heavy Lifting," Geoffrey is twenty-two and Tobias is on the cusp of sixteen. Ultimately, this will prove the last time Geoffrey sees his father, who died alone nine years later in a tiny Southern California apartment near the beach—two weeks before the milkman found him, writes Wolff in The Duke of Deception, "after smelling something unpleasant."

Heavy Lifting

On the hot, breathless, soft, fragrant afternoon of my graduation from Princeton it seemed that everything good was not merely latent but unavoidable, folded and in the bag. I'd worked like a Turk those past years, and my labors had been rewarded and then some with fancy Latin on my fancy diploma, *summa* it said and summit I believed. Not one but two ex-girlfriends had come to the ceremony in front of lovely tree-shaded Nassau Hall, and so resolutely happy was I that it didn't even stain my pride to sweat through my shirt and gray worsted suit, to be capped like a monkey in tasseled mortarboard.

Each of my exes had brought me the same gift, a suitcase. It occurred to me that unarticulated longings were expressed by these mementos, and coming to them for visits wouldn't have answered their prayers. Sending me off solo on a long voyage would have been in the ballpark, Godspeed would have done their fantasies justice, *adiós* was more like it.

And that too was as I wished it! All was jake, A-OK, on the come and coming! Admitted, I had no money, but a job was waiting nigh September, far, far away, teaching in Turkey, which was even farther from my father in California than I was now in the Garden State, and the farther the better. The last time I had intersected with him, two years before, he had swept through Princeton in a car sought for repossession, charging clothes and books and jazz records to my accounts. My stepmother, having just left him again and for good, gave me unwelcome word of him a year later; he was in Redondo Beach, in trouble.

For me, that June, what was trouble? A college friend with a different kind of daddy, the kind who owned a fifty-foot paid-for ketch, had invited me to spend the summer with him on that boat in Massachusetts Bay, Buzzards Bay, Nantucket Sound, Vineyard Sound, Narragansett Bay. It was our onus to sail that *Sea Witch* from snug harbor to snug harbor, cleaning and polishing and varnishing, making the boat ready for his parents' pleasure if they wanted to come aboard, which they wouldn't because they had better places to play that summer, as though there could be a better place to play than where we were to be fed and paid to play. I was warned that sunburn was a lively danger, likewise hangovers from the free consumables at coming-out parties in Nonquitt and Nantucket, Newport and Edgartown. Dark and lonely work, but somebody had to do it.

Now, a few days after graduation, doing it, we were embarked. My suitcases and diploma were stored ashore with my passport and vaccination certificates and Greek tragedies in translation; we tugged at anchor off Cuttyhunk, drinking a rum drink to celebrate our third day at sea. There were four of us, two happy couples laughing and watching the sun fall, when my father got through on the radiotelephone. Writing about that conversation thirty-four years later I feel foggy dread, as though I've sailed on a cloudless day through deep clear water bang onto a reef. It's the nature of a radiotelephone conversation that everyone aboard can hear it, not to mention anyone else aboard any vessel within miles who wants to listen in.

This conversation mortified me. My dad stuttered flamboyantly. He did everything abundantly, elaborately, extravagantly, but his stuttering was grandiose. Moreover, he couldn't get the hang of the turn-and-turn-about of a radio conversation, in which one either speaks or listens. Listening was not my dad's thing, so I heard myself shouting at him, and worse, I heard myself stammering back, so that it must have seemed I was mocking the poor fellow, when in fact I was falling, as abruptly as a boat may fetch up on a shoal, into the speech defect I had inherited from him—nature or nurture, who cares?

While my friends, helplessly obliged to eavesdrop, pretended to have a conversation in the cockpit, I was below, where it was dark and close, as if the clean, salty air had been sucked from the cabin. I stretched the mike on its snaky cord as far from my friends as possible, but the loudspeaker stayed put, broadcasting his invitation:

My father wanted me to come to him for the summer, in La Jolla.

I said I wouldn't.

My father said he missed me.

I said nothing.

My father tried to tell me he had a j-j-j-job.

I said, really, how nice. (I thought, how novel, what a piquant notion, my dad working for a living.)

My father said congratulations on the degree.

I wondered how he'd guessed I had one.

He said congratulations on the job in Turkey, did I remember he'd lived there once upon a time?

I said I remembered.

He asked did I have a "popsie" aboard with me?

I reddened; it was quiet in the cockpit; I said I had to get off now, this was too expensive, far too complicated.

He said my brother was coming to La Jolla to visit from

Washington State. Learned boy that I was, I didn't believe my father. I hadn't seen Toby for seven years.

My father said it again, Toby was right now on the road from Concrete, Washington, arriving in a couple of days.

I listened to static while gentle waves slapped the *Sea Witch*. He said he'd send airfare.

I said sure. I thought fat chance.

I borrowed ticket money from the yachtsman dad and hopped a hound (more accurately a Trailway—cheaper) in New York. This would be the place to detail the squalor of a cross-country summer bus journey from the noxious flats of Jersey to the uncompromising wasteland of Death Valley—you know the drill, you've ridden a bus, you've read about the Joads. Assume I was sad, hungry, and as funky as everyone else aboard our land yacht, our prairie schooner. The one constant in addition to the diesely whine while successive drivers went up through the gearbox—do-re-me-fa-sol-la-ti-do—and down—do-ti-la-sol . . . —was the question I kept asking myself: *How had this happened to me? Why was I here?*

You might think—noticing the books I was conspicuously reading and annotating, and I'm afraid you were meant to notice them and me—that the question *Why was I here?* was a Big Question and that I was questing for a vision from Sophocles, Erich Auerbach, Sartre, George Steiner. Boy oh boy, you think you know your aliens! I felt so apart from my fellow passengers that I believed I needed a visa to visit Earth. But at some point west of Gila Bend and east of El Centro, with the air-conditioning on the blink again, I commenced to reflect on the situation of La Jolla—seaside, wasn't it? Even a martyr had to take time off for a swim.

Hedonism, taking care of fun before taking care of business, was a legacy from my father. For this he had been thrown out of one boarding school after another, to the theatrical dismay of his mother and father, a Hartford, Connecticut, surgeon. For this he had also been thrown out of two colleges, neither of which, despite his testimony to the contrary, were fancy and ancient universities. For buying what he could not afford—sports cars and sports coats, Patek-Philippe wristwatches, dinners at Mike Romanoff's and 21, Leicas and Bolexes, Holland & Holland shotguns, whatever nice thing was around—he'd been fired from jobs. These jobs as an airplane designer (I know, I know: he was audacious) he had conned his way into with faked-up resumes. Getting fired would put him in a bad mood, so he'd buy more stuff; buying stuff intoxicated him, and so did booze. Drunk, he'd turn on his first wife, my mother and Toby's. After fourteen years of this, she told Dad to get lost, and I moved in with him. When I was seventeen, his second wife—her fortune and good mood seriously depressed by my old man—took a hike on him, and soon after that he took one on me. In the Wolff nuclear family, fission was all the rage.

Dad met me at the same bus station where he'd met Toby more than a week earlier. Visiting San Diego recently I was hard-pressed to find any site downtown as melodramatically seedy as my memory of that place, a garishly lit set dressed with tattoo parlors, bucket-of-blood bars, pawnshops, and, under the hard light of noon, my dad looking bewildered and lost. I had for many childhood years loved him recklessly, investing him with achievements and wisdom and powers beyond the reach of any mortal, and only a pinch less magnificent than the history and potential he had bestowed upon himself. Spare any father such impulsive love as I showered on that man. Later, when I became disillusioned, when I imagined that I understood Duke Wolff for what he really was—a deadbeat bullshit artist with a veneer of charm rubbed right through from negligent overexercise—I hated him, and like the love before it, that hate too was indulgent, exorbitant.

This June afternoon outside the bus depot, examining my father blinking behind the thick lenses of owlish Goldwater specs, I was too wary to indulge contempt. The eyeglasses, out of register with Duke's formerly stylish presentations, were the least of it. Even at his lowest he'd enjoyed flamboyant temperamental resources: flash and spritz and nonchalance. Now he seemed timid, dulled, hungover. No: that wasn't it either; I was all too inured to his hangovers, which used to provoke in my dad a manic snap, as though he'd decided that if this was as bad as it got, bring it on, let's start another IV Mount Gay rum drip. What I was seeing lumbering toward me was a crummy linenish jacket. This wasn't what I'd have expected: seersucker, maybe, or the soiled white linen suit that Sydney Greenstreet might sport—tits-up in the tropics and all that—but not this, some thing on whose behalf a thousand polyesters had lost their lives, some rag that needed a cleaning the day it was sold, tarted up with cheapjack brass crested buttons. From Duke's good old bad old days of smart tailoring, what a fall was here! Halting toward me was a zombie. Dad Wolff looked as though he'd been shot smack in the heart with about 500 cc of Thorazine. Talk about taking the edge off! He looked like they'd sawed through his brain.

My brother, Toby, fifteen, was with him, hanging back gingerly, vigilant. I felt like someone to whom something bad would soon happen; Toby looked like someone to whom it had already happened. This was the more alarming because he looked so wakeful and sharp. He had a strong, bony face, with steady eyes and a jutting chin. He was tall and lean, handsome, like our mother. He didn't appear vulnerable; he gave an impression of competence, but after all, he was a kid.

I hadn't seen Toby during the past seven years, but we'd recently been in touch by telephone and letter, and I knew that he'd had a rocky time of it with his stepfather. Coming across the country to see my only sibling, I'd phoned from a roadside diner to tell Duke which bus to meet and I'd reached Toby. He didn't know where our father had disappeared to. No sooner had Toby arrived than Dad had taken off with a woman friend in a fancy Italian car. He had left his teenaged son with a hotel phone number and a vague assurance that he'd return to La Jolla in a few days.

Behind the wheel of the hubby-mummy rented Pontiac, driving to La Jolla, Duke was stiff and tentative. This was unlike him. I remembered him as a bold driver, fast and cocksure, every little journey to the grocery store a high-octane adventure in squealing tires and red-lined rpms. Now Dad held to the slow lane, glancing anxiously in the rearview. His face had once been imposing, Mussolini-monumental; now his nose was bulbous, stippled with burst blood vessels. The few times he spoke, I saw that his false teeth, what he used to call China clippers, were loose against his gums. I had questions: Where had he gone, leaving Toby alone? How could he take time off from his job? Asking this question I gave the impression, meant to give it, that I didn't believe he had a job. How soon could he give me cash (I came down hard on *cash*, to distinguish it from a check or an IOU) to repay my yachtsman classmate's yachtsman daddy? These questions immediately returned us to our fundamental relationship: I was the hectoring (and mind-dullingly dull) parent; Duke was the irresponsible (and charmingly fun-loving) kid. The exchange didn't leave much for Toby to do, except sit in the backseat and study his fingers, as though he might be looking hard at his hole cards.

Duke was miserly with basic information—what exactly he did for a living, where he had gone "in the desert" (as he put it) or why. But as we approached La Jolla he became effusive about his "lady friend." This conversation had the effect of making Toby visibly uncomfortable, inasmuch as it had been my father's stated ambition, made explicit to Toby, to re-up with our mom if everything this summer went swimmingly, as of course it had to. This nutty scheme had (no, wonders never do cease) a certain appeal to my mother, who has had a lifelong weakness for nutty schemes. Her marriage to her second husband, like her marriage to Duke before that, was a disaster, and Duke after all did live in Southern California, and my mom, freezing up near the Canadian border, had always had, as she put it, "sand between my toes." But even this quixotic woman—who had decided a few years earlier that it was a sage idea to drive from Florida to Utah to explore for uranium without knowing what uranium was or why anyone wanted it—was on hold as far as a reenrollment in Dad's program was concerned, waiting to get a report card from Toby on Duke's attendance and comportment.

When we rolled up in front of a tiny bungalow east of Girard Avenue, my befuddlement increased. The woman who greeted us, as warily as Toby and I greeted her, was nothing like my father's type. He was drawn to palefaces, to blue eyes, to understated clothes. This woman was sunburnt brown, her leathery skin set off with much jangly jewelry. She wore many, many rings of the turquoise family, accessorizing showy peasant duds from south of the border, busy with appliqué and bold stitching. She wore, for God's sake, cowgirl boots ornamented with horsehair.

We stood beside the car shaking her ringed hand and listening to her bracelets ring like chimes; we admired her cactus garden; she got to listen to my father—and not, I suspected, for the first time—inflate my achievements at college and Toby's in high school; she didn't invite Toby or me inside. She didn't invite Dad inside either, but it was clear that inside was where he was going, and without his only children. He gave us rudimentary instructions to "my flat near the beach." Toby, manifestly eager to get away from where we were, assured me he knew the way. Duke said he'd be along soon, he'd bring home a nice supper. I asked how he'd get home from there, and he waved vaguely, mumbled "taxi." His lady friend seemed as unhappy as a person can be without flooding the earth with tears. Duke, by contrast, had abruptly come awake to joy; he was peppy, full of beans.

"Don't you two rascals go getting in t-t-t-trouble," he warned. "And if the manager badgers you about the rent, tell him to go f-f-f-f . . . "

"Go f-f-fish," I s-s-s-said.

Driving south through the attractive neighborhoods to our little second-floor studio apartment on Playa del Sur, fifty yards from the beach, I was mostly preoccupied with Toby, glad for the chance to be alone with him. He too relaxed, lit a Lucky Strike expertly with his lighter, inhaled intemperately, remarked that it had been an oddball visit so far. I asked him to steer while I lit a Camel expertly with my lighter, inhaled intemperately, and warned him that smoking was bad for his wind, especially if he planned to make a name for himself playing football at the Hill School back in Pennsylvania, where he was beginning on full scholarship in September.

My avuncular manner surprised me. I prided myself on being a laissez-faire kind of guy, I'll look out for me, you look out for you. Maybe I was practicing to become a teacher. Maybe I was out of my depth.

I unpacked my worldly goods—mostly books, a few jazz LPs (Bessie Smith, Bud Powell, the Miles Davis Quintet, with Coltrane) I carried with me everywhere—and Toby wanted to show me the beach. This generosity was all Wolff—sharing the good news, keeping alert to fun. By then it was late afternoon, and I worried that Dad might come home to an empty apartment, but Toby argued soberly that he didn't imagine Duke would be rushing home from his friend's house. I saw the wisdom in this hunch.

And so, dressed in long trousers and boat shoes and a white Lacoste tennis shirt, I accompanied Toby across Vista del Mar and Neptune Place to the Pump House, and down concrete steps to the beach. The first things I noticed were not the bitchin' sets of waves breaking way offshore, nor the surfers paddling way out there waiting to ride, nor the surfers with lots of white hair waxing their boards near the water's edge. I noticed, of course, the babes, and so did Toby.

"Hubba hubba," he said with reassuring irony, a family vice.

So we sat for a long time on a couple of hand towels, talking about the future, with our eyes cocked on the very here and now, avoiding the subject of our father. Toby was witty, resourceful, a hit parade of corny songs, which he was willing to sing out loud: "On the Wings of a Dove" and "Calendar Girl." He could do Chuck Berry's "Sweet Little Sixteen" and Hank Williams—"Hey, hey good-lookin', whatcha got cookin', howsabout cookin' something up with me?" He could do a Jimmy Rogers yodel in caricature of a locomotive whistle, and he knew the gospel classics, "The Old Rugged Cross." He did tenor lead, I did baritone. Even then, he remembered the words I'd forgot. The dynamite chicks stared frankly at us and our noise, with what I imagined that afternoon—but never imagined again— was interest.

It didn't get dark till nine or so. We waited. The landlord came asking for rent. He was kind, patient, pretended to believe that we didn't know where our old man could be found. He said it had gone on too long now, that Duke was months behind, that he had no choice. . . .

"Do what you have to do," I said, thinking about a sailboat waiting for me back east.

"Such a shame," he said and sighed, "a man of his attainments, with his education!"

"Uh-huh," I said.

When the landlord left, Toby said, "Tell me something. Did Dad really go to Yale?"

"What do you think?"

"So that would pretty much rule out his graduate degree from the Sorbonne?"

We laughed together, bless us.

Sometime after midnight we quit talking, stopped listening to my jazz records and Dad's Django Reinhardt and Joe Venuti. We'd eaten a couple of cans of Dinty Moore stew, knocked back some Canadian Club we'd found on a high shelf of the mostly bare cupboard. We'd each asked aloud where the other thought Duke might be. We'd wondered aloud whether we should look for him, but I was sure he was drunk, and he had always been a mean drunk, and I didn't want to find him. I didn't trust myself to keep my hands to myself while he sat on the edge of his bed in his boxers, snarling about how ungrateful I was, how grievously I had kicked him in the ass when he was down: *You're a real piece of work, aren't you?* I'd heard it; I didn't think I could hear it again, especially if it came to be Toby's turn.

A couple of hours before dawn his lady friend phoned. She was hysterical, said she didn't know what to do, he wouldn't leave, wouldn't move, wouldn't speak. He'd rock back and forth weeping.

"You've got to get him out of here. I can't take this. What if my husband comes snooping around?"

So I phoned the police. By the time Toby and I got there, the police had called for an ambulance. Dad was breathing, but save for the technicality of being alive, he was gone from this world. His lady friend too said, as so many ex-bosses, ex-friends, ex-wives, creditors, teachers, doctors, parole officers before and after had said, *A man with his educational attainments, what a pity!*

They checked him into Scripps Memorial Hospital. The police had investigated his wallet and he had Blue Cross. Now *this* was a shock, because he had Blue Cross owing to the fact that he also had a job! Just as he'd said. He worked for General Dynamics Astronautics. By sunup I knew this, and knew as well that he was catatonic, and roughly what catatonia was. He would be removed that afternoon to a "more appropriate facility," and I could guess what that would be. As obdurately as my heart had hardened, I heard myself telling the doctor to tell Dad his sons were here for him, we were behind him all the way. Toby nodded.

"Well," the doctor said, "he has said a few words. He keeps asking for a woman who lives in town. Could you help out with this, maybe let her know he wants to see her?"

"No," I said.

That morning I worked out a deal with the landlord. On principle he wouldn't let us stay in the apartment on which so much rent was due, but he'd let me lease, in my name, an identical unit down the exterior hall, same monthly rent but this time he required an up-front security deposit, first and last month in cash or by cashier's check by the end of business tomorrow.

I borrowed it from a classmate, the roommate of the son of the yachtsman dad from whom I'd borrowed my bus fare. Tangled, wot? It took a boy of my educational attainments to keep all those debts straight, all the lines of credit, but a boy of my educational attainments also knew how to cash in on sympathy. My classmate friend cabled the money from New York that afternoon, and that night Toby and I moved our father's entirely unpaid-for worldly goods to our new residence.

Drunk on resourcefulness, I bought a car and found a job the very next day. The car caught my eye on the lot of Balboa

Auto Sales. I'm confident of the name of the dealer because I still have a copy of my stiff reply from Istanbul to a bill collector in San Diego (Hi there, Mr. Ben D. Warren!) begging for the final $150 of the $300 purchase price on a '52 Ford convertible, cream, with torn red vinyl upholstery and bald whitewall tires and an appetite for oil that gave my jaunty wreck a range of about three miles between lube-stops, which made the drive to Tijuana, a popular excursion in the coming weeks, a hardship that only the senoritas of the rowdier cantinas could ameliorate. Ask Toby: he was in charge of oil changing, while I was in charge of drinking and whoring.

The job was easier to cop than the automobile. I simply went to Dad's employer, on the theory that they needed to replace him, and offered my services. A few weeks before in Princeton, getting my diploma, I'd suspected life was going to go smoothly for me, but this . . . *this* was silky! To build rockets during the age of the putative missile gap, the government had contracted with General Dynamics Astronautics to supply Atlas ICBMs at cost-plus. Now cost-plus, I don't have to tell you, is one sweet deal. The greater the cost, the greater the plus, so personnel basically threw money at me when I walked through its door with a bachelor's degree in English Literature. Every time I opened my mouth to mention courses I'd taken—history, American civilization, Spanish—they tossed in another jackpot, so that by day's end I was an engineering writer for more than eight hundred a month, with an advance from the credit union and a complete understanding of how my father had found a job with these cheerful jokers. Don't you miss the Cold War!

Dad was embalmed in an academy of laughter down in Chula Vista, not much of a detour from my weekend line of march to Tijuana. Toby and I were permitted to visit only on Saturdays, which suited my schedule fine, and when we visited he behaved like his old self, which, on the best day of his life, did not display a mastery of your everyday parenting skills. He seemed oblivious to any inconvenience he might have caused his sons, made no mention of the carnage of Toby's first week in La Jolla. Quotidian challenges were beneath his notice: whether he'd lost his job (he had), how much longer his insurance would support his treatment (not long enough), by what transport we'd conveyed ourselves to our audience with him (he did fret about a car "I had to desert in the desert," a play on words that amused him so exceedingly that he neglected the situation's starker implication, soon enough to weigh heavily on him).

We met a few of his new friends, men and women jollier than I would have expected, but their serenity might have been an outcome of the electric shock therapy Duke resolutely and justly resisted. He was busy with workshop therapy, making a leather portfolio into which he burned my initials. This was a difficult gift to receive, and to hold now.

Not least because it fell into a category of assets—personalized keepsakes—that opened a painful fissure between Toby and me. One thing, and it was a *thing,* was uppermost on my father's mind when my brother and I visited his asylum in Chula Vista. This was a silver cigarette lighter inscribed to him in London after the blitz by friends in the RAF when he was in England on behalf of North American to deliver P-51 Mustangs. He wanted that lighter; jeepers, did he *desire* that silver lighter; did we grasp that the lighter MATTERED to him? He decided that we had lost it during our move from one apartment to another. Oh, was he disappointed! His new friends would like to see that inscribed silver lighter, and he'd like to show it to them. Why didn't we just run back to La Jolla and find it, "chop-chop"?

It's amazing what kids—even kids as old as I was then, old enough to buy a car on the installment plan and to sign a lease—will accept as the way of the world. I don't mean merely that kids are subject to arbitrary tyrannies, though they are; I mean that until I had sons I never really understood how emotionally derelict my father was. I judged the cost of his selfishness on an empirical scale, by the measurable havoc he inflicted on me. It wasn't till I had sons that I began to understand that such lunatic solipsism as Duke's shook the rudiments of his sons' worlds, misaligned the paths connecting us, upset proportion, priority, ratio, reason itself.

How else explain us searching together the fifty-foot walkway connecting those two apartments, as well as the shrubs below that walkway, as well as our new apartment? What warped sense of duty provoked us to knock on the door of the new tenants' apartment during the dinner hour to persuade them that we needed to search every inch of their abode for a lost cigarette lighter? And failing to find it, to phone the car rental company, the very company that was seeking payment from our father, to ask if a silver cigarette lighter had been found in one of their Pontiacs?

I think now, considering my own dear sons, beginning at last to fathom how difficult it is to be anyone's son, that our father drove us insane that summer. I'll speak for myself: he pushed me to the edge and over it.

My life with Toby seemed on the surface, subtracting weekend visits to the loony bin in Chula Vista and the brothels of Tijuana, workaday. After staring at my pencils and at my colleagues staring at their pencils for six of the eight hours I "worked" in a hangar, the Ford would stumble up the coast to La Jolla, trailing cloud banks of exhaust, a whole weather system. I drove with the torn top up to shelter myself from the black fog that swirled around me when I was stopped in traffic.

But there I go, looking at the dark side, getting gothic on you. At day's end there was home, simple but clean. And the beach. Ah, Windansea! Remember my first visit there, my eyes as big as plates, those surfer chicks, what Dad called popsies?

Well, I hadn't completed my second walk from the Pump House south toward Big Rock Reef when a teen approached me.

"Hey!" she said. Her toenails were painted vivid red. Her hair was ... guess what color. She was ... (Did you guess pretty?)

I cradled my paperback. "Hey, yourself," I came back.

"You from around here?" she asked.

I chuckled. "No. No, not at all, just visiting on my way to Istanbul."

"Is that on the beach?" (No, of course she didn't ask that. There's no call to get snotty here, just because I was about to have my heart broken.) "Huh?" (*That's* what she said.)

"Are you from around here?" was my trenchant rejoinder.

She was, she said, she was. And her business with me was to invite me to a keg party that night down in Pacific Beach. She was glad I could make it. We'd have a lot of fun. Was I sure I had the address written down? She checked what I'd written on the title page of Camus's *The Stranger*.

"Thing is, me and my friends need some cash to front the keg."

Thing was, I didn't have any cash in my bathing suit. Could I bring it when I came? No? Okay, hang on, don't go anywhere, I'll just run home and get it, which I did. She was waiting by a VW van, pretty much holding her pretty hand out.

I don't have to tell you how the party went. What party, eh? What Surf Boulevard in Pacific Beach?

Seven years later, reading Tom Wolfe's title essay in *The Pump House Gang*, I felt a full flush of shame rise from my toes. The keg scam was a chestnut among the surfers and surfer-babes at Windansea. But that was the least of my mortification there. Frank laughter was the worst of it. Back home at the Jersey shore or on the beach at Watch Hill, blinking contemplatively behind my groundbreaking round, silver-framed glasses (so far ahead of the curve that the nickname "granny glasses" hadn't yet been invented), in my navy polo shirt to hide my chubby tits, in my Brooks Brothers madras bathing costume, by George I was a stud muffin! Here, carrying a Great Book past those hep longboarders in their nut-hugger nylon suits with competition stripes, I was a freaking joke!

So where, during these humiliating hours after work, was Toby? Safe inside, at his books, writing essays I assigned him. It took him a while to forgive me for practicing my apprentice teaching skills on him. To prepare him for the exactions of a classical education at the Hill School, I obliged him to do a day's work while I did a day's work, to read a book a day and write an essay every week: "Blindness and Insight in *King Lear* and the *Oedipus Tyrannus*"; "The Boundaries of Sea and River: Liberty and Bondage in *Moby Dick* and *Huckleberry Finn*." I guess what I knew best came in pairs. It was crazy the hoops I made my beleaguered, injured, perplexed little brother jump through. He wrote them; he was a better reader and writer for them. But I was a tin-pot despot, as arbitrary in my edicts as Duke sending us on a treasure hunt for his fire-stick. No wonder Toby stole from his father and lied to me.

Did you guess he'd had the sacred lighter all along? Used it to spark up that Lucky during our ride in the Pontiac from the leathery, jangly lady's bungalow to Dad's sea-near studio apartment.

He slept on a pull-out sofa bed in our one-roomer, and mid-August, when the alarm clock woke me for work, I saw the stupid, pretty thing on the floor beneath his blue jeans. In the sullen light of dawn, I made out an inscription engraved on it. My father's initials in elegant sans serif. No RAF boys, of course, but another name for sure, a new engraving, commissioned up on Girard Avenue, TOBY. I remembered the hours we'd spent together hunting for that costly goddamned thing, Toby's helpful suggestions where next to search: the beach, Dad's suit pockets, maybe it had fallen out of Dad's trouser pocket into one of the shoes in his closet?

That morning was awful, and I want to pull a curtain across it. Duke was coming "home" from Chula Vista that afternoon; I was meant to pick him up after work. I didn't know what we'd all do, where we'd live, how we'd sit together in a room, how we'd look at one another, what in the world we were supposed to do now. What I knew for sure: Toby hated us both, his father and his brother. I knew why he hated the one, but not the other. Now I think I know all I'll ever know about that aspect of that summer, and all I want to say to Toby is, Forgive me. Even though he has pardoned me, and himself, just this last time, Forgive me.

I fetched Duke; he raged at Toby. We sent my brother home to my mother on a bus. As bad as it was between my father and me, after Toby left it got worse. My father wasn't allowed to drink—all that medication—but of course he drank. How many days did the nightmare last? Few, I think. He tried to talk me into staying with him instead of going to Turkey. I managed not to laugh in his face. My work at Astro was a mercy, got me out of the apartment. My infamy on the beach was a joy, got me away from him. And I'd invited a couple of visitors, Princeton friends. One was coming up from Mexico in a Cadillac hearse, the other, from whom I'd borrowed the money to rent our apartment, was in the navy, coming to San Diego to join his aircraft carrier. I'd paid him back; breaking a Wolff family tradition, I'd repaid all my debts to friends that summer.

While my erstwhile classmate with the hearse was visiting, Duke was arrested in San Diego. For a wonder, he wasn't drunk and he wasn't up to mischief. He was buying breakfast food at a late-hours store and he'd made a U-turn in my Ford. He'd stuttered when the policeman stopped him. They took him downtown. It went hard on him. By the time my friend and I arrived in the hearse, they were ready to let him go. This was the old police station, gone now, surrendered to gentrification down near Seaport Village. Back then it had a holding tank, and my father was in it, stone terrified. Before they let him go they checked with Sacramento. They got back a complicated story. It went very hard on him, grand theft auto for the Abarth-Allemagne roadster in the desert, burned and sand-blasted by a desert storm. My father wanted me to go bail for him, but he wouldn't promise to show up in court, or even to stay in California.

I didn't go bail; I went to Istanbul.

Then was then. I try to explain to my wife, to my sons. They try to understand, and they've done a good job of it. The only way I know how to explain is on the page. It's a bitch getting the tone right. Now, writing this, I feel jumpy again after many years of feeling a warm embrace of resignation. That's okay. These shifts aren't spurious, I believe. Family stories are always fluid, and to be emotionally exact is to be inconsistent. Toby and I have talked a lot about this. We've talked a lot about a lot. We talk all the time, and as good as a friendship can get, that's how good I think ours is. When I told him I'd found the apartment where we spent the summer of '61, he seemed interested enough, but not *too* interested. When I told him I'd taken snapshots of the apartment, he didn't ask for copies.

He lifted a trinket that summer, my father lifted a car. Stealing: Jesus, Princeton had an honor code, it seemed like a really big deal, where could stealing lead? Where did it send my dad? That pal who loaned me money? The one I'd invited to visit just about the time my dad disappeared into the system and I fled to Asia Minor? He stole my dad's best shoes. He told me this in an expensive automobile driving to a fancy dinner party at a gentlemen's club on Society Hill in Philadelphia. We were purring along in his Mercedes, snug in our navy blue topcoats and leather gloves and cashmere scarves. It was snowing. I had mentioned a few hours earlier to my old chum that I'd been back in La Jolla after all these years, back to the apartment at Playa del Sur. He'd seemed uncomfortable to hear this, and I understood his discomfort to stem from the disgrace visited on my family name that summer.

"I've been in that apartment," my friend said.

"I don't think so," I said. "You were supposed to visit me there, but then Dad went to jail and I went to . . ."

". . . to Istanbul," my amigo finished. "No, I've been there."

"I don't believe . . ."

"Hush," he said. "Let me tell you."

We were purring along the Schuylkill River now, and the headlights from cars on the expressway dimly lit the black water. Big wet flakes flew at our windshield; the dash glowed greenly. The car was heavy and solid; we were heavy and solid. My friend had been successful in business, investing prudently but shrewdly the inheritances of people who trusted his judgment and honor. His voice was measured. He told me. He told me how he had got the landlord at Playa del Sur, who didn't yet know I'd run out on him just after running out on my father, to let him in. How he had waited there. How he had had a beer or two from the fridge, and then a glass or two or three of the Wild Turkey I was drinking back then. How he had listened to the record player. How he had stretched out and taken a nap. How he had wanted to walk down to the beach, but the landlord wouldn't give him a key. How he had waited and waited for me to come back from work. How he began to feel pissed off, put-upon. How he couldn't wait any longer; the *Saratoga* was cruising west; he was due aboard. How he had noticed my dad's shoes in the closet, really nice shoes, beautifully cared for, Church shoes, dark brown cap-toes. How something—boredom?—had urged him to try those shoes on his own feet. How they had fit as though they were made for him. How he had stolen them.

"And there was a jacket, too. Nice tweed job. I don't think it was your jacket. I didn't recognize it from college."

"What color?" I wanted to know.

"Greenish, heather, I guess you'd call it. Nubby but *soft*, a really nice tweed sport coat."

"It wouldn't have been mine," I said. "I didn't own a jacket that fits that description," I lied.

"How about that," my old friend said.

"What the hell," I said, "that was a long time ago."

You see, in Philadelphia, so far from Windansea that winter night, at last, I was finished with all this, who stole what from whom, who borrowed and who paid, who was owed what. I'm finally at the end of all that. This time I mean it. This time, again, I really mean it.

TOBIAS WOLFF

Like his brother, Geoffrey, Tobias Wolff (1945–) has had a productive and distinguished career as both writer and teacher. He is the author of three highly praised short story collections, and his work has appeared in such publications as the Atlantic Monthly, Harper's, The New Yorker, *and the* New York Times Magazine. *The recipient of numerous awards, prizes, and fellowships, Wolff became a professor of English at Stanford University in 1997.*

Tobias Wolff has written two brilliant memoirs. The first, This Boy's Life, *was published in 1989 and tells the story of the childhood he spent with his mother after his parents' divorce. While the more prominent figure in* This Boy's Life *is Wolff's volatile and abusive stepfather, his father, Arthur, makes several brief appearances and there is no mistaking the similarity between father and son in the boy's developing character: he lies to everyone, steals from friends, and, in a breathtaking act of self-invention, fabricates transcripts and letters of recommendation so as to gain admission and a scholarship to an exclusive East Coast prep school —a school from which he was later expelled, just as his father had been expelled from a similar school in his youth.*

In 1994 Tobias Wolff published in Pharaoh's Army: Memories of the Lost War, *which picks up where his earlier memoir left off and describes his experiences as an army lieutenant in the Vietnam War. Unlike his father, whose inflated claims of wartime service were oft-repeated, Wolff fails even to mention in* Pharaoh *that he was a member of the Green Berets.*

"Civilian," first published in the Threepenny Review *and included as the next-to-last chapter of* In Pharaoh's Army, *illustrates even more pointedly Tobias's growing resolve to contrast his life with that of his father, to replace with solidity what his father had spun only from words. The events of "Civilian" take place in the summer of 1968; a year earlier Wolff had spent an awkward and uncomfortable night with his father when he dropped in to see him unannounced on his way overseas—the first time in six years the two had seen each other. The chronograph mentioned in the text is treated more fully by Geoffrey in* The Duke of Deception, *wherein he reveals that his father paid for the watch with a bad check and two years in prison. As did Geoffrey in "Heavy Lifting," Tobias is also describing in "Civilian" the last time he saw his father—who died almost literally in a house upon the sand.*

Civilian

I was discharged in Oakland the day after I stepped off the plane. The personnel officer asked me if I would consider signing up for another tour. I could go back as a captain, he said. Captain? I said. Captain of *what?*

He didn't try to argue with me, just made me watch him take his sweet time fiddling with the file folders on his desk before handing over my walking papers and separation pay. I went back to the bachelor officers quarters and paced my room, completely at a loss. For the first time in four years I was absolutely free to follow my own plan. The trouble was, I didn't have one. When the housekeeping detail asked me to leave I packed up and caught a taxi to San Francisco.

For over a week I stayed at a hotel in the Tenderloin, hitting the bars, sleeping late, and wandering the city, sharply aware that I was no longer a soldier and feeling that change not the way I'd imagined, as freedom and pleasure, but as aimlessness and solitude.

It wasn't that I missed the army. I didn't. But I'd been a soldier since I was eighteen, not a good soldier but a soldier, and linked by that fact to other soldiers, even those long dead. When, browsing through a bookstore, I came across a collection of letters sent home by Southern troops during the Civil War, I heard their voices as those of men I'd known. Now I was nothing in particular and joined to no one.

In the afternoons I put myself through forced marches down to the wharf, through Golden Gate Park, out to the Cliff House. I walked around the Haight, seedier than a year before, afflicted like the faces on the street with a trashed, sullen quality. Sniffling guys in big overcoats hunched in doorways, hissing at passersby, though not at me: a clue that I was radiating some signal weirdness of my own. No hug patrols in evidence. I went there once and didn't go back.

As I walked I kept surprising myself in the windows I passed, a gaunt hollow-eyed figure in button-down shirt and khakis and one of my boxy Hong Kong sport coats. Without cap or helmet my head seemed naked and oversized. I looked newly hatched, bewildered, without history.

There might have been some affectation in this self-imposed quarantine. I didn't have to stay in a seedy room in San Francisco, broodingly alone; I could have gone on to Washington. My mother and brother gave every sign of wanting to welcome me home, and so did my friends, and my ex-fiancée Vera. She had parted ways with my successor, Leland, soon after they took up together, and her most recent letters had spoken of her wish to try again with me. All I had to do was get on a plane and within hours I would be surrounded by the very people I'd been afraid of not seeing again. But I stayed put.

I thought of my friends and family as a circle, and this was exactly the picture that stopped me cold and kept me where I was. It didn't seem possible to stand in the center of that circle. I did not feel equal to it. I felt morally embarrassed. Why this was so I couldn't have said, but a sense of deficiency, even blight, had taken hold of me. In Vietnam I'd barely noticed it, but here, among people who did not take corruption and brutality for granted, I came to understand that I did, and that this set me apart. San Francisco was an open, amiable town, but I had trouble holding up my end of a conversation. I said horrifying things without knowing it until I saw the reaction. My laugh sounded bitter and derisive even to me. When people asked me the simplest questions about myself I became cool and remote. Lonesome as I was, I made damn sure I stayed that way.

One day I took a bus over to Berkeley. I had the idea of applying for school there in the fall and it occurred to me I might get a break on admission and fees because of my father being a California resident. It wasn't easy to collect hard intelligence about the old man, but since the state had kept him under lock and key for over two years, and on parole ever since, I figured his home of record was one thing we could all agree on.

I never made it to the admissions office. There was some sort of gathering in Sproul Plaza, and I stopped to listen to one speaker and then another. Though it was sunny I got cold in the stiff bay breeze and sat down by a hedge. The second speaker started reading a list of demands addressed to President Johnson. People were walking around, eating, throwing Frisbees for dogs with handkerchiefs around their necks. On a blanket next to me a bearded guy and a languorous Chinese girl were passing a joint back and forth. The girl was very beautiful.

Microphone feedback kept blaring out the speaker's words, but I got the outline. Withdrawal of our troops from Vietnam. Recognition of Cuba. Immediate commutation of student loans. Until all these demands were met, the speaker said he considered himself in a state of unconditional war with the United States government.

I laughed out loud.

The bearded guy on the blanket gave me a look. He said something to the Chinese girl, who turned and peered at me over the top of her sunglasses, then settled back on her elbows. I asked him what he thought was so interesting and he said something curt and dismissive and I didn't like it, didn't like this notion of his that he could scrutinize me and make a judgment and then brush me off as if I didn't exist. I said a few words calculated to let him know that he would be done with me when I was done with him, and then he stood up and I stood up. His beautiful girlfriend pulled on his hand. He ignored her. His mouth was moving in his beard. I hardly knew what he was saying, but I understood his tone perfectly and it was intolerable to me. I answered him. I could hear the rage in my voice and it pleased me and enraged me still more. I gave no thought to my words, just said whatever came to me. I hated him. If at that moment I could have turned his heart off, I would have. Then I saw that he had gone quiet. He stood there looking at me. I heard the crazy things I was saying and realized, even as I continued to yell at him, that he was much younger than I'd thought, a boy with ruddy cheeks his beard was too sparse to hide. When I managed to stop myself I saw that the people around us were watching me as if I were pathetic. I turned away and walked toward Sather Gate, my face burning.

I got to Manhattan Beach just after sundown, and surprised my father once again. He was in his bathrobe, about to pop some frozen horror into the oven. I told him to keep it on ice and let me stand him to dinner at the restaurant where we'd eaten the year before. He said he wasn't feeling exactly jake, thought he might be coming down with something, but after we had a few drinks he let himself be persuaded of the tonic potential of a night on the town.

So we gave it another try, and this time we got it right. Again we stuffed ourselves with meat and drink, and again my father grew immense with pleasure and extended his benevolence to everyone in range. The old rich rumble entered his voice; the stories began, stories of his youth and the companions of his youth, rioters whose deeds succeeded in his telling to the scale of legend. He found occasion to invoke the sacred names (Deerfield; New Haven; Bones; the Racquet Club), but this time I managed to get past the lyrics and hear his music, a formal yet droll music in which even his genuine pretensions sounded parodic. I let him roll. In fact I egged him on. I didn't have to believe him; it was enough to look across the table and see him there, swinging to his own beat.

I had come back to Manhattan Beach, I surely understood even then, because there could no longer be any question of judgment between my father and me. He'd lost his claim to the high ground, and so had I. We could take each other now without any obligation to approve or disapprove or model our virtues. It was freedom, and we both grabbed at it. It was the best night we'd ever had.

I paid the next morning. So did he, and then some. Late into the day he was still in bed, flushed and hot, and I finally realized that he really had been coming down with something. I called his doctor, who stopped by the apartment on his way home that evening, diagnosed the flu, and prescribed something to bring the fever down. He wouldn't let me pay, not after my father sneaked it in that I was just back from Vietnam. I followed the doctor to the door, insisting, wagging my wallet, but he wouldn't hear of it. When he left I went back to the old man's bedroom and found him laughing, and then I started laughing too. Couple of crooks.

That night and the next day he was too sick to do much of anything but sleep. In his sleep he moaned and talked to himself. I came into his room now and then and stood over him in the dim slatted light cast by the street lamp. Big as he was, he looked as if he'd been toppled, felled. He slept like a child, knees drawn up almost to his chest. Sometimes he whimpered. Sometimes he put his thumb in his mouth. When I saw him like that he seemed much older than his sixty years, closer to the end and more alone than I wanted to think about.

Then he started coming out of it. He liked being babied, so he wore his invalid droop and mopery as long as I let him. When I helped him in and out of bed he groaned and mewed and walked as if his joints had rusted shut. He had me buy him an ice bag, which he wore like a tam-o'-shanter, his eyes tremulous with self-pity. All day long he called out his wishes in a small desolate voice—cheese and crackers, please, some Gouda on stone-ground Wheat Thins would be swell, with a little Tabasco and red onion, if I wouldn't mind. Palm hearts with cream cheese, *por favor,* and this time could I skip the paprika and just sprinkle a little onion salt on them? Thanks a mil! Ginger ale, old son, over ice, and would it be too much trouble to *crush* the ice?

He was relentless and without shame. Once he pushed me too far and I said, "Jesus, Duke, suffer in silence awhile, okay?" This was the first time in my life I'd called him by that name, and the sound of myself saying it made me cringe. But he didn't object. It probably reassured him that I was ready to vacate any outstanding claims on him as his child and accept a position as his crony. I never called him Duke again. I wanted to feel as if I still had a father out there, however singular the terms.

He started feeling better after the second day, and I was almost sorry. I liked taking care of him. I'd blitzed the apartment with cleansers, stocked his cabinets with cans of stew and hash and clam chowder and the treats he favored—Swedish flatbread, palm hearts, macadamia nuts. I had a new muffler put on the Cadillac. While he was laid up sick the smallest acts felt purposeful and worthwhile, and freed me from the sodden sensation of uselessness. Out running errands, I found myself taking pleasure in the salt smell and hard coastal light, the way the light fired the red-tiled roofs and cast clean-edged shadows as black as tar. In the afternoons I brought a chair and a book out to the sidewalk and faced the declining sun, chest bared to the warmth, half listening for the old man's voice through the open window at my back. I was reading *Portnoy's Complaint.* Geoffrey had sent it to me some time before and I'd never been able to get past the first few pages, but now it came to life for me. I read it in a state of near collapse, tears spilling down my cheeks. It was the first thing I'd finished in months.

My father took note of my absorption. He wanted to know what was so fascinating. I let him have it when I was through, and that evening he told me he'd never read anything so disgusting—not that he'd finished it. Come on, I said. He had to admit it was funny. Funny! How could such a thing be funny? He was baffled by the suggestion.

"Okay," I said. "What do you think *is* funny, then?"

"What b-book, you mean?"

"Book. Movie. Whatever."

He looked at me suspiciously. He was stretched out on the couch, eating a plate of scrambled eggs. "*Wind in the Willows,*" he said. Now there was a book that showed you didn't have to be dirty to be humorous. He happened to have a copy on hand and would be willing to prove his point.

More than willing; I knew he was dying to read it aloud. He'd done this before, to Geoffrey and me, one night in La Jolla seven years earlier. It was a dim memory, pleasant and rare in that it held the three of us together. Of the book itself I recalled nothing except an atmosphere of treacly Englishness. But I couldn't say no.

He started to read, smiling rhapsodically, the ice bag on his head. I was bored stiff until Toad of Toad Hall made his entrance and began his ruinous love affair with the automobile.

"What dust clouds shall spring up behind me as I speed on my reckless way!" he cried. "What carts shall I fling carelessly into the ditch in the wake of my magnificent onset!" Toad had my attention. I found him funny, yes, but also familiar in a way that put me on alert.

Toad is arrested for stealing a car, and in the absence of any remorse is sentenced to twenty years in a dungeon. He escapes dressed as a washerwoman and manages to commandeer the very car he was imprisoned for stealing, after the owner offers a lift to what he thinks is a weary old crone. Toad pins the Samaritan with an elbow and seizes the wheel. "Washerwoman indeed!" he shouts. "Ho, ho! I am the Toad, the motorcar snatcher, the prison-breaker, the Toad who always escapes! Sit still, and you shall know what driving really is, for you are in the hands of the famous, the skillful, the entirely fearless Toad!"

By now I knew where the déjà vu came from. My father was Toad. He wasn't playing Toad, he *was* Toad, and not only Toad the audacious, Toad the shameless and incorrigible, but, as the story gave occasion, good-hearted Toad, hospitable Toad, Toad for whom his friends would risk their very lives. I'd never seen my father so forgetful of himself, so undefended, so confiding.

He read the whole book. It took hours. I got up now and then to grab a beer and refill his glass of ginger ale, stretch, fix a plate of crackers and cheese, but quietly, so he wouldn't break stride. The night deepened around us. Cars stopped going by. We were entirely at home, alone in an island of lamplight. I didn't want anything to change.

But Toad couldn't keep up the pace. The hounds of respectability were on his neck, and finally they brought him down. He had no choice but to make a good act of contrition and promise to keep the peace, live within his means, be good.

My father closed the book. He put it down and looked over at me, shaking his head at this transparent subterfuge. He wasn't fooled. He knew exactly what Toad's promise was worth.

I'd meant only to touch down in Manhattan Beach, but day followed day and I was still there. In the afternoons I sat by the water and read. At night I went to a bar down the road, then came home and sat up with the old man, listening to music and shooting the breeze. We talked about everything except Vietnam and prison. Only once did he mention his life there, when I asked about a livid scar on his wrist. He told me he'd been cut in a fight over which television program to watch, and that stupid as it sounded he'd had no choice, and didn't regret it. I never heard him mention another inmate, never heard him say "the joint" or even "Chino." He gave the impression it hadn't touched him.

I was drinking too much. One night he asked me if I didn't want to give the old noggin a breather, and I stalked out and came back even drunker than usual. I wanted it understood that he could expect nothing of me, as I expected nothing of him. He didn't bring it up again. He seemed to accept the arrangement, and I found it congenial enough that I could even imagine going on in this way, the two of us in our own circle, living on our own terms. I had nearly six thousand dollars in the bank, a year's worth of unspent salary and hazardous duty pay. If I enrolled in the local community college I could milk another three hundred a month from the GI Bill. They didn't check to see if you actually went to class—all you had to do was sign up. I could get a place of my own nearby. Start writing. By the time my savings and subsidies ran out, I'd have a novel done. Just a thought, but it kept coming. I mentioned it to the old man. He seemed to like the idea.

It was a bad idea, conceived in laziness and certain to end miserably for both of us. Instead of masquerading as a student I needed to *be* a student, because I was uneducated and lacked the discipline to educate myself. Same with the novel. The novel wouldn't get written, the money would all get spent, and then what? I had intimations of the folly of this plan, though I persisted in thinking about it.

I'd been in town about a week when I met a woman on the beach. She was reading and I was reading, so it seemed natural to compare notes. Her name was Jan. She did speech therapy in the local schools. She had four or five years on me, maybe more. Her nose was very long and thin and she wore her blond hair mannishly close. She was calm, easy to talk to, but when I asked her out she frowned and looked away. She picked up a handful of sand, let it run through her fingers. "All right," she said.

Grand Illusion was showing at the local art theater. We got there early and strolled to the end of the street and back until they opened the doors. Jan wore a white dress that rustled as she walked and made her skin look dark as chocolate. She had the coolness and serenity of someone who has just finished a long swim. As we were going inside I noticed that her zipper had slipped a few inches. Hold on, I said, and slowly pulled it up again, standing close behind her, my nose almost in her hair.

I had seen *Grand Illusion* before, many times. My friend Laudie and I had memorized Pierre Fresnay's death scene with Erich von Stroheim and used to play it out to impress our dates. But that night I couldn't even follow the plot, I was so conscious of this woman beside me, her scent, the touch of her shoulder against mine, the play of light on her bare arms. At last I figured do or die and took her hand. She didn't pull away. A little while later she laced her fingers through mine.

When the lights came on I was awkward and so was she. We agreed to stop somewhere for a drink. She didn't have any place in mind so I took her to the bar where I'd been going, an alleged discotheque frequented by former servicemen and some still in uniform. The moment I saw Jan inside the place, in her white dress and cool, manifest sanity, I saw it for what it was—a hole. But she claimed she liked it and insisted on staying.

We'd just gotten our drinks when a hand fell on my shoulder.

"Hey, Cap'n, you trying to keep this lovely lady all to yourself? No fuckin way, man."

Dicky. Dicky and his sidekick, Sleepy.

Chairs scraped. Lighters and cigarettes and glasses descended on the table, a pitcher of beer. They were with us. Jan kept trying not to stare at Dicky, and kept failing. Dicky was clean-shaven but he had a big curly mustache tattooed above his lip. I couldn't tell whether his intention was serious or jocular, if he actually thought he resembled a person with a mustache or was just riffing on the idea. He claimed to have been with a marine recon team near the DMZ, even to have operated in North Vietnam. I didn't know what Sleepy's story was.

They were there every night, hopping tables. The last time I'd seen them they were trying to break into Sleepy's car after he'd locked the keys inside. Dicky rigged up a wire of some kind and when that didn't work right away he went into a rage and smashed out the driver's window, but not before he'd kicked some dents into the door panel and broken off the radio antenna. Sleepy stood there with the rest of us who'd come out of the bar to watch, and didn't say a word.

Dicky caught Jan looking at him. He looked back at her. "So," he said, "how'd you get to know this carbon? Hey, just kidding, the cap'n here's numero fuckin uno."

I told him we'd been to see a film together.

"*Film?* You saw a *film?* What happen, your specs get dirty? Hey, Sleepy, you hear that? The cap'n says he saw a film, I say, What happen, your specs get dirty?"

"I laughed," Sleepy said, "didn't you hear me laugh?"

"No, I didn't hear you laugh. Speak up, asshole! So what film did you see, Cap'n?" For some reason sweat was pouring out of his hair and down his face.

I gave Dicky the short description of *Grand Illusion*.

He was interested. "That was some bad shit, man, Whirl War One. All that bob wire and overcoats and shit, livin like a buncha moles, come out, take a look around, *eeeeeeeerrr, boom,* your fuckin head gets blown off. No way, man. No fuckin way. I couldn't get behind that shit *at all*. I mean, millions of assholes going south, right? Millions! It's like you take the whole city of L. A., tell em, Hey, muchachos, here's the deal, you just run into that bob wire over there and let those other fuckers put holes in you. Big Bertha, man. And poison gas, what about that mustard shit, you think you could handle that?"

Jan had her eyes on me. "Were you a captain?"

I'd told her I'd just come back from Vietnam, but nothing else. I shook my head no.

"But I tell you straight," Dicky said, "no bullshit. If they'd of had me and my team back in Whirl War One we coulda turned that shit around *real* fast. When Heinrich starts waking up in the morning with Fritzy's dick in his hand, maybe they decide to do their yodeling and shit at home, leave these other people the fuck alone, you hear what I'm saying?"

Sleepy's chin was on his chest. He said, "I hear you, man."

"What were you, then?" Jan said to me.

"First lieutenant."

"Same thing," Dicky said. "Lieutenant, cap'n, all the same—hang you out to dry every fuckin one of em."

"That's not true."

"The fuck it isn't. Fuckin officers, man."

"I didn't hang anybody out to dry. Except maybe another officer," I said. "A captain, as a matter of fact."

Dicky ran a napkin over his wet face and looked at it, then at me. Jan was also looking at me.

As soon as I started the story I knew I shouldn't tell it. It was the story about Captain Kale wanting to bring the Chinook into the middle of the hooches, and me letting him do it. I couldn't find the right tone. My first instinct was to make it somber and regretful, to show how much more compassionate I was than the person who had done this thing, how far I had evolved in wisdom since then, but it came off sounding phony. I shifted to a clinical, deadpan exposition. This proved even less convincing than the first pose, which at least acknowledged that the narrator had a stake in his narrative. The neutral tone was a lie, also a bore.

How do you tell such a terrible story? Maybe such a story shouldn't be told at all. Yet finally it will be told. But as soon as you open your mouth you have problems, problems of recollection, problems of tone, ethical problems. How can you judge the man you were now that you've escaped his circumstances, his fears and desires, now that you hardly remember who he was? And how can you honestly avoid judging him? But isn't there, in the very act of confession, an obscene self-congratulation for the virtue required to see your mistake and own up to it? And isn't it just like an American boy, to want you to admire his sorrow at tearing other people's houses apart? And in the end who gives a damn, who's listening? What do you owe the listener, and which listener do you owe?

As it happened, Dicky took the last problem out of my hands by laughing darkly when I confessed that I'd omitted to offer Captain Kale my ski goggles. He grinned at me, I grinned at him. Jan looked back and forth between us. We had in that moment become a duet, Dicky and I, and she was in the dark. She had no feel for what was coming, but he did, very acutely, and his way of encouraging me was to show hilarity at every promissory detail of the disaster he saw taking shape. He was with me, even a little ahead of me, and I naturally pitched my tune to his particular receptivities, which were harsh and perverse and altogether familiar, so that even as he anticipated me I anticipated him and kept him laughing and edgy with expectation.

And so I urged the pilot on again, and the Chinook's vast shadow fell again over the upturned faces of people transformed, by this telling, into comic gibbering stickmen just waiting to be blown away like the toothpick houses they lived in. As I brought the helicopter down on them I looked over at Jan and saw her watching me with an expression so thoroughly disappointed as to be devoid of reproach. I didn't like it. I felt the worst kind of anger, the anger that proceeds from shame. So instead of easing up I laid it on even thicker, playing the whole thing for laughs, as cruel as I could make them, because after all Dicky had been there, and what more than that could I ever hope to have in common with her?

When I got to the end Dicky banged his forehead on the table to indicate maximum mirth. Sleepy leaned back with a startled expression and gave me the once-over. "Hey," he said, "great shirt, I used to have one just like it."

I called Vera the next morning from a pancake house, my pockets sagging with quarters. It was the first time I'd heard her voice in over a year, and the sound of it made everything in between seem vaporous, unreal. We began to talk as if resuming a conversation from the night before, teasing, implying, setting each other off. We talked like lovers. I found myself shaking, I was so maddened not to be able to see her.

When I hung up, the panic of loneliness I'd come awake to that morning was even worse. It made no sense to me that Vera was there and I was here. The others too—my mother, my friends, Geoffrey and Priscilla. They had a baby now, my nephew Nicholas, born while I was in Vietnam. I still hadn't laid eyes on him.

I made up my mind to fly home the next day.

That last night, the old man and I went out to dinner. For a change of pace we drove down to Redondo Beach, to a stylish French restaurant where, it turned out, they required a coat and tie. Neither of us had a tie so they supplied us with a pair of identical clip-ons, mile-wide Carnaby Street foulards with gigantic red polka dots. We looked like clowns. My father had never in his life insulted his person with such a costume and it took him a while to submit to it, but he came around. We had a good time, quietly, neither of us drinking much. Over coffee I told him I was leaving.

He rolled with it, said he'd figured it was about time I checked in with my mother. Then he asked when I'd be coming back.

"I'm not sure," I said.

"If you're thinking of going to school here, you'll want to give yourself plenty of time to look around, find some digs."

"Dad, I have to say, I've been giving that a lot of thought."

He waited. Then he said, "So you won't be going to school here."

"No. I'm sorry."

He waved away the apology. "All for the b-best, chum. My view exactly. You should aim higher." He looked at me in the kindest way. He had beautiful eyes, the old man, and they had remained beautiful while his face had gone to ruin all around them. He reached over and squeezed my arm. "You'll be back."

"Definitely. That's a promise."

"They all come back for Doctor Wolff's famous rest cure."

"I was thinking maybe next summer. As soon as I get myself really going on something."

"Of course," he said. "Filial duty. Have to look in on your old pop, make sure he's keeping his nose clean." He tried to smile but couldn't, his very flesh failed him, and that was the closest I came to changing my mind. I meant it when I said I'd be back but it sounded like a bald-faced lie, as if the truth was already known to both of us that I would not be back and that he would live alone and die alone, as he did, two years later, and that this was what was meant by my leaving. Still, after the first doubt I felt no doubt at all. Even that brief hesitation began to seem like mawkish shamming.

He was staring at my wrist. "Let's have a look at that watch."

I handed it over, a twenty-dollar Seiko that ran well and looked like it cost every penny. My father took off his Heuer chronograph and pushed it across the table. It was a thing of beauty. I didn't hold back for a second. I picked it up, hefted it, and strapped it on.

"Made for you," he said. "Now let's get these g-goddamned ties off."

Geoffrey noticed the chronograph a few nights after I got home. We were on his living room floor, drinking and playing cards. He admired the watch and asked how much it set me back. If I'd had my wits about me I would have lied to him, but I didn't. I said the old man had given it to me. "The old man gave it to you?" His face clouded over and I thought, Ah, nuts. I didn't know for sure what Geoffrey was thinking, but I was thinking about all those checks he'd sent out to Manhattan Beach. "I doubt if he paid for it," I said. Geoffrey didn't answer for a while. Then he said, "Probably not," and picked up his cards.

Vera's family owned a big spread in Maryland. After a round of homecoming visits, I left Washington and moved down there with her to help with the haying and see if we couldn't compose ourselves and find a way to live together. We did not. In the past she'd counted on me to control my moods so that she could give free rein to her own and still have a ticket back. Now I was as touchy and ungoverned as Vera, and often worse. She began to let her bassett hound eat at the table with her, in a chair, at his own place setting, because, she said, she had to have *some* decent company.

We were such bad medicine together that her mother, the most forbearing of souls, went back to Washington to get away from us. That left us alone in the house, an old plantation manor. Vera's family didn't have the money to keep it up, and the air of the place was moldy and regretful, redolent of better days. Portraits of Vera's planter ancestors hung from every wall. I had the feeling they were watching me with detestation and scorn, as if I were a usurping cad, a dancing master with oily hair and scented fingers.

While the sun was high we worked outside. In the afternoons I went upstairs to the servants' wing, now empty, where I'd set up an office. I had begun another novel. I knew it wasn't very good, but I also knew that it was the best I could do just then and that I had to keep doing it if I ever wanted to get any better. These words would never be read by anyone, I understood, but even in sinking out of sight they made the ground more solid under my hope to write well.

Not that I didn't like what I was writing as I filled up the pages. Only at the end of the day, reading over what I'd done, working through it with a green pencil, did I see how far I was from where I wanted to be. In the very act of writing I felt pleased with what I did. There was the pleasure of having words come to me, and the pleasure of ordering them, re-ordering them, weighing one against another. Pleasure also in the imagination of the story, the feeling that it could mean something. Mostly I was glad to find out that I could write at all. In writing you work toward a result you won't see for years, and can't be sure you'll ever see. It takes stamina and self-mastery and faith. It demands those things of you, then gives them back with a little extra, a surprise to keep you coming. It toughens you and clears your head. I could feel it happening. I was saving my life with every word I wrote, and I knew it.

In the servants' quarters I was a man of reason. In the rest of the house, something else. For two months Vera and I tied knots in each other's nerves, trying to make love happen again, knowing it wouldn't. The sadness of what we were doing finally became intolerable, and I left for Washington. When I called to say my last good-bye she asked me to wait, then picked up the phone again and told me she had a pistol in her hand and would shoot herself if I didn't promise to come back that same night.

"Vera, really, you already pulled this."

"When?"

"Before we got engaged."

"That was you? I thought it was Leland." She started to laugh. Then she stopped. "That doesn't mean I won't do it. Toby? I'm serious."

"Bang," I said, and hung up.

A week later I traveled to England with friends. When they returned home I stayed on, first in London, then in Oxford, reading, hitting the pubs, walking the countryside. It was restful: the greenness, the fetishized civility, the quaint, exquisite class consciousness I could observe without despair because as a Yank I had no place in it. My money stretched double and nobody talked about Vietnam. Every afternoon I went back to my room and wrote. I saw little to complain of in this life except that it couldn't go on. I knew I had to make a move, somehow buy into the world outside my window.

Some people I'd met encouraged me to take the Oxford entrance exams in early December. That left four and a half months to prepare myself in Latin, French, English history and literature. I knew I couldn't do it alone, so I hired university tutors in each of the test areas. After they'd made it clear how irregular this project was, how unlikely, they warmed to it. They took it on in the spirit of a great game, strategizing like underdog coaches, devising shortcuts, second-guessing the examiners, working me into the ground. After the first few weeks my Latin tutor, Miss Knight, demanded that I take a room in her house so she could crack the whip even harder. Miss Knight wore men's clothing and ran an animal hospital out of her kitchen. When she worked in the garden birds flew down and perched on her shoulder. She very much preferred Greek to English, and Latin to Greek, and said things like, "I can't *wait* to set you loose on Virgil!" She cooked my meals so I wouldn't lose time and drilled me on vocabulary and grammar as I ate. She kept in touch with my other tutors and proofread my essays for them, scratching furiously at the pompous locutions with which I tried to conceal my ignorance and uncertainty. All those months she fed her life straight into mine, and because of her I passed the examination and was matriculated into the university to read for an honors degree in English Language and Literature.

Oxford: for four years it was my school and my home. I made lifelong friends there, traveled, fell in love, did well in my studies. Yet I seldom speak of it, because to say "When I was at Oxford . . . " sounds suspect even to me, like the opening of one of my father's bullshit stories. Even at the time I was never quite convinced of the reality of my presence there. Day after day, walking those narrow lanes and lush courtyards, looking up to see a slip of cloud drifting behind a spire, I had to stop in disbelief. I couldn't get used to it, but that was all right. After every catch of irreality I felt an acute consciousness of good luck; it forced me to recognize where I was, and give thanks. This practice had a calming effect that served me well. I'd carried a little bit of Vietnam home with me in the form of something like malaria that wasn't malaria, ulcers, colitis, insomnia, and persistent terrors when I did sleep. Coming up shaky after a bad night, I could do wonders for myself simply by looking out the window.

It was the best the world had to give, and yet the very richness of the offering made me restless in the end. Comfort turned against itself. More and more I had the sense of avoiding some necessary difficulty, of growing in cleverness and facility without growing otherwise. Of being once again adrift.

I was in the Bodleian Library one night, doing a translation from the West Saxon Gospels for my Old English class. The assigned passage was from the Sermon on the Mount. It came hard, every line sending me back to the grammar or the glossary, until the last six verses, which gave themselves up all at once, blooming in my head in the same words I'd heard as a boy, shouted from evangelical pulpits and the stages of revival meetings. They told the story of the wise man who built his house upon a rock and the foolish man who built his house upon the sand. "And the rain descended, and the floods came, and the winds blew, and beat upon that house; and it fell; and great was the fall of it."

I'd forgotten I'd ever known these words. When they spoke themselves to me that night I was surprised, and overcome by a feeling of strangeness to myself and everything around me. I looked up from the table. From where I sat I could see the lights of my college, Hertford, where Jonathan Swift and Evelyn Waugh had once been students. I was in a country far from my own, and even farther from the kind of life I'd once seemed destined for. If you'd asked me how I got here I couldn't have told you. The winds that had blown me here could have blown me anywhere, even from the face of the earth. It was unaccountable. But I *was* here, in this moment, which all the other moments of my life had conspired to bring me to. And with this moment came these words, served on me like a writ. I copied out my translation in plain English, and thought that, yes, I would do well to build my house upon a rock, whatever that meant.

ROBERT BENSON

*For more than two decades, Robert Benson (1941–) has taught at
the University of the South, in Sewanee, Tennessee, where he is a
professor of English and chair of the medieval studies program.
Born and raised in New Orleans, he is author or coeditor of five
scholarly books.*

*In the mid-1990s Benson became interested in the personal es-
say, and he has since written about listening as a child to lions in
the night, roaring in the nearby zoo, about working as a teenager
on a survey crew in the swamps, and about fishing expeditions as
a boy with his brother and parents—including the time his father
caught a seven-foot shark on the family's first deep-sea outing in
the Gulf. It was on that trip, recalls Benson, that he first realized
that his father, a lawyer whom he otherwise rarely saw without
coat and tie, had a past and an interior life of which he had been
previously unaware. It was watching the ease and skill with which
his father moved about the boat that afforded him this realization,
and that first glimpse, he writes, "was more exciting than not being able to see land."*

Lawrence Benson was a man who worked six days a week, six

and a half if he could sneak it in. He was a man of formal bearing, who "preserved old civilities and kept others, including members of his own family, on their mettle and at a distance." He slept, ate, and worked on a schedule, did not admit of spontaneity, and was in some ways, says Robert, "not easy to live with, but the world of my childhood was stable and predictable largely because of the order my father imposed and insisted upon."

It was the hint of another side to his father that had so excited the young Robert that day on the Gulf, and over the years he reveled as he made further similar discoveries. Most came as a result of listening to conversations between his father and an old friend who stopped by unannounced for dinner every fall during duck-hunting season. The friend was a swamp guide and trapper, who elicited from Lawrence Benson stories that otherwise went untold. These revealed him to be a man of knowledge about the marsh and its inhabitants—both human and animal—and they made Robert realize that his father had not always been a lawyer and lived in the city. Rather, he was a child of the rural South, and "he had hunted and fished and gone barefoot, had milked cows and plucked chickens, had caught lightning bugs and gigged frogs."

That carefree childhood came to an abrupt end with the events described in "Rising to the Light"—events that taught Lawrence to guard his emotions, that affected the father he became to Robert and, with time, the father Robert became to his children. The essay was first published in the Sewanee Review in 1995.

Rising to the Light

My father believed that the only good snake was a dead snake, and he had better reasons than most people for this conviction. In the summer of 1918, he was twelve years old. In his yard near a sluggish creek, he was pushing his baby sister in the swing that hung from the lowest branch of an enormous live oak. He was barefooted, of course, and each time he pushed he stepped out of the way, usually stepping out from the tree. The swing rose higher, and his sister squealed happily and threw her head back to watch clouds, branches, and bright sky flying past. The boy who would be my father enjoyed her delight and worked up a sweat trying to get the swing higher. The effort absorbed him, and in his own yard he grew incautious. As he danced out of the way of the rushing swing and swiped at his sister's auburn hair, he brought his bare foot down among the roots of the oak squarely onto a rattlesnake. The small pit viper put both fangs into his right foot just above his big toe.

It took Grandmother several minutes to get from him a reasonable idea of what had happened, and because she had another child, she thought first to kill the snake. In the time it took to dispatch the snake, my father's foot turned a grayish green to the ankle, and his toes began to round as if filling with water.

Grandfather did not cut but he did suck. He put his mouth to the darkening wound, again and again sucking blood and venom from his son's swollen foot. The doctor from town would not see the boy for twenty-four hours. That night, trying to do the right thing, his parents wrapped the foot in hot towels to draw the poison, and the skin split across the top of the swollen foot. The bite of pit vipers hurts like a kidney stone, and rattlesnake venom is especially painful. The boy's fever rose, and he tossed on his bed and shook his head, knotting and unknotting his fingers, biting his lip and his forearm, not crying much. In August heat, he shook with cold and asked for more cover, but as a patchwork comforter was laid across him he screamed with fear. He experienced what he referred to for the rest of his life as "the horrors." Each patch on the comforter was a writhing snake coiling and striking repeatedly. He could not explain his horrors then, and the quilt stayed on. Blood poisoning, loving but primitive treatment, and the natural restlessness of a boy confined to the indoors added up to nearly four months of recuperation. He remembered for the rest of his life the hemotoxic venom burning in his flesh, but another event in what should have been his childhood gave snakes their full mythic and symbolic weight.

Some things you never get over. Some terrible memories enter the blood and become almost genetic, touching even the lives of people who have no recollection of them. My father was never reluctant to speak of his snakebite. With little prompting he would re-create the incident in language plain and grim. But there was something worse that he would not talk about, not even with my mother, to whom he told nearly everything. It is an unruly and disproportionate matter, one of life's dark extravagances that can bring clarity to the lesser confusion of all our stories.

When he was eight, my father saw his older brother beheaded in a mine shaft in Colorado. I recently came across an old photograph of a handsome sandy-haired boy, tie slightly askew, double-breasted jacket buttoned. The boy is smiling a pleasant, slightly smart-aleck smile. The picture seems well composed and complete, but the right side has been neatly torn away. On the back in my father's hand is this inscription: "Geo. Powell Benson—Lawrence's older brother—killed in Colorado 6/30/14." When we were children, without drama or self-conscious fanfare of any kind, my father told my brother and me the story that contained few more details than the writing on the picture, told us once as if it were part of his obligation to the truth and never spoke of it again. The telling can't have taken five minutes, and all that I remember is Powell had been decapitated. No parent ever recovers from the death of a child. My brother may have been old enough to hear such a tale, and he has told me other things about the accident and its aftermath that I do not remember. My childish imagination could find nothing to hold, and the telling sank within me like a polished steel weight. But in my fifty-third year that picture of Powell coupled with the fears fathers have about their children brought it all back, and I have tried to visualize the grim details of what my father suffered.

The train ride from Louisiana in 1914 must have taken a week, but the boys had never been on a train, and they didn't care how long it took. Everything was fun. Grandmother was glad to see the country, relieved to have convinced my grandfather that the boys needed such a trip, that travel, as her mother had always said, was important to a child's education. She believed in expanding horizons literally. My grandfather grumbled some about their going and stayed home. Two days out of Kansas City, when the adventure had begun to flatten with the country, they caught sight of the Rockies. My father and Powell were thrilled, and Grandmother forgot the fatigue and the dust. She was convinced again that it was all worth it. The high country was delightful and exciting. Elevated vistas are not common in south Louisiana, nor is cool weather in June.

In Idaho Springs they rode a buckboard to their hotel. On the way Powell, who was eleven or twelve, saw a sign advertising tours of a played-out gold mine. "Can we please go, Mother? We might find some gold. It wouldn't take long. Please." My father took his cue from his brother. "Can we? Please? It's a real gold mine! Let's go see. Please." Grandmother was sweet-natured and liked to indulge the boys, and they knew if they kept begging that she would agree. Two days later Grandmother finally said yes. They would go to the mine on the next to last day of the trip. The boys danced and whooped in the hotel lobby, and Powell frogged my father's arm.

The mine itself was not much of an attraction, but the idea of going down into the earth greatly appealed to the children. The shaft cut into solid rock was not neatly squared, but four huge timbers supported the shaft and provided a frame to which the elevator was attached. The vertical supports, banded and bolted to the dark rock, were squared at the top and every fifty or sixty feet down by horizontal beams. Between each set of horizontal timbers, the bare rock, cool and wet in some places, dry in others, came close enough to touch. The elevator itself was a heavy wooden platform with an angled iron railing around it at waist height. It was raised and lowered by an old steam generator that the boys could hear grinding and slapping even near the bottom of the shaft.

The day was brilliant and clear, and looking up as they descended, they could see the huge pulley wheel that moved the elevator, and beyond that the blue sky. A vivid piece of the bright world they had left. The shaft itself was dimly lit by a string of bare lightbulbs that hung straight down on one side.

The opposite side was either totally dark or shadowed and vague. The boys could tell when the rock walls were almost against the sides of the elevator by the sound of the clanking cable and the pulleys. Once or twice on the way down the platform even touched the rock. On the dark side the boys felt the fenders on the lower edge scrape by. They leaned over and tried to touch the cool rock. The elevator operator and tour guide was no more than seventeen, but he was growing a moustache and enjoyed his authority.

"Keep your hands off that rock," he said with worldly irritation. "This ain't the playground. Gold mine's no place for kids." He said "kids" with deliberate disdain. My father giggled at the young man's accent and poked Powell in the ribs. Powell grinned back, and both boys leaned out for the wall again, leaning this time further than they'd intended because the uneven rock had opened slightly.

"You'd best look to your kids, lady. They's ways to get bad hurt down here."

"Lawrence, keep your hands down," Grandmother said. "Powell, you boys settle down." The close rock walls and the deepening gloom made her a little anxious. She looked at her shoes and wondered if she had done the right thing.

It didn't take long to see the mine, nor did it take long to see why it had been abandoned. The boys' notion of finding gold lying about on the ground vanished in the dull gray horizontal tunnel. The guide walked slightly ahead with a coal-oil lantern, and Grandmother brought up the rear with another. The guide recited a string of dates dealing with the discovery of gold in the area and the construction of several of the local mines. His recitation on the mining process was as boring to the children as repetition had made it to him. Grandmother feigned interest so that the young man would not be offended, and she tried to ask questions she thought the boys might like to ask. The guide did not like having his speech interrupted by questions. It was hard enough remembering it all anyway. The boys made faces behind the guide's back and said they wanted to go. The elevator ride had been fun.

Going up, Grandmother spoke to the guide, not for his sake or hers but for the edification of her family, about the hopes and fears that had brought men to these dark places. My father said you couldn't pay him to work in a hole in the ground, no matter what, and he fixed his eyes on the growing patch of sky overhead. He and Powell reached out to see if they could touch the rock. The elevator operator had stopped paying any attention to them. The platform rose with surprising speed, and near the top, Powell leaned over the railing to see if he could still see the bottom. As he leaned out, the platform passed through one of the sets of horizontal supports near the top. The sudden appearance of the timbers startled him, and he pulled his head back for an instant, smiled at my father, and leaned out again. Just above those supports a rock shelf came nearly to the iron railing. Powell's head and neck were between the rock and the railing as my father turned to him mocking the guide. "This ain't the playground." He was still forming the words when the platform lurched and his brother's body fell at Grandmother's feet. The elevator rocked back and forth, its cable groaning as the platform settled. There was blood on my father's high leather shoes. He tried to look away, but his eyes could not find the sky. The charged air was full of his mother's screams.

In the summer of 1914 my father was eight. He was bitten by the rattler four summers later, but the two events became in some ways a single horror for him. He could never talk about Powell's death, for his own childhood was over from that moment. Four years later his sense of the uncertainty of life in the world was confirmed, and snakes became for him the embodiment of evil, darkness, and the promise of pain and loss, "evocative," as Faulkner says, "of all knowledge and an old weariness and of pariah-hood and of death."

From early childhood my brother and I enjoyed hunting and fishing, hiking and camping, and we occasionally encountered snakes without disastrous results. Our father encouraged our outdoor interests, taking us fishing, teaching us to shoot rifles and shotguns, and whenever we encountered snakes, he killed them all regardless of name or reputation. When we walked in the woods, we had to walk behind him, follow single file in his footsteps. He was an enthusiastic fisherman most of his life, but he never forgot the danger that waited on the banks of blackwater bayous. We never saw him as reluctant to go fishing or to be in the woods, but he was minutely careful, and we sensed that even a simple fishing trip was an adventure, fraught with real peril. It was very exciting. He was uneasy though on family vacations. If we went to Biloxi or Gulf Shores, we were made fearfully conscious of the dangers of the undertow. Once in Tennessee, we went to Rock City, probably at my insistence. I was ten. I remember running to the edge of the scenic overlook where I was supposed to be able to see seven states. I was stung and puzzled by my father's sudden anger. Neither of us enjoyed the afternoon. Mother described herself as a death-watch Mary because of her anxiety about her children's safety, but my father's sense of life's tragic potential was vivid if unspoken in painful and bloody memory.

My interest in snakes must have been a particularly heavy cross for him to bear. Early fascination he expected to pass, but as fascination deepened and began to take on the look of science, he must have felt haunted, must have wondered what he'd done to deserve such a strange child. By the time I was thirteen, I had determined to become a herpetologist. Friends with a fondness for amateur psychology suggested that my father's loathing of snakes actually caused my interest, that knowing and not fearing snakes was a way of asserting my adolescent independence, a more civilized and acceptable way than juvenile delinquency, with which I had only a slight brush. As a second son, they said, I reveled in the other side of my father's fear. However that may be, I was conscious only of the fact that herpetology offered me an opportunity to combine academic matters with love of the outdoors. I read every snake book I could get my hands on, my favorite being Raymond Ditmars's *Snakes of the World* (1931), which contained a gory and precise account of Marlin Perkins's reaction to being bitten by a gaboon viper. I learned the scientific names for all of the common southeastern snakes and for many of the exciting snakes from faraway places: the king cobra, the bushmaster, the Australian tiger snake. Being able to see a garter snake and say *Thamnophis sirtalis* was great fun of what I took to be a very mature sort.

A friend of my brother's got a job one summer working in the snake house in the Audubon Park Zoo, and I immediately volunteered to be his assistant—at no salary. That summer I spent nearly every day at the snake house. I helped clean exhibits, washed windows, replaced gravel and water in the smaller tanks. My position was never official though I acted as though it were, moving confidently and with studied disdain through squeamish crowds, going nonchalantly in and out of the door marked POISONOUS SNAKES. NO ADMITTANCE. EMPLOYEES ONLY. I am certain now that no one noticed, but the summer after my eighth-grade year I believed I ruled at least a part of the world, and I remember being mystified that the girls I longed to date remained unimpressed. When school started again in September, I spent three or four afternoons a week at the zoo doing whatever needed doing, delighted for the chance to observe and enjoy the snakes.

Although the snake house was small, dim, and damp, we saw and cared for an interesting variety of snakes, including some snakes that were rare even in grander zoos. During nearly eighteen months of my devoted service, we received and displayed two African cobras, a large and ill-tempered western diamondback (*Crotalus atrox*), a Mexican moccasin, an anaconda, and two Russell's vipers. The diamondback never adjusted to captivity, and we were not able to keep him on display because he would not accept the presence of people, striking repeatedly at the glass at the front of his tank until his nose and lips bled freely. He refused to eat and for several months he was force-fed. He struck the wire walls of the holding cages with such force that his fangs would occasionally get caught in the hardware cloth. We turned him over to one of the herpetologists at Tulane. The cobras, on the other hand, adjusted quickly to their circumstances. We received two adult African cobras from another zoo, and for a day or two in the holding cages they would "hood up" and hiss loudly when anyone walked by. But they soon ignored all human activity, and we opened the door to their cage casually to freshen their water or to drop in the rats they fed on. My recollection of the offhanded way I moved among dangerous snakes now makes me a little nervous. Youthful reflexes and some knowledge yield only an illusion of invulnerability. My world held no horrors to moderate my confidence.

The snake house also had a good collection of local snakes: canebrake and pigmy rattlesnakes, water moccasins and copperheads, king snakes, rat snakes, ribbon snakes, a mud snake, a hognosed snake, and an assortment of water snakes. My first nonpoisonous snake bite was from a large diamondback water snake. I was cleaning one of the walk-in exhibits. It was the job I liked best. I wore red-soled rubber boots with my jeans tucked down inside and brought in a garden hose with a trigger-controlled nozzle. Visitors were always impressed by seeing a person in a snake tank (a "pit" they liked to say), even if the snakes were nonpoisonous. I hosed out the enclosure and cleaned the glass front with a squeegee. The bigger the crowd, the more nonchalant I tried to be, reaching down to move knots of snakes out of the corners with my hands. All snakes have rows of recurved teeth for holding and swallowing prey, and the larger the snake, the larger the recurved teeth. Diamondback water snakes are not only large, but they are intractable and ornery. As I reached for the tail of one snake, another snake that I had ignored bit the back edge of my right hand. Because the snake's teeth are recurved, the best response is not to jerk your hand away, but to allow the snake time to free his teeth and pull back. The best response, however, takes a lot more self-control than I possessed. As soon as I felt the bite, I jerked my hand, dislodged several of the snake's teeth, and helped him make a rather spectacular if superficial wound.

I was embarrassed to have been so careless in front of an audience and pleased to have been publicly wounded. "No m'am, I'm fine. Thanks. It's part of the job. Really. I'll be fine." A week later at school, I pulled a perfect recurved tooth from my hand. It came out just like a splinter.

My activities in the zoo and as an aspiring herpetologist did not escape my father's notice, but he was generous and tried not to interfere. He had over the years built several cages to house the generations of hamsters that had once interested me, and he did not pay too much attention to the fact that these cages provided temporary housing for snakes, and he never saw the copperhead that escaped from one of these cages in our garage. I'm still not sure how it got out, but snakes are adept at improbable escapes. I never mentioned it. Now and then, in the arrogance of youthful knowledge, I presumed to instruct my father concerning his attitude toward snakes. One Saturday morning my mother woke me up saying, "Son, go see what kind of snake that is your father killed in the yard." I was angry before my feet hit the floor. Why couldn't they have called me before he killed it? Why should I get up now? It wouldn't be any deader in an hour or two. Pulling on my jeans, I walked into the backyard still rubbing the sleep from my eyes. My father had put the hoe away and was spraying the insects on the camellia bushes.

"Where's the snake?" I asked. He gestured with the hose on the stirrup pump toward the roots of the magnolia tree. There I found a black racer cut into three sections. The tail was lifting and turning slowly. "It's a blacksnake, *Coluber constrictor constrictor*," I announced. My father paid no attention. He didn't need to have his adversary named. "Dad, it's just a blacksnake. They eat mice. It's not poisonous. They're good to have around."

"No live snake's good to have around." He smiled, glanced at the three pieces of snake, and went back to spraying the flowers.

I said shit under my breath and started back to the house.

"Son, when I walked out past the magnolia, that snake came towards me," he offered in explanation to dignify my position.

I knew too much to let it pass. "Blacksnakes are aggressive like that sometimes. But he couldn't have hurt you. His pupils are round. He's nonpoisonous. You didn't have to kill him." My tone was smug and instructional.

"Who do you think you're talking to?" he said. Herpetology was no longer the subject. "I don't intend to get close enough to check the shape of his pupils. Anything I can't see from the end of the hoe, I don't need to see. And I don't need a lecture from you. Is that clear?" When I muttered yessir, he turned deliberately away and walked back to the flowers.

Occasionally I rescued nonpoisonous snakes from his wrath. In fact I thought he almost admired a green snake, *Opheodrys aestivus,* he watched me catch, but when I mentioned it to him later he just laughed. "They're all ugly as sin, every kind there is." Nothing I said or did ever saved a venomous one. The truth is I didn't try often. Canebrake rattlesnakes, *Crotalus horridus atricaudatus,* are not numerous over much of their range; and although I had seen others catch them, I had never collected one. My father had asked my brother and me to help him clear brush from the banks of a muddy creek that ran behind the house. It was August, and even though we had started before six in the morning, we had sweated through our shirts and jeans by seven. My brother said, "Let's sit a minute after I knock this privet down."

"You got it," I responded. I never had to be told twice to stop working.

As Larry swung his brush hook into the tangle of privet, we immediately heard a rattler buzz. We probed gingerly at the sound and discovered a twenty-four-inch canebrake. When we prodded the snake, he assumed an impressive posture, raising the front third of his length in a striking loop and trying in vain to retreat against a wall of cut brush. He rattled continuously. My father had been twenty or thirty feet down the creek bank when the rattling started. He was moving closer as I started up to the house for my potato rake and a pillowcase.

"Watch him. I'll be right back," I called to Larry.

As I moved past my father, he caught my left arm in his left hand and spun me towards him. "No," he said.

"Daddy, I've never caught a rattlesnake. This one's a perfect size for the collection. We've got a medium tank that's empty now anyway." I pulled my arm free, and I started to the house. I took a step and saw him pick up my brush hook and move closer to the snake.

"Please, Dad," I said with more anger than supplication.

He looked from the snake to me. I took one step in his direction, and he raised his left hand with his index finger pointing up at my face. His own face was flushed. His lips did not move much.

"Not another word." Each word was louder than the one before.

I stopped. The first swing took the snake six inches behind the head and cut him neatly in two. The rattling continued until there were not enough connected muscles left to move the tail.

My father's feelings toward snakes never changed. As he grew older he was outdoors less, and encounters with snakes were unlikely. My enthusiasms moderated some, and time made both of us more good-humored about matters herpetological. In June after my freshman year in college, we went bank fishing on Bayou Lacombe on the north shore of Lake Pontchartrain, and I watched him kill a large cottonmouth that swam into the roots of a cypress tree near our stringer of bream. He went to the task with purpose and warmth, losing his cap in the process. As he flung the dead snake from the end of a heavy stick, he looked over as if he expected me to intercede belatedly on the snake's behalf.

"Protecting our fish?" I asked. We both laughed.

Coral snakes (*Micrurus fulvius fulvius*) are the rarest of Louisiana's poisonous snakes, or at least the most rarely encountered. They are slender and brightly colored little snakes which are sometimes mistaken for harmless snakes by those Ditmars calls misguided persons. In his *Field Book of North American Snakes* (1939) Ditmars describes the coral snake as "a very dangerous snake from combination of deceptiveness in appearance and actions and the high toxicity of its bite. . . . Of coral snake bites that the author has heard of, two out of three were fatal." The neurotoxic venom is, Ditmars writes, "drop for drop more lethal than that of a cobra." I had collected or observed nearly every species of native poisonous snake in my herpetological ramblings, but I had never seen a coral snake in the field. Only one of the experts I knew had ever collected one.

I fished a lot the summer after my freshman year in college, and on several Saturdays my father went with me. One morning, however, when I proposed fishing, he declined.

"You go on," he said. "Your mother and I are going to transplant a couple of those smaller camellia bushes, and I want to do it before it gets too hot."

"Do you need some help?" I asked without enthusiasm.

"No, thanks. Go fish. Just don't catch 'em all."

I was gone most of the day, but I have almost no recollection of fishing. When I pulled into the driveway around four-thirty, Mother ran down from the porch to greet me. She was excited. I turned off the key and stepped out as she announced, "Your father's caught a coral snake!" And then, more modestly, "At least that's what we think it is. Come and see."

We walked around the house toward the garage. In the back-yard my father was watering the bushes that he had moved while I fished. Near the door to the garage was a big glass jar with a piece of two-by-six lying across the top. In the bottom of the jar were leaf litter and moss. I knelt down to look closely.

"I figured if there wasn't enough air in there with that board on top, to hell with him," Daddy said as he turned off the hose and walked over.

There was a coral snake in the jar, and for several minutes all I could do was look. "Where was it? Who saw it first? What did you say? How on earth did you get it in the jar?" The questions rushed out. My father smiled.

"I saw it when I got ready to dig out that second bush. It was just there, inside hoe range too. I was ready to smack him, but your mother stopped me. She had just seen the snake and said, 'Lawrence, wait. Don't kill it. I think it might be a coral snake. They're rare. And very poisonous, Bob says.' You can imagine how impressed I was."

"Anyhow, your mother made me keep the damned thing at bay while she went looking for one of your books. It took her forever, but then she appeared with a picture and stood there looking first at the book then at the snake. 'Yes,' she concluded, 'it's a coral snake all right. I think we should try to catch it.' I don't recall agreeing to anything, but she found that jar in the garage."

"Your father was magnificent," Mother offered. "He looked

like he'd been catching coral snakes all his life. I put the jar down and your father lifted him on the shovel and dropped him in and then shoveled that moss and stuff in for him."

"For him nothing," my father said. "On him sounds better. I thought it might kill him." He smiled and touched my shoulder.

While I listened to this remarkable narration, I lifted the jar and turned it around to look at the small bright snake. My father never looked at the jar, showed absolutely no interest in its contents. Throughout the account of this adventure that he never could have imagined, his tone was cheerful and matter-of-fact. But he only looked at me, occasionally at Mother when she offered some detail or correction, and every now and then he looked off as if he were listening to something faint and far away that only he could hear. That evening he looked tired and old, but he was relaxed, and went to bed earlier than usual and slept soundly.

It's been more than seventy years since Powell was killed and my father was bitten, and I have tried to find a place in memories that are not mine. I have tried to imagine the horror of an elevator ride out of a gold mine I have never seen. I have tried to look at snakes as he saw them all his life without trying: still bright with a child's fear and bewildering pain. Some things are clear now, but much of what I remember puzzles me. I also know that I have said and done much that puzzles my sons.

Daddy caught the coral snake when he was a year or so younger than I am now. My children have played with and learned a lot about snakes, and my wife has been a patient if not an enthusiastic home zookeeper for thirty years, but when I passed fifty I grew uneasy about many things. Age brings caution, and I am more or less constantly aware of what might at any moment be lost. I have never worried much about my sons being harmed by poisonous snakes. I worry because they live in a world more dangerous than the Honey Island Swamp ever was, a landscape of burnt-out gold mines, tawdry and dark places that promise what they cannot pay. When I can deal with threats directly, I am grateful. Recently an old friend and I were walking with our children on his land along the Alabama River. We walked through the open river-swamp woods in single file, at my suggestion. Jack led the way, his son and daughter behind him followed by my sons and me. I have always walked in the woods paying as much attention to the ground as to anything else, an old habit of my father's solidified by my years of snake collecting. We saw a few deer, flushed a wild turkey hen from her nest, and watched pileated woodpeckers and a variety of songbirds. We were nearly back to the truck when I looked ahead and noticed that Jack and his daughter had just stepped over, and his son was about to step on, a thirty-inch rattlesnake. I lunged by my two sons and grabbed Jack's ten-year-old and pulled him back.

"Snake," I said loudly.

"Where," Jack said.

When I pointed to the snake coiled in the leaves, Jack said, "Damn. I stepped right over him. So did Liddell." He shuddered. "Good eyes." The snake had not moved since I first saw it. It neither rattled nor attempted to escape. I shot it once with a small .38, and watched as it knotted and rattled. I told myself that I was protecting the children.

I have an old black-and-white photograph of my father steering an outboard motor on a cypress skiff down Bayou Lacombe. He is laughing and looks young and confident. At forty-seven he could enjoy some of the things he had missed. For a time after the accident in Colorado, his mother, nearly mad with grief and guilt, held seances in the dining room to bring Powell back. Night after night my father heard his parents pleading with the dead, terrified that his brother's mangled body would move through the house. Having come out of the gold mine alive, he also felt guilt and saw reproach in his mother's eyes. The year before he was snake-bit he was sent away to military school. The grace and courage with which he lived into his seventies are apparent in his laughter and most vivid for me in his improbable encounter with the coral snake—a reckless act of love, unimaginable until performed. When he died two months before his seventy-fifth birthday, he smiled like a housebound boy given permission to go and play.

SAM PICKERING

Born and raised in Nashville, Sam Pickering (1941–) has been on the faculty at the University of Connecticut since 1978. As a young man Pickering once taught at a Nashville prep school, where he used such tactics as lecturing from desktops and outside windows to gain the attention of students—of whom one later became a writer and used Pickering as the model for the character played on film by Robin Williams in Dead Poets Society. *An authority on children's literature and the author of many scholarly works, Pickering has also written nearly a dozen collections of personal essays.*

Many of Pickering's essays circle back to his native Tennessee and are laced with the doings of such characters as Googoo Hooberry, Slubey Garts, and Proverbs Goforth. That Tennessee should so permeate his writing is hardly surprising. His father, born in 1909, grew up in the town of Carthage, home to Pickerings from the time of the Civil War, and spent virtually his entire life in Tennessee.

Samuel F. Pickering Sr. was a man to whom both humor and story were important, and he combined the two as often as possible. He once served on a jury, says his son in the essay "Home

Again, Home Again," hearing the case of a woman who was suing a large Nashville hotel after an apple pie fell on her head from an overhead window. She claimed the falling pie made her blink, which she did continuously throughout the trial. But the elder Pickering had occasion to discover that her affliction went away outside the courtroom; keeping the information to himself, he nonetheless persuaded his fellow jurors to find for the woman but to make an award less generous than might otherwise have been expected. This "cured the woman," said the father, "but did serious damage to her lawyer"—she stopped blinking and he started.

Clearly, Pickering shares his father's loves. "I am a chip off my father's DNA," he says, and up until the time of his father's death in 1990 he even used for himself the diminutive of his father's name: Samuel F. Pickering Jr. Shortly after his father died, however, he received a phone call from a reporter asking if he wanted to change his preference. "Drop the Junior," *said Pickering, "it's time for a new me." While he was at it he also dropped the middle initial and shortened* Samuel.

"Son and Father" *was first published in the* Virginia Quarterly Review *in 1986, four years before the death of Samuel F. Pickering Sr. In 1987 the essay was included in Pickering's collection* The Right Distance.

Son and Father

"The more I see of old people," my father said in the last letter he wrote me, "the greater my feeling is that the bulk of them should be destroyed."

"Not you," I thought when I read the letter, "at least not yet."

For years I imagined that I was different from, even better than, my father. Then one evening I walked into his room to ask about a book and found him asleep on his bed. Although I had seen him sleeping countless times, I was startled. His pajamas were inside out, as mine invariably are, and I noticed that we slept in the same position, left arm bent under the pillow, hand resting on the headboard; right leg pulled high toward the chest, and left thrust back and behind with the toes pointed, seemingly pushing us up and through the bed. Suddenly I realized Father and I were remarkably alike, the greatest difference being only the years that lay between us. At first I was upset. I had never consciously rejected family, but like the bottom of the bed against which I appeared to be pushing at night, my father and his life provided a firmness against which I could press and thrust myself off into something better.

As I looked at the old man lying on the bed, his thin ankles and knobby feet sticking out of his pajamas like fallen branches, I felt warm and comfortable. Instead of being parted by time and youth's false sense of superiority, we were bound together by patterns of living. His life could teach me about my future and my past, but, I thought, how little I knew about him. How well, I wondered, did any son know a father—particularly an only son, the recipient of so much love and attention that he worried about having a self and turned inward, often ignoring the parents about him and responding aggressively to concern with a petulant "leave me alone."

In his letter Father said that he and Mother disagreed about the past. "I tell her," he wrote, "that her recollections are remarkable, albeit not necessarily accurate." My memories of Father are ordinary and consist of a few glimpses: such things, for example, as his running alongside and steadying me when I learned to ride a bicycle and his fondness for chocolate. Mother liked chocolate too, and whenever Father was given a box of candy, he hid it in his closet where Mother could not reach it. The closet was dark, and as he grew older and his sight failed, he kept a flashlight in a shoebox. In a way, I suppose, past events resemble leaves on a tree. A multitude of little things make up life in full bloom, but as time passes, they fall and disappear without a trace. A few seeds blow into the garage, or memory, and get wedged behind spades, axes, and bits of lumber. If found or remembered, they are usually swept aside. Does it matter that Father rolled and chewed his tongue while telling a story or that after having drinks before dinner he would talk with his mouth full and embarrass me? Particular place is often necessary if the seeds lodged in memory are to sprout and grow green. Sadly, places vanish almost as quickly as leaves in October.

The Sulgrave Apartments, where I lived for eight years, and the long alley behind stretching through neighborhoods and drawing gangs of children to its treasures have vanished. When

I was five I entered Ransome School. For the first months, Father walked all the way to school with me: along West End; across Fairfax, where Mr. Underwood the policeman waved at us; under the railway trestle and up Iroquois; past three small streets, Howell, Harding, and Sutherland. Slowly, as I grew surer, Father walked less of the distance with me; one morning he did not cross Sutherland; sometime later, he stopped at Harding, then Howell. Eventually he left me at the corner of Fairfax and I made my own way to Ransome under the watchful eye of Mr. Underwood. What I did when I was five, I can do no longer. The trestle and tracks with their caches of spikes, Iroquois, Harding, Howell, Sutherland, and Ransome itself, a scrapbook of small faces, have disappeared. All the associations that would freshen memory have been torn down for an interstate, going to Memphis or Birmingham, I am not sure which. Great washes of cars and trucks pour down ramps and rush through my old neighborhood. Traffic is so heavy that I rarely drive on West End, and when I must, the congestion makes me so nervous and the driving takes such concentration that I never think of Ransome, Mr. Underwood, or a little boy and a tall, thin man holding hands as they walked to school.

Father grew up in Carthage, Tennessee, a town of some two thousand people set high above the Cumberland River on red clay bluffs fifty-five miles east of Nashville. Since Carthage was the seat of Smith County, sidewalks ran along Main Street, and Father and his brother Coleman used to roller-skate from their house to Grandfather's insurance agency, downtown over the bank. Life in Carthage was slow and from my perspective appealingly unsophisticated. On the front page of the weekly newspaper alongside an ad for Tabler's Buckeye Pile Ointment were excerpts from the sermons of the Reverend Sam P. Jones, the local Methodist minister. "I wouldn't give whiskey to a man until he had been dead for three days," Jones said. "When an old red-nosed politician gets so he isn't fit for anything else," he declared, "the Democrat Party send him to the Legislature." When a resident went away, a notice duly appeared on the front page. "D. B. Kittrell," the paper informed readers, "went to Nashville last week with about 40 fat hogs and has not yet returned."

Not much money was to be made in Carthage, and people lived comfortably. Every morning Grandpa Pickering walked downtown and had coffee with friends, after which he came home for breakfast. Only then did he go to his office. Grandfather's house was a white, clapboard, two-story Victorian with a bright tin roof. A porch ran around two sides; at one corner of the porch was a cupola; on top was a weathervane. Huge sugar maples stood in the front yard, and about the house were bushes of white hydrangeas; in spring they seemed like mountains of snow to me. In back of the house was the well, sheds, fields, a tobacco barn, and then a long slope down to the river. Bessie the maid cooked Grandfather's breakfast. She made wonderful shortcake, and whenever I was in Carthage, she gave me sweet coffee to drink. Bessie's first marriage had not been a success; James, her husband, was unfaithful, and one night when he returned from gallivanting, she shot him. Although James lost a leg, he did not die, and Grandfather got Bessie off with a suspended sentence. Later, after Grandfather's death, Bessie married a preacher and moved to Nashville. On Thanksgiving and Christmas she often came to our house and cooked. The last time she came she asked me if I was still catching bugs and snakes.

I don't remember any snakes in Carthage, and the only bugs I recall catching are tobacco worms. I took a bucket from the back porch and after walking down to the tobacco patch filled it with worms. Then I drew a big circle in the dust on the road and in the middle dumped the worms. The first worm to detach itself from the squirming green pile and to crawl out of the circle I returned to the bucket and carried back to the field. The others

I crushed. Tobacco worms are big and fat, and if I lined up worm and sole just right and put my foot down quickly heel to toe, I could occasionally squirt a worm's innards two feet.

Grandfather died when I was young, and I have few memories of him. During the last months of his life, he was bedridden. Beside his bed was always a stack of flower magazines. All seemed to have been filled with pictures of zinnias, bright red and orange and occasionally purple zinnias, the only flower Father ever grew. Grandma Pickering outlived her husband, and I have clearer memories of her. She was strong-willed and opinionated, once confessing to me that she voted for Roosevelt the first time. In some ways Carthage may have been too small for her; she was interested in literature, and after her death I found scrapbooks filled with newspaper clippings, poems, reviews, and articles. Most of the poems were conventionally inspirational or religious and were typically entitled "Symbols of Victory" and "Earth Is Not Man's Abiding Place." Occasionally, though, I found other kinds of poetry, poems for the dreamer, not the moralist, poems which did not teach but which sketched moods. Pasted on the bottom of a page containing an article on "Shakespeare's Ideals of Womanhood" and a review of *For Whom the Bell Tolls* were two lines:

> I've reached the land of Golden-rod,
> Afar I see it wave and nod.

Much as it is hard to think of Father skating along the sidewalks of Carthage, so it is difficult to think of Grandma Pickering as a dreamer. Instead of bright, beckoning goldenrod, I associate her with a rusting red Studebaker. Almost until the day she died, she drove, and whenever she left Carthage for Nashville, the sheriff radioed ahead to the highway patrol, warning, "Mrs. Pickering's on the road." Along the way, patrolmen watched out for her, and when she reached Lebanon, one telephoned Father and then he and Mother and I drove out to a Stuckey's near the city limits and waited. After what seemed forever, she eventually appeared, inevitably with cars backed up behind her by the score, something that embarrassed me terribly.

Father told me little about his childhood in Carthage. I know only that he had an Airedale named Jerry; that on Rattlesnake Mountain, the hill just outside town, he once saw a huge snake; that he almost died after eating homemade strawberry ice cream at a birthday party; and that Lucy, the talented little girl next door, died from trichinosis. Report cards provided most of what I know about Father's childhood, and in Grandmother's scrapbooks I found several. Father entered first grade in 1915; Lena Douglas taught him reading, spelling, writing, arithmetic, and language; his average for the year in all subjects was ninety-nine and a half; for his first two years he was remarkably healthy and only missed three days of school. The Carthage schools proved too easy, and for a year in high school Father attended KMI, Kentucky Military Institute, a place about which he never spoke except to say, "Children should not be sent to military schools." After KMI Father returned to Carthage, skipped two grades, graduated from high school, and in 1925 entered Vanderbilt.

One of my undergraduate nicknames was "Machine," and once or twice when I walked into class intent on an A, people made whirring or clanking sounds. Father, it seems, rarely attended class; every semester at Vanderbilt his quality credits were reduced because of absences. In 1927 he skipped so many classes that the dean called him in for a conference. Story had it that if the dean got out of his chair and put his arm around a student's shoulders, the student was certain to be dismissed from school. Midway through the interview, the dean rose and approached Father. Swiftly Father got up and walked around the desk, and thus conversation proceeded in circular fashion, with the dean lecturing and pursuing and Father explaining and running. The result was probation, not expulsion. It was a wonder that Father had enough energy to elude the dean, because he never attended gym class, a required course. Before graduation one of Father's physician friends wrote a letter, urging the suspension of the requirement in Father's case, explaining, "Pickering has a lameness in his back." After reading the letter, the dean said, "No more lies, Pickering; out of my office." Father left silently and graduated.

Although Father majored in English during the great years of Vanderbilt's English department—the years of the Fugitives and the Agrarians—his college experiences were personal, not intellectual. From Carthage he brought with him the small-town world of particulars and familial relationships. For him, as for me, reality was apparent and truth clear, and he had little interest in hidden structures or highly wrought reasoning, making Ds in psychology and philosophy. In later years he rarely talked about classroom matters unless there was a story attached. When John Crowe Ransom assigned two poems to be written, Father exhausted his inspiration and interest on the first and got his roommate, who had a certain lyrical ability, to write the other. The week following the assignment, Professor Ransom read Father's two poems to the class, remarking, "It is inconceivable to me that the same person could have written these poems."

"A matter of mood, Mr. Ransom," Father explained, and he was right. Whose mood seems beside the point, especially when the nonpoetic have to write verse. I inherited Father's poetic skills, and in sixth grade when I was assigned a poem, I turned to him and he turned out "The Zoo," a very effective piece for twelve-year-olds, featuring, among other animals, a polar bear with white hair, a chimp with a limp, an antelope on the end of a rope, and a turtle named Myrtle. Despite his lack of poetic talent, Father read a fair amount of poetry and was fond of quoting verse, particularly poems like Tennyson's "The Splendour Falls," the sounds of which rang cool and clear like bells. Father's favorite poet was Byron; and the dying gladiator was a companion of my childhood, while the Coliseum seemed to stand not in faraway Rome but just around the corner of another day. College, however, probably had little to do with Father's enjoyment of Byron; the source was closer to home, Father's grandfather William Blackstone Pickering. On a shelf in our library I found *The Works of Lord Byron in Verse and Prose,* published in Hartford in 1840 by Silas Andrus and Son. The book was inscribed "Wm. B. Pickering from his father." Over the inscription a child wrote, "Sammie F. Pickering." Under that in a firm, youthful handwriting was written "Samuel Pickering, Beta House, Vanderbilt University, 1926."

Often holding three jobs at once, Father worked his way through Vanderbilt and simply did not have much time for classes. Yet he was always a reading man, and at times I suspected that there was nothing he had not read. Years later at his office, he kept books in the top drawer of his desk. When business was slow, he pulled the drawer out slightly, and after placing a pad and pencil in front of himself for appearances, he read. Despite the college jobs, such a reader should have done better than the B's, C's, and D's Father made in English. In part the small-town world of Carthage may have been responsible for his performance. Carthage was a world of particulars, not abstractions, a place in which Tabler's Buckeye Pile Ointment "Cures Nothing but Piles," a town in which Mrs. Polk, a neighbor, could burst into Grandfather's kitchen crying that her daughter Mary, who had gone to Nashville, was "ruined."

"Oh, Lord," Grandfather exclaimed, "was she taken advantage of?"

"Yes," Mrs. Polk answered, "she had her hair bobbed."

At Vanderbilt during the 1920s literary criticism was shifting from the personal and anecdotal to the intellectual and the abstract. Instead of explaining ordinary life, it began to create an extraordinary world of thought far from piles and bobbed hair. For Father such a shift led to boredom and the conviction that although literary criticism might entertain some people, it was ultimately insignificant. In the sixty years that have passed since Father entered Vanderbilt, criticism has become more rarefied, and the result is, as a friend and critic wrote me, "we write books that even our mothers won't read."

Carthage influenced more than Father's schoolwork; it determined the course of his career. Although Grandmother dreamed of the land of goldenrod, she stayed in Carthage and joined the Eastern Star. After graduating from Vanderbilt in 1929, Father went to work in the personnel department of the Travelers Insurance Company. Years later, he told me that he had made a mistake. "I did what my father did," he said; "I should have done something different, even run off to sea." An old man's thoughts often wander far from the path trod by the young man, and running away to sea is only accomplished in books and dreamed about when the house is quiet and the children asleep. For his insurance business, Grandfather traveled about Smith County in a buggy; occasionally he took the train to Nashville. Once when he was trying to settle a claim over a mule which had been struck by lightning (no mule ever died a natural death in Tennessee; mules were the lightning rods of the animal world), he stayed overnight at Chestnut Mound with Miss Fanny and Godkin Hayes. The next morning after breakfast, when he was climbing into his buggy, Miss Fanny asked Grandfather if he ever went to Difficult Creek, Tennessee, saying she had heard he was quite a traveler and had been to Nashville.

"Yes, ma'am," Grandfather answered. "I go there right much."

"Well, the next time you go," Miss Fanny said, "will you please say hello to Henry McCracken; he's my brother and I haven't seen him in over twenty years."

"What!" my grandfather exclaimed; "Difficult Creek is only

twelve miles away, just on the other side of the Caney Fork River. Roane's Ferry will take you across in eight minutes."

"Oh, Mr. Sam," Miss Fanny answered wistfully, "I do want to see my brother, but I just can't bring myself to cross the great Caney Fork River."

Father crossed the Caney Fork, but he didn't travel far. After working in Washington and Richmond, he was sent to Nashville in the late thirties. From that time on he refused to be transferred. Beyond Difficult Creek lay the little town of Defeated Creek, and for most of his life Father was content to meander through a small circle of miles and visit with the Miss Fannys he met. Personnel, however, may have been too easy for him. Reading books in the office, he became a character, albeit a competent one. "He was a bumblebee," a man told me; "he shouldn't have been able to fly, but he did. What's more he did things that couldn't be done." By the 1960s, though, the topography of Father's world changed. The wild growth of wealth changed the course of Defeated Creek, making it swing closer to home. People suddenly became not who they knew or what they were but how much money they made. Strangers appeared, and instead of being identified by a rich string of anecdotes, they became bank accounts or corporations. It was almost impossible not to be swept up by the wash of money, and as Father's friends grew wealthy and began to possess the glittering goods of the world and to take trips beyond simple goldenrod to lands where orchids hung heavy from trees and butterflies bigger than fans waved in the sun, Father became envious. Although he occasionally criticized the affluence of certain groups—physicians, for example—he was not resentful. What troubled him most, I think, was how wealth changed conversation. Despite his wide reading, there was little room for him or Miss Fanny in talk about Bali or Borneo.

Disregard for possessions tempered Father's resentment of wealth. Although he liked shoes, both good and bad, and as a handsome man was vain on occasions like Christmas, when he wore a red vest, clothes, for example, mattered little to him. Outside the office he wore khaki trousers and checkered shirts that he bought at Sears. So long as the interior of the house was tasteful, something he knew Mother managed well, Father paid no attention to it. If a visitor admired something, Father was likely to offer it to him, especially, it seemed, if it was a family piece: an envelope of Confederate money or a Bible published in 1726 and listing forgotten generations of ancestors. As a child, I learned to hide things. When I found a box of old letters in a storeroom at Aunt Lula's house, I hid them in the attic. When the day came, as I knew it would, when Father asked for them, saying he had a friend who would like to have them, I lied and said that I lost them. Of course saving everything was beyond me, and I once resented his forays through my things. Even today when I want a good tricycle for my children, I resent his giving away the English trike that Mother's father bought me in New York. Now, though, I understand Father's desire to rid himself of possessions. I behave similarly. I wear Sears trousers and shirts from J. C. Penney's. I have turned down positions that would greatly increase my salary because I like the little out-of-the-way place where I live. I, too, alas, give away possessions. "You are the only teacher I have ever met," a graduate student told me recently, "who has two offices and not a single book." I don't have any books because I have given them away, out of, I think, the same compulsion that led Father to give away things and that kept him from becoming wealthy: the desire to keep life as clean and as simple as possible.

Wealth clutters life, bringing not simply possessions but temptation. Money lures one from the straight and clear into the darkly complex. The sidewalks in Carthage ran in narrow lines to the courthouse. Skating along them, a boy was always aware of where he was: in front of the Reeds' house, then the Ligons', the Fishers', the McGinnises', and then by the drugstore, the five and ten, King's barbershop, and finally the bank and post office. Wealth bends lines and makes it difficult for even the most adept skater to roll through life without losing his way or falling into the dirt. Instead of enriching, wealth often lessens life. At least that's the way I think Father thought, for he spurned every chance to become wealthy. For some twenty years he managed the affairs of his Aunt Lula, Grandmother's widowed sister. Father being her nearest relative, Aunt Lula called upon him whenever anything went wrong. For three summers in a row, Aunt Lula fell ill during Father's two-week summer vacation, and we hurried back to Nashville from the beach to put her in the hospital. Aunt Lula owned a farm, 750 acres of land just outside Nashville in Williamson County. The farm had been in the family for generations, and when I came home from college at Christmas, I spent mornings roaming over it rabbit hunting.

Aunt Lula did not have a will, and when Father's closest friend, a lawyer, learned this, he urged Father to let him draw one up for her. "For God's sakes, Sam," he said; "you have nursed her for years. She would want you to have the farm. I will make out the will tonight and you have her sign it tomorrow." Father demurred, and when Aunt Lula died, two relatives who had never met her shared the estate. Father put the land up for sale and received a bid of seventy-five thousand dollars.

"Borrow the money," Mother advised, "and buy the land yourself. Nashville is growing by leaps and bounds, and the farm is worth much more."

"That would not be right," Father answered, and the land was sold. Six years later it was resold for over a million dollars. Father kept the lines of his life straight and his temptations few, and I admire him for it; yet at night when I think about the three teaching jobs I have taken this summer so the house can be painted and dead oaks felled in the yard, I sometimes wish he had not sold the farm. This is not to say that Father did not understand the power of money. He thought it important for other people and urged me to make the most of my chances, citing his younger brother Coleman as a warning. According to Father, Coleman was the talented Pickering and could have done practically anything; yet, Father recounted, he refused to grasp opportunities. Satisfied to live simply, Coleman was in truth Father's brother, a man wary of complexity, determined to remain independent and free from entangling responsibilities.

After forty most people I know realize that their actions and thoughts are inconsistent. Worried about gypsy moths, a child's stuttering, or slow-running drains, they have little time for principle and not simply neglect but recognize and are comfortable with the discrepancy between words and deeds. To some extent Father's attitude toward wealth reflected this state of mind. Behind his behavior, however, also lay the perennial conflict between the particular and the abstract or the general. From infancy through school people are taught the value of general truths or principles, the sanctity, for example, of honor and truth itself. As one grows older and attempts to apply principles to real human beings, one learns that rules are cruelly narrow and, instead of bettering life, often lead to unhappiness. The sense of principle or belief in general truth is so deeply ingrained, however, that one rarely repudiates it. Instead, one continues to pay lip service to it and actually believe in its value while never applying it to particular individuals. Thus during the turmoil over integration in Nashville during the 1950s and early '60s, Father sounded harshly conservative. One day, though, while he and Mother and I were walking along Church Street, we came upon four toughs, or hoods as they were then called, harassing a black woman. "You there," Father bellowed, all 136 pounds of him swelling with his voice; "who do you think you are?" Then as mother and I wilted into a doorway, he grabbed the biggest tough and, shaking him, said, "Apologize to this lady. This is Tennessee, and people behave here."

"Yes, sir, yes, sir," the man responded meekly and apologized.

Father then turned to the woman, and while the toughs scurried away, took off his hat and said, "Ma'am, I am sorry for what happened. You are probably walking to the bus stop; if you don't mind, my wife and I and our son would like to walk with you."

Although Father expounded political and moral generalities during the isolation of dinner, he never applied them to the hurly-burly of his friends' lives. He delighted in people too much to categorize and thus limit his enjoyment of them. Not long after the incident on Church Street, Father was invited to join the Klan. Around ten or eleven each morning, a man appeared outside the Travelers building, selling doughnuts and sweet rolls. As could be expected from a man who did not have to work too hard and who loved candy, Father always bought a doughnut and a cup of coffee and then chatted a bit. On this occasion, the man said, "Mr. Pickering, I have known you for some time, and you seem a right-thinking man. This Friday there is going to be a meeting of the Klan at Nolensville, and I'd like for you to attend and become a member."

"That's mighty nice of you to invite me," Father replied, "but I believe I will just continue to vote Republican."

As could be expected, Father was inconsistent toward me. Of things he thought comparatively unimportant—sports, for example—he rarely said much, except to moan about the Vanderbilt football team. When I was in high school, he picked me up after football practice, and unlike some boys' fathers, who filmed practices, had conferences with the coaches, and caused their sons untold misery, Father never got in the way. About social matters he behaved differently, urging me to do the things he never did—join service clubs, for example. "They will help your career," he explained. When he heard me taking a political stance that was not generally accepted and thereby safe, he intervened. Ten years ago I spent three months in the Soviet Union. On my return people often asked me questions; once during a discussion with businessmen Father overheard me say something "risky." "Pay no attention to my son," he interrupted; "he has been brainwashed." That ended the conversation.

Of Father's courtship of Mother, I know and want to know little. Toward the end of his life, he refused to tell me family stories, saying, "You will publish them." Quite right—I would publish almost anything except an account of his and Mother's love affair. Theirs was a good and typical marriage with much happiness and sadness during the early and middle years and with many operations at the end. They were very different, but they stumbled along in comparative harmony.

"When I first met him," Mother told me, "I thought him the damnedest little pissant."

"Your mother," Father often said, "does not appreciate my sense of humor." That was a loss, because laughing was important to Father, and for much of his life, he played practical jokes. Practical jokes are an almost implicit recognition of the foolishness of man's endeavors. Involving actual individuals rather than comparative abstractions like wordplay, for example, such humor flourishes in stable communities in which people's positions remain relatively constant and clearly defined. The popularity of practical jokes waned as the South grew wealthy. Money undermined community both by making people more mobile and by changing the terms by which position was defined. As people became financial accomplishments, not neighbors, cousins, sons, and daughters, they took themselves more seriously. When they, rather than a web of relationships over which they had comparatively little control, determined what they were, their actions grew increasingly significant. No more could the practical joker be seen as a friend; no more was his laughter benign, even fond. Instead, threatening the basis of identity by mocking, he undermined society. By the late 1960s Father had stopped playing practical jokes; before then, though, the going was good.

After selling some rocky, farmed-out land to a company that wanted to construct a shopping center, one of Father's acquaintances, Tuck Gobbett, built a twenty-room house outside Nashville. Known locally as the Taj Mahal, the house had everything: sauna bath, swimming pool, Japanese shoji screens around the garage, and even a pond with swans purchased from a New York dealer. In its garishness the house was marvelous, and Father enjoyed it, saying only, "The birds were a mistake. As soon as snapping turtles find the pond, it's good-bye swans." He was right; two years later the turtles came, and the swans disappeared. Father decided Gobbett went too far, however, when he got rid of the off-brand beagles he had always owned and bought an Afghan hound. The dog had a royal pedigree, and when Gobbett advertised in a kennel-club magazine that the dog was standing at stud, Father saw his chance. "Why is it," he asked me years later, "that mongrel people always want purebred dogs." Father then read about Afghans, learning quite a bit about bloodlines. Able to disguise his voice, he telephoned Gobbett, explaining that he lived in Birmingham and was the owner of a champion bitch. He had, he said, seen the advertisement in the kennel-club magazine and wondered about the possibility of breeding the animals. Of course, he continued, he would first have to scrutinize the pedigree of Gobbett's dog. After Gobbett detailed his dog's ancestry, Father then supplied that of the bitch, which, not surprisingly, came from the best Afghan stock in the nation. Saying he would need time to investigate the Gobbetts' dog, Father hung up, promising to call within a week. During the week Father visited Gobbett. When asked about news, Gobbett excitedly described the telephone call, saying the bitch had "an absolutely first-class pedigree" and the puppies would be worth a thousand dollars apiece.

The next week Father telephoned, saying he looked into the dog and thought the pedigree would do. Although the owner of the bitch usually received all the puppies except for one from a breeding, Father said he did not want a single puppy. After this remark, he said he had pressing business and would call the following week to make arrangements for the mating. Gobbett was ebullient. "What fools there are in the world," he said; "there is money to be made in these dogs. The puppies will make me a man to be reckoned with in Afghan circles." As could be expected, completing the arrangements was not easy, but after a month and a half of conversations, the date and place were set. Then at the end of the final telephone call, almost as an afterthought, Father said, "There is just one thing though."

"What's that?" Gobbett asked.

"Oh, nothing important," Father said; "my dog has been spayed, but I don't suppose that will make a difference."

Father's humor was rarely bawdy, and the jokes he told were usually stories, gentle tales about foolishness. My favorite, one that I have often told, was called "Edgar the Cat." Two bachelor brothers, Herbert and James, lived with their mother and James's cat Edgar in a little town not unlike Carthage. James was particularly attached to Edgar, and when he had to spend several days in Nashville having work done on his teeth, he left Herbert meticulous instructions about Edgar. At the end of his first day away from home, James telephoned Herbert. "Herbert," he said, "how is Edgar?"

"Edgar is dead," Herbert answered immediately.

There was a pause; then James said, "Herbert, you are terribly insensitive. You know how close I was to Edgar and you should have broken the news to me slowly."

"How?" Herbert said.

"Well," James said, "when I asked about Edgar tonight, you should have said 'Edgar's on the roof, but I have called the fire department to get him down.'"

"Is that so?" said Herbert.

"Yes," James answered, "and tomorrow when I called you could have said the firemen were having trouble getting Edgar down but you were hopeful they would succeed. Then when I called the third time you could have told me that the firemen had done their best but unfortunately Edgar had fallen off the roof and was at the veterinarian's, where he was receiving fine treatment. Then when I called the last time you could have said that although everything humanly possible had been done for Edgar he had died. That's the way a sensitive man would have told me about Edgar. And, oh, before I forget," James added, "how is Mother?"

"Uh," Herbert said, pausing for a moment, "she's on the roof."

There was an innocence in Father's humor, perhaps a sign of softness, something that contributed to his not grabbing Aunt Lula's farm. In the eighteenth and early nineteenth centuries, Pickerings were Quakers and, so far as I call tell, gentle people who did not struggle or rage against life but who took things as they came, people who copied poems into family Bibles while recording the deaths of children. When seven-year-old Marthelia died in 1823, her father wrote:

> When the Icy hand of death his sabre drew!
> To cut down the budding rose of morn!!
> He held his favorite motto full in view—
> The fairest Bud must the tomb adorn!!!

In general Pickerings lived quiet lives, cultivating their few acres and avoiding the larger world with its abstractions of honor, service, and patriotism. For them country meant the counties in which they lived, not the imperial nation. Years ago I knew

John Kennedy had things backwards when he said, "Ask not what your country can do for you, but what you can do for your country." The great excuse for country, with its borders dividing brothers, was that it bettered the life of the individual.

With the exception of the Civil War, the struggles of the nation have not touched us. Coming of age between battles, few Pickerings have looked at the dark side of man's heart. Perhaps because of this, we are soft and, in our desires, subconscious or conscious, to remain free, have become evasive. Few things are simple, though, and this very evasiveness may be a sign of a shrewd or even tough vitality. Aware that those who respond to challenges and fight for a cause or success often are ground under, we have learned to live unobtrusively and blossom low to the ground and out of sight. Even when a Pickering does respond to a call, it's usually not for him. In 1942 the navy rejected Father's application for Officers' Training School because he was too thin. In 1944 Father was drafted; two days before he was slated to leave for training camp and after a series of farewell parties, he received a telegram instructing him not to report, explaining that he was too thin.

Not long ago my daughter Eliza McClarin Pickering was born. She was born, fittingly enough, in a hospital in a relatively small town. For four days she was the only baby in the maternity ward and the nurses let me wander in and out at my convenience. With little to do, the nurses drank coffee, ate doughnuts, and talked. One night as I stood looking at Eliza in her crib, I overheard a conversation at the nurses' station around the corner. "I have worked at four hospitals," one nurse declared confidentially, "but this is the worst for poking I have ever seen. There's Shirley," she said, warming to the subject, "she runs out to the parking lot and gets poked every chance she gets. And Kate, there's not a bed on the third floor that she hasn't been poked in." Like Homer's account of those slain at the sack of Troy, the nurse's list of fallen was long and colorful. During the recital, the second nurse was silent. Finally, though, she spoke. "My word," she said in mild astonishment, "it's just a whirlwind of festivities."

Although few strong breezes blow through the lives of Pickerings, there are festivities, not shining affairs strung with bright lights but quiet events lit by words. After being married on my grandfather's farm in Hanover, Virginia, Father and Mother spent their first night together in the Jefferson Hotel in Richmond. Early the next morning they started for Nashville in Father's Ford coupe. On the outskirts of Richmond, they stopped for gas, and Mother bought a newspaper to look at the wedding pictures. She spread the paper out on the front seat and was looking at the pictures with Father when the man who was cleaning the windshield spoke up, saying, "It's a pity about that wedding. I feel so sorry for the girl."

"What do you mean," Father answered, jumping in before Mother could respond.

"Well," the man said, "she didn't marry the man she wanted to. She was in love with a poor insurance man but her father made her marry a rich fellow."

"Who told you that?" Father asked.

"Oh," the man answered, "a colored preacher that comes through here told me all about it. He preaches up in Hanover, and some of the members of his congregation work at her father's farm."

"Hmmm," Father said, "I hate to ruin your story, but look at the picture of the groom, and then look at me. This," he said gesturing toward Mother after the man had a good look, "is that unfortunate girl, and I am the poor insurance man. The preacher was wrong; sometimes in life poor folks carry off the prizes." And that's what Father did in a quiet way all his days. No prize of his was mentioned in an obituary; his name was not associated with any accomplishment; yet in the few acres he tilled and even beyond, at least as far as Carthage, he was known.

While at Vanderbilt, Father bought an old car. On a trip to Carthage it broke down, and, having to hurry back to Nashville to take an examination, one of the few times he attended class, Father left the car in Carthage and took the train. For a modest fee George Jackson, a black man, agreed to drive the car to Nashville once it was repaired. Father wrote out careful instructions and drew a map. Alas, George lost both, but this did not deter him. On arriving in Nashville, he stopped in a residential area, went up to a house, and asked where "young Mr. Samuel Pickering" lived. Amazingly, the people in the house knew Father. They gave George clear directions, and he delivered the car. When Father learned that the map had gone astray and George had lost his way, he asked him how he knew whom to ask for instructions. "Mister Sam," George answered, "everybody knows you." The one time Father told this story, he laughed, then said, "What a world we have lost. Not a better world," he added, "but a different one. At times I miss it." Not, old man, so much as I miss you—not so much as I miss you.

SCOTT RUSSELL SANDERS

*Author of more than twenty books, Scott Russell Sanders (1945–)
has written works that range from science fiction to children's sto-
rybooks. He is best known, however, for his personal essays, which
regularly appear in such publications as* Audubon, Orion, *and
the* Georgia Review. *Sanders, who holds a Ph.D. from Cam-
bridge, has since 1971 been on the faculty of Indiana University,
where he serves as Distinguished Professor in the Department of
English.*

*Sanders has written that he was born in the backwoods of Ten-
nessee and "came to consciousness" in the backwoods of Ohio. Before him, his father, Greeley Ray Sanders, grew up on a red-dirt
cotton farm in Mississippi. After a failed attempt at a boxing career, Greeley spent World War II working in a Mississippi muni-
tion plant—experience that in 1951 led him and his young family
to northeastern Ohio and the Ravenna Arsenal, a thirty-square-
mile military reservation littered with ordnance and old weap-
ons. There, Greeley supervised the "loadline"—the place where
bombs, artillery shells, and land mines were filled and the floor*

was so saturated with TNT that a dropped tool could spark an explosion and cost a worker a leg.

But the Arsenal was also a de facto game preserve. The family took evening excursions to count deer, and it was here that Greeley began instilling his own love of nature into his son. In his essay "News of the Wild," Sanders writes, "When I think of my father I see him outdoors. Whether in a garden, pasture, or woods, on a river or lake, he was always looking around, sniffing the air, listening, and he always seemed utterly at ease." On fishing trips, hikes, and outings his father would cry out repeatedly with delight, "Will you look at this." And later, when Scott was old enough to venture out on his own, his father would ask on his return, "What did you find?"—meaning what fossil or feather or patch of ripe berries. Later still, when Sanders began taking his own children to the woods, he'd ask them the same question: "What did you find?"

But Greeley taught his son about more than nature. He taught him to throw a baseball, to use tools, to fix a faucet, to carpenter. And he taught him to feel shame. For Greeley was an alcoholic and there was a constant pressure in the family for everyone to keep what they knew a secret.

Scott Russell Sanders has woven bits of his father's life story through many of his essays; in the selection presented here, he writes about his father's drinking. "Under the Influence" was first published in Harper's Magazine in 1989. Sanders later included the essay in his collection Secrets of the Universe.

Under the Influence

My father drank. He drank as a gut-punched boxer gasps for breath, as a starving dog gobbles food—compulsively, secretly, in pain and trembling. I use the past tense not because he ever quit drinking but because he quit living. That is how the story ends for my father, age sixty-four, heart bursting, body cooling and forsaken on the linoleum of my brother's trailer. The story continues for my brother, my sister, my mother, and me, and will continue so long as memory holds.

In the perennial present of memory, I slip into the garage or barn to see my father tipping back the flat green bottles of wine, the brown cylinders of whiskey, the cans of beer disguised in paper bags. His Adam's apple bobs, the liquid gurgles, he wipes the sandy-haired back of a hand over his lips, and then, his bloodshot gaze bumping into me, he stashes the bottle or can inside his jacket, under the workbench, between two bales of hay, and we both pretend the moment has not occurred.

"What's up, buddy?" he says, thick-tongued and edgy.

"Sky's up," I answer, playing along.

"And don't forget prices," he grumbles. "Prices are always up. And taxes."

In memory, his white 1951 Pontiac with the stripes down the hood and the Indian head on the snout jounces to a stop in the driveway; or it is the 1956 Ford station wagon, or the 1963 Rambler shaped like a toad, or the sleek 1969 Bonneville that will do 120 miles per hour on straightaways; or it is the robin's-egg blue pickup, new in 1980, battered in 1981, the year of his death. He climbs out, grinning dangerously, unsteady on his legs, and we children interrupt our game of catch, our building of snow forts, our picking of plums, to watch in silence as he weaves past into the house, where he slumps into his overstuffed chair and falls asleep. Shaking her head, our mother stubs out the cigarette he has left smoldering in the ashtray. All evening, until our bedtimes, we tiptoe past him, as past a snoring dragon. Then we curl in our fearful sheets, listening. Eventually he wakes with a grunt, Mother slings accusations at him, he snarls back, she yells, he growls, their voices clashing. Before long, she retreats to their bedroom, sobbing—not from the blows of fists, for he never strikes her, but from the force of words.

Left alone, our father prowls the house, thumping into furniture, rummaging in the kitchen, slamming doors, turning the pages of the newspaper with a savage crackle, muttering back at the late-night drivel from television. The roof might fly off, the walls might buckle from the pressure of his rage. Whatever my brother and sister and mother may be thinking on their own rumpled pillows, I lie there hating him, loving him, fearing him, knowing I have failed him. I tell myself he drinks to ease an ache that gnaws at his belly, an ache I must have caused by disappointing him somehow, a murderous ache I should be able to relieve by doing all my chores, earning A's in school, winning baseball games, fixing the broken washer and the burst pipes, bringing in money to fill his empty wallet. He would not hide the green bottles in his tool box, would not sneak off to the barn with a lump under his coat, would not fall asleep in the daylight, would not roar and fume, would not drink himself to death, if only I were perfect.

I am forty-two as I write these words, and I know full well now that my father was an alcoholic, a man consumed by disease rather than by disappointment. What had seemed to me a private grief is in fact a public scourge. In the United States alone some ten or fifteen million people share his ailment, and behind the doors they slam in fury or disgrace, countless other children tremble. I comfort myself with such knowledge, holding it against the throb of memory like an ice pack against a bruise. There are keener sources of grief: poverty, racism, rape, war. I do not wish to compete for a trophy in suffering. I am only trying to understand the corrosive mixture of helplessness, responsibility, and shame that I learned to feel as the son of an alcoholic. I realize now that I did not cause my father's illness, nor could I have cured it. Yet for all this grown-up knowledge, I am still ten years old, my own son's age, and as that boy I struggle in guilt and confusion to save my father from pain.

Consider a few of our synonyms for *drunk:* tipsy, tight, pickled, soused, and plowed; stoned and stewed, lubricated and inebriated, juiced and sluiced; three sheets to the wind, in your cups, out of your mind, under the table; lit up, tanked up, wiped out; besotted, blotto, bombed, and buzzed; plastered, polluted, putrefied; loaded or looped, boozy, woozy, fuddled, or smashed; crocked and shit-faced, corked and pissed, snockered and sloshed.

It is a mostly humorous lexicon, as the lore that deals with drunks—in jokes and cartoons, in plays, films, and television skits—is largely comic. Aunt Matilda nips elderberry wine from the sideboard and burps politely during supper. Uncle Fred slouches to the table glassy-eyed, wearing a lamp shade for a hat and murmuring, "Candy is dandy but liquor is quicker." Inspired by cocktails, Mrs. Somebody recounts the events of her day in a fuzzy dialect, while Mr. Somebody nibbles her ear and croons a bawdy song. On the sofa with Boyfriend, Daughter giggles, licking gin from her lips, and loosens the bows in her hair. Junior knocks back some brews with his chums at the Leopard Lounge and stumbles home to the wrong house, wonders foggily why he cannot locate his pajamas, and crawls naked into bed with the ugliest girl in school. The family dog slurps from a neglected martini and wobbles to the nursery, where he vomits in Baby's shoe.

It is all great fun. But if in the audience you notice a few laughing faces turn grim when the drunk lurches on stage, don't be surprised, for these are the children of alcoholics. Over the grinning mask of Dionysus, the leering mask of Bacchus, these children cannot help seeing the bloated features of their own parents. Instead of laughing, they wince, they mourn. Instead of celebrating the drunk as one freed from constraints, they pity him as one enslaved. They refuse to believe *in vino veritas,* having seen their befuddled parents skid away from truth toward folly and oblivion. And so these children bite their lips until the lush staggers into the wings.

My father, when drunk, was neither funny nor honest; he was pathetic, frightening, deceitful. There seemed to be a leak in him somewhere, and he poured in booze to keep from draining dry. Like a torture victim who refuses to squeal, he would never admit that he had touched a drop, not even in his last year, when he seemed to be dissolving in alcohol before our very eyes. I never knew him to lie about anything, ever, except about this one ruinous fact. Drowsy, clumsy, unable to fix a bicycle tire, throw a baseball, balance a grocery sack, or walk across the room, he was stripped of his true self by drink. In a matter of minutes, the contents of a bottle could transform a brave man into a coward, a buddy into a bully, a gifted athlete and skilled carpenter and shrewd businessman into a bumbler. No dictionary of synonyms for *drunk* would soften the anguish of watching our prince turn into a frog.

Father's drinking became the family secret. While growing up, we children never breathed a word of it beyond the four walls of our house. To this day, my brother and sister rarely mention it, and then only when I press them. I did not confess the ugly, bewildering fact to my wife until his wavering walk and slurred speech forced me to. Recently, on the seventh anniversary of my father's death, I asked my mother if she ever spoke of his drinking to friends. "No, no, never," she replied hastily. "I couldn't bear for anyone to know."

The secret bores under the skin, gets in the blood, into the bone, and stays there. Long after you have supposedly been cured of malaria, the fever can flare up, the tremors can shake you. So it is with the fevers of shame. You swallow the bitter quinine of knowledge, and you learn to feel pity and compassion toward the drinker. Yet the shame lingers in your marrow, and, because of the shame, anger.

For a long stretch of my childhood we lived on a military reservation in Ohio, an arsenal where bombs were stored underground in bunkers, vintage airplanes burst into flames, and unstable artillery shells boomed nightly at the dump. We had the feeling, as children, that we played in a mine field, where a heedless footfall could trigger an explosion. When Father was drinking, the house, too, became a mine field. The least bump could set off either parent.

The more he drank, the more obsessed Mother became with stopping him. She hunted for bottles, counted the cash in his wallet, sniffed at his breath. Without meaning to snoop, we children blundered left and right into damning evidence. On afternoons when he came home from work sober, we flung ourselves at him for hugs, and felt against our ribs the telltale lump in his coat. In the barn we tumbled on the hay and heard beneath our sneakers the crunch of buried glass. We tugged open a drawer in his workbench, looking for screwdrivers or crescent wrenches, and spied a gleaming six-pack among the tools. Playing tag, we darted around the house just in time to see him sway on the rear stoop and heave a finished bottle into the woods. In his good-night kiss we smelled the cloying sweetness of Clorets, the mints he chewed to camouflage his dragon's breath.

I can summon up that kiss right now by recalling Theodore Roethke's lines about his own father in "My Papa's Waltz":

> The whiskey on your breath
> Could make a small boy dizzy;
> But I hung on like death:
> Such waltzing was not easy.

Such waltzing was hard, terribly hard, for with a boy's scrawny arms I was trying to hold my tipsy father upright.

For years, the chief source of those incriminating bottles and cans was a grimy store a mile from us, a cinder block place called Sly's, with two gas pumps outside and a moth-eaten dog asleep in the window. A strip of flypaper, speckled the year round with black bodies, coiled in the doorway. Inside, on rusty metal shelves or in wheezing coolers, you could find pop and Popsicles, cigarettes, potato chips, canned soup, raunchy postcards, fishing gear, Twinkies, wine, and beer. When Father drove anywhere on errands, Mother would send us kids along as guards, warning us not to let him out of our sight. And so with one or more of us on board, Father would cruise up to Sly's, pump a dollar's worth of gas or plump the tires with air, and then, telling us to wait in the car, he would head for that fly-spangled doorway.

Dutiful and panicky, we cried, "Let us go in with you!"

"No," he answered. "I'll be back in two shakes."

"Please!"

"No!" he roared. "Don't you budge, or I'll jerk a knot in your tails!"

So we stayed put, kicking the seats, while he ducked inside. Often, when he had parked the car at a careless angle, we gazed in through the window and saw Mr. Sly fetching down from a shelf behind the cash register two green pints of Gallo wine. Father swigged one of them right there at the counter, stuffed the other in his pocket, and then out he came, a bulge in his coat, a flustered look on his red face.

Because the Mom and Pop who ran the dump were neighbors of ours, living just down the tar-blistered road, I hated them all the more for poisoning my father. I wanted to sneak in their store and smash the bottles and set fire to the place. I also hated the Gallo brothers, Ernest and Julio, whose jovial faces shone from the labels of their wine, labels I would find, torn and curled, when I burned the trash. I noted the Gallo brothers' address, in California, and I studied the road atlas to see how far that was from Ohio, because I meant to go out there and tell Ernest and Julio what they were doing to my father, and then, if they showed no mercy, I would kill them.

While growing up on the back roads and in the country schools and cramped Methodist churches of Ohio and Tennessee, I never heard the word alcoholism, never happened across it in books or magazines. In the nearby towns, there were no addiction treatment programs, no community mental health centers, no Alcoholics Anonymous chapters, no therapists. Left alone with our grievous secret, we had no way of understanding Father's drinking except as an act of will, a deliberate folly or cruelty, a moral weakness, a sin. He drank because he chose to, pure and simple. Why our father, so playful and competent and kind when sober, would choose to ruin himself and punish his family, we could not fathom.

Our neighborhood was high on the Bible, and the Bible was hard on drunkards. "Woe to those who are heroes at drinking wine, and valiant men in mixing strong drink," wrote Isaiah. "The priest and the prophet reel with strong drink, they are confused with wine, they err in vision, they stumble in giving judgment. For all tables are full of vomit, no place is without filthiness." We children had seen those fouled tables at the local truck stop where the notorious boozers hung out, our father occasionally among them. "Wine and new wine take away the understanding," declared the prophet Hosea. We had also seen evidence of that in our father, who could multiply seven-digit numbers in his head when sober, but when drunk could not help us with fourth-grade math. Proverbs warned: "Do not look at wine when it is red, when it sparkles in the cup and goes down smoothly. At the last it bites like a serpent, and stings like an adder. Your eyes will see strange things, and your mind utter perverse things." Woe, woe.

Dismayingly often, these biblical drunkards stirred up trouble for their own kids. Noah made fresh wine after the flood, drank too much of it, fell asleep without any clothes on, and was glimpsed in the buff by his son Ham, whom Noah promptly cursed. In one passage—it was so shocking we had to read it under our blankets with flashlights—the patriarch Lot fell down drunk and slept with his daughters. The sins of the fathers set their children's teeth on edge.

Our ministers were fond of quoting St. Paul's pronouncement that drunkards would not inherit the kingdom of God. These grave preachers assured us that the wine referred to during the Last Supper was in fact grape juice. Bible and sermons and hymns combined to give us the impression that Moses should have brought down from the mountain another stone tablet, bearing the Eleventh Commandment: Thou shalt not drink.

The scariest and most illuminating Bible story apropos of

drunkards was the one about the lunatic and the swine. Matthew, Mark, and Luke each told a version of the tale. We knew it by heart: When Jesus climbed out of his boat one day, this lunatic came charging up from the graveyard, stark naked and filthy, frothing at the mouth, so violent that he broke the strongest chains. Nobody would go near him. Night and day for years this madman had been wailing among the tombs and bruising himself with stones. Jesus took one look at him and said, "Come out of the man, you unclean spirits!" for he could see that the lunatic was possessed by demons. Meanwhile, some hogs were conveniently rooting nearby. "If we have to come out," begged the demons, "at least let us go into those swine." Jesus agreed. The unclean spirits entered the hogs, and the hogs rushed straight off a cliff and plunged into a lake. Hearing the story in Sunday school, my friends thought mainly of the pigs. (How big a splash did they make? Who paid for the lost pork?) But I thought of the redeemed lunatic, who bathed himself and put on clothes and calmly sat at the feet of Jesus, restored—so the Bible said—to "his right mind."

When drunk, our father was clearly in his wrong mind. He became a stranger, as fearful to us as any graveyard lunatic, not quite frothing at the mouth but fierce enough, quick-tempered, explosive; or else he grew maudlin and weepy, which frightened us nearly as much. In my boyhood despair, I reasoned that maybe he wasn't to blame for turning into an ogre. Maybe, like the lunatic, he was possessed by demons. I found support for my theory when I heard liquor referred to as "spirits," when the newspapers reported that somebody had been arrested for "driving under the influence," and when church ladies railed against that "demon drink."

If my father was indeed possessed, who would exorcise him? If he was a sinner, who would save him? If he was ill, who would cure him? If he suffered, who would ease his pain? Not ministers or doctors, for we could not bring ourselves to confide in them; not the neighbors, for we pretended they had never seen him drunk; not Mother, who fussed and pleaded but could not budge him; not my brother and sister, who were only kids. That left me. It did not matter that I, too, was only a child, and a bewildered one at that. I could not excuse myself.

On first reading a description of delirium tremens—in a book on alcoholism I smuggled from the library—I thought immediately of the frothing lunatic and the frenzied swine. When I read stories or watched films about grisly metamorphoses—Dr. Jekyll becoming Mr. Hyde, the mild husband changing into a werewolf, the kindly neighbor taken over by a brutal alien—I could not help seeing my own father's mutation from sober to drunk. Even today, knowing better, I am attracted by the demonic theory of drink, for when I recall my father's transformation, the emergence of his ugly second self, I find it easy to believe in possession by unclean spirits. We never knew which version of Father would come home from work, the true or the tainted, nor could we guess how far down the slope toward cruelty he would slide.

How far a man *could* slide we gauged by observing our backroad neighbors—the out-of-work miners who had dragged their families to our corner of Ohio from the desolate hollows of Appalachia, the tightfisted farmers, the surly mechanics, the balked and broken men. There was, for example, whiskey-soaked Mr. Jenkins, who beat his wife and kids so hard we could hear their screams from the road. There was Mr. Lavo the wino, who fell asleep smoking time and again, until one night his disgusted wife bundled up the children and went outside and left him in his easy chair to burn; he awoke on his own, staggered out coughing into the yard, and pounded her flat while the children looked on and the shack turned to ash. There was the truck driver, Mr. Sampson, who tripped over his son's tricycle one night while drunk and got so mad that he jumped into his semi and drove away, shifting through the dozen gears, and never came back. We saw the bruised children of these fathers clump onto our school bus, we saw the abandoned children huddle in the pews at church, we saw the stunned and battered mothers begging for help at our doors.

Our own father never beat us, and I don't think he ever beat Mother, but he threatened often. The Old Testament Yahweh was not more terrible in his wrath. Eyes blazing, voice booming, Father would pull out his belt and swear to give us a whipping, but he never followed through, never needed to, because we could imagine it so vividly. He shoved us, pawed us with the back of his hand, as an irked bear might smack a cub, not to injure, just to clear a space. I can see him grabbing Mother by the hair as she cowers on a chair during a nightly quarrel. He twists her neck back until she gapes up at him, and then he lifts over her skull a glass quart bottle of milk, the milk running down his forearm, and he yells at her, "Say just one more word, one goddamn word, and I'll shut you up!" I fear she will prick him with her sharp tongue, but she is terrified into silence, and so am I, and the leaking bottle quivers in the air, and milk slithers through the red hair of my father's uplifted arm, and the entire scene is there to this moment, the head jerked back, the club raised.

When the drink made him weepy, Father would pack a bag and kiss each of us children on the head, and announce from the front door that he was moving out. "Where to?" we demanded, fearful each time that he would leave for good, as Mr. Sampson had roared away for good in his diesel truck. "Someplace where I won't get hounded every minute," Father would answer, his jaw quivering. He stabbed a look at Mother, who might say, "Don't run into the ditch before you get there," or, "Good riddance," and then he would slink away. Mother watched him go with arms crossed over her chest, her face closed like the lid on a box of snakes. We children bawled.

Where could he go? To the truck stop, that den of iniquity? To one of those dark, ratty flophouses in town? Would he wind up sleeping under a railroad bridge or on a park bench or in a cardboard box, mummied in rags, like the bums we had seen on our trips to Cleveland and Chicago? We bawled and bawled, wondering if he would ever come back.

He always did come back, a day or a week later, but each time there was a sliver less of him.

In Kafka's *The Metamorphosis,* which opens famously with Gregor Samsa waking up from uneasy dreams to find himself transformed into an insect, Gregor's family keep reassuring themselves that things will be just fine again, "When he comes back to us." Each time alcohol transformed our father, we held out the same hope, that he would really and truly come back to us, our authentic father, the tender and playful and competent man, and then all things would be fine. We had grounds for such hope. After his weepy departures and chapfallen returns, he would sometimes go weeks, even months without drinking. Those were glad times. Joy banged inside my ribs. Every day without the furtive glint of bottles, every meal without a fight, every bedtime without sobs encouraged us to believe that such bliss might go on forever.

Mother was fooled by just such a hope all during the forty-odd years she knew this Greeley Ray Sanders. Soon after she met him in a Chicago delicatessen on the eve of World War II, and fell for his butter-melting Mississippi drawl and his wavy red hair, she learned that he drank heavily. But then so did a lot of men. She would soon coax or scold him into breaking the nasty habit. She would point out to him how ugly and foolish it was, this bleary drinking, and then he would quit. He refused to quit during their engagement, however, still refused during the first years of marriage, refused until my sister came along. The shock of fatherhood sobered him, and he remained sober through my birth at the end of the war and right on through until we moved in 1951 to the Ohio arsenal, that paradise of bombs. Like all places that make a business of death, the arsenal had more than its share of alcoholics and drug addicts and other varieties of escape artists. There I turned six and started school and woke into a child's flickering awareness, just in time to see my father begin sneaking swigs in the garage.

He sobered up again for most of a year at the height of the Korean War, to celebrate the birth of my brother. But aside from that dry spell, his only breaks from drinking before I graduated from high school were just long enough to raise and then dash our hopes. Then during the fall of my senior year—the time of the Cuban missile crisis, when it seemed that the nightly explosions at the munitions dump and the nightly rages in our household might spread to engulf the globe—Father collapsed. His liver, kidneys, and heart all conked out. The doctors saved him, but only by a hair. He stayed in the hospital for weeks, going through a withdrawal so terrible that Mother would not let us visit him. If he wanted to kill himself, the doctors solemnly warned him, all he had to do was hit the bottle again. One binge would finish him.

Father must have believed them, for he stayed dry the next fifteen years. It was an answer to prayer, Mother said, it was a miracle. I believe it was a reflex of fear, which he sustained over the years through courage and pride. He knew a man could die from drink, for his brother Roscoe had. We children never laid eyes on doomed Uncle Roscoe, but in the stories Mother told us he became a fairy-tale figure, like a boy who took the wrong turning in the woods and was gobbled up by the wolf.

The fifteen-year dry spell came to an end with Father's retirement in the spring of 1978. Like many men, he gave up his identity along with his job. One day he was a boss at the factory, with a brass plate on his door and a reputation to uphold; the next day he was a nobody at home. He and Mother were leaving

Ontario, the last of the many places to which his job had carried them, and they were moving to a new house in Mississippi, his childhood stomping grounds. As a boy in Mississippi, Father sold Coca-Cola during dances while the moonshiners peddled their brew in the parking lot; as a young blade, he fought in bars and in the ring, seeking a state Golden Gloves championship; he gambled at poker, hunted pheasants, raced motorcycles and cars, played semiprofessional baseball, and, along with all his buddies—in the Black Cat Saloon, behind the cotton gin, in the woods—he drank. It was a perilous youth to dream of recovering.

After his final day of work, Mother drove on ahead with a car full of begonias and violets, while Father stayed behind to oversee the packing. When the van was loaded, the sweaty movers broke open a six-pack and offered him a beer.

"Let's drink to retirement!" they crowed. "Let's drink to freedom! to fishing! hunting! loafing! Let's drink to a guy who's going home!"

At least I imagine some such words, for that is all I can do, imagine, and I see Father's hand trembling in midair as he thinks about the fifteen sober years and about the doctor's warning, and he tells himself *Goddamnit, I am a free man,* and *Why can't a free man drink one beer after a lifetime of hard work?* and I see his arm reaching, his fingers closing, the can tilting to his lips. I even supply a label for the beer, a swaggering brand that promises on television to deliver the essence of life. I watch the amber liquid pour down his throat, the alcohol steal into his blood, the key turn in his brain.

Soon after my parents moved back to Father's treacherous stomping ground, my wife and I visited them in Mississippi with our five-year-old daughter. Mother had been too distraught to warn me about the return of the demons. So when I climbed out of the car that bright July morning and saw my father napping in the hammock, I felt uneasy, for in all his sober years I had never known him to sleep in daylight. Then he lurched upright, blinked his bloodshot eyes, and greeted us in a syrupy voice. I was hurled back helpless into childhood.

"What's the matter with Papaw?" our daughter asked.

"Nothing," I said. "Nothing!"

Like a child again, I pretended not to see him in his stupor, and behind my phony smile I grieved. On that visit and on the few that remained before his death, once again I found bottles in the workbench, bottles in the woods. Again his hands shook too much for him to run a saw, to make his precious miniature furniture, to drive straight down back roads. Again he wound up in the ditch, in the hospital, in jail, in treatment centers. Again he shouted and wept. Again he lied. "I never touched a drop," he swore. "Your mother's making it up."

I no longer fancied I could reason with the men whose names I found on the bottles—Jim Beam, Jack Daniel—nor did I hope to save my father by burning down a store. I was able now to press the cold statistics about alcoholism against the ache of memory: ten million victims, fifteen million, twenty. And yet, in spite of my age, I reacted in the same blind way as I had in childhood, ignoring biology, forgetting numbers, vainly seeking to erase through my efforts whatever drove him to drink. I worked on their place twelve and sixteen hours a day, in the swelter of Mississippi summers, digging ditches, running electrical wires, planting trees, mowing grass, building sheds, as though what nagged at him was some list of chores, as though by taking his worries on my shoulders I could redeem him. I was flung back into boyhood, acting as though my father would not drink himself to death if only I were perfect.

I failed of perfection; he succeeded in dying. To the end, he considered himself not sick but sinful. "Do you want to kill yourself?" I asked him. "Why not?" he answered. "Why the hell not? What's there to save?" To the end, he would not speak about his feelings, would not or could not give a name to the beast that was devouring him.

In silence, he went rushing off the cliff. Unlike the biblical swine, however, he left behind a few of the demons to haunt his children. Life with him and the loss of him twisted us into shapes that will be familiar to other sons and daughters of alcoholics. My brother became a rebel, my sister retreated into shyness, I played the stalwart and dutiful son who would hold the family together. If my father was unstable, I would be a rock. If he squandered money on drink, I would pinch every penny. If he wept when drunk—and only when drunk—I would not let myself weep at all. If he roared at the Little League umpire for calling my pitches balls, I would throw nothing but strikes. Watching him flounder and rage, I came to dread the loss of control. I would go through life without making anyone mad. I vowed never to put in my mouth or veins any chemical that would banish my everyday self. I would never make a scene, never lash out at the ones I loved, never hurt a soul. Through hard work, relentless work, I would achieve something dazzling—in the classroom, on the basketball floor, in the science lab, in the pages of books—and my achievement would distract the world's eyes from his humiliation. I would become a worthy sacrifice, and the smoke of my burning would please God.

It is far easier to recognize these twists in my character than to undo them. Work has become an addiction for me, as drink was an addiction for my father. Knowing this, my daughter gave me a placard for the wall: WORKAHOLIC. The labor is endless and futile, for I can no more redeem myself through work than I could redeem my father. I still panic in the face of other people's anger, because his drunken temper was so terrible. I shrink from causing sadness or disappointment even to strangers, as though I were still concealing the family shame. I still notice every twitch of emotion in the faces around me, having learned as a child to read the weather in faces, and I blame myself for their least pang of unhappiness or anger. In certain moods I blame myself for everything. Guilt burns like acid in my veins.

I am moved to write these pages now because my own son, at the age of ten, is taking on himself the griefs of the world, and in particular the griefs of his father. He tells me that when I am gripped by sadness he feels responsible; he feels there must be something he can do to spring me from depression, to fix my life. And that crushing sense of responsibility is exactly what I felt at the age of ten in the face of my father's drinking. My son wonders if I, too, am possessed. I write, therefore, to drag into the light what eats at me—the fear, the guilt, the shame—so that my own children may be spared.

I still shy away from nightclubs, from bars, from parties where the solvent is alcohol. My friends puzzle over this, but it is no more peculiar than for a man to shy away from the lions' den after seeing his father torn apart. I took my own first drink at the age of twenty-one, half a glass of burgundy. I knew the odds of my becoming an alcoholic were four times higher than for the sons of nonalcoholic fathers. So I sipped warily.

I still do—once a week, perhaps, a glass of wine, a can of beer, nothing stronger, nothing more. I listen for the turning of a key in my brain.

ROBERT B. STEPTO

Robert Stepto (1945–) grew up in Chicago, where he received his early education at the University of Chicago's Laboratory School. At sixteen he left home for college and in 1974 he received his Ph.D. from Stanford, after which he joined the faculty at Yale, where he is now a professor of English, American studies, and African-American studies. Stepto is a frequent contributor to scholarly journals and the author or editor of several books on Afro-American literature; in 1998 he published Blue as the Lake, *a collection of personal essays that trace his family's history from the time of his great-great-great-grandparents, who in 1860 bought their freedom from slavery in Virginia and moved to Missouri to start a farm.*

Stepto's educational attainment continues a long family legacy. His grandfather, by virtue of a then-rare high school diploma, became a member of the 351st Field Artillery, one of the few black combat units to serve in World War I. His father, Robert Charles, received a medical degree in 1944 at the age of twenty-four; in 1948 he added a Ph.D. from the University of Chicago, where he later became a professor.

As a private practitioner, Dr. Stepto's first office was on the second floor over a pharmacy, not far from the South Side home he, his wife, and his young son shared with his in-laws. As his practice began to thrive, the fruits of success began to accrue: the family moved into its own "two-flat," there were vacations at the summer cottage, and there were the arrivals home at night of Dr. Stepto, a jazz fan, with a sack full of Chinese food and five or ten new records. It brought him pleasure, recalls Stepto, to play Provider in this fashion—and "What better provisions are there than Chinese food and a new stack of sides?"

But another measure of Robert Charles Stepto's rise in the world was his decision to abandon the neighborhood barbershop he'd frequented for years in favor of "a barber with whom he could make an appointment." It was a move that valued expediency over social decorum, and it is likely not the only time he made such a judgment. Blue as the Lake is rich in sympathetic characterizations of Stepto's family and forebears, but with the exception of the selection presented here there are relatively few references to his father. One is a recollection of a cold and windy September day when Stepto was a child and he and his father built a driftwood fire on the beach; his father then had the idea of cooking a meal and he fixed a "grand lunch" for the two of them. It was only the second time his father had ever cooked for him, remembers Stepto, and it was "as good as it would ever be."

"Hyde Park" describes Stepto's last visit with his father before his death in 1994. First published in 1997 in Callaloo, the essay suggests that things had not much changed since the cookout.

Hyde Park

All my flights from the East to Chicago end this way. After an indifferent run across uniform southern Michigan farmland, we burst upon the blue expanse of Lake Michigan, momentarily as big as any sea one must cross to get to a place completely unknown. Then the pilot comes on the intercom: We're descending, we're arriving soon, the wind is windy, the Cubs are losing, have a good day. Some passengers moan and wonder: Descent? Did he say descent? Good God we're over water. I thought we were going to Chicago.

While they shift and lurch and try to remember the instructions half-heard two hours before about flotation devices, I ease back and almost say out loud: the Lake looks good to me. A hit of the Lake before landing in the prairie's drift and then driving into the humid heft of the city is just what I need. I romanticize the Lake. Even though I know and even dream the tales of the Lake's dangers—ore ships vanishing, nice people like my fourth-grade teacher drowning—I still want to be out there, nudging through the Lake's waves. Riding to nowhere with my dad in Dr. Calloway's powerboat at six in the morning with only a sack of chocolate donuts for breakfast and only a thin White Sox jacket to shell off the fog and breeze—that's where I want to be. Riding the ferry from Milwaukee to Ludington on a sunny childhood day, playing shuffleboard during the few intervals the ship's captain doesn't need my helmsmanship—that's not bad, either. Aching with hope that the one man in my father's crowd with a sailboat, a fast yawl no less, might ask me to help crew in the next Chicago to Mackinac race—that's a first-rate might-have-been, an outstanding almost-happened.

But then we land and it's time to get down to business, the business of getting out to the South Side. Years ago, provided that I wasn't traveling with my wife—who is deeply suspicious of my homegrown itineraries—I'd plan elaborate schemes of travel, with transfers, double-transfers, and the like. It was just no fun and much too adult simply to hail a cab and debark at home forty-five minutes later. I'd claim that I couldn't afford a cab, but what I really couldn't afford was depriving myself of a short wade into the city's essences.

These days, I grab a cab more and more, chiefly because the cabdrivers are more interesting. Gone, it seems, are the sullen rednecks who resent driving you anywhere; gone, too, are the tiresome black cabbies who want to know "How many coloreds are up to that college you go to?" or want to borrow ten dollars—"I know your address and everything, you know I'll pay you back." No, these days you get the West Indian and East Indian and even West African types: brothers with cabs like living rooms, smelling like sweet flowers, decked out with photographs, doilies, little national flags and no smoking signs in three languages. These brothers have coolers with sodas and iced cappuccinos; when they offer a cold drink they add, "Would you like my business card, too?" I like these dudes because they make you think uplift and hustle are still the order of the day. But these guys are new to Chicago. There's another reality, too, dancing not to the hustle but to the blues.

The "blues ride," the "nachal" ride full of testiness and style and eruptions of funk, comes not in the rolling parlors of the new American dreamers but instead in the utilitarian vans of the A2B Coach Company, a black-owned outfit that serves the University of Chicago by way of stopping half a dozen places where black folks might want to go. There's a published route with designated times, but like a Gershwin tune that's caught the eye of Sonny Rollins, it's a score about to be improvised upon. Frankly, I don't worry any more when the van gets to Twenty-second Street and then suddenly veers west for blocks. The driver ain't crazy, ain't lost; someone's slipped him a five to drop them off in Chinatown, and that's what's happening. And don't let a doe-eyed stewardess sweetly step aboard, show some leg, and let it drop that she lives in an apartment in Lake Meadows. Lake Meadows never was on the schedule—but it is now.

The last time I rode out to the South Side before my father died, I deliberately took an A2B van, even though the next one wasn't going to leave for almost an hour. My father had been acting oddly—had even sent me a postcard the week before suggesting I not come—and so I actually welcomed the delay. Why rush things? Why beat a path to his apartment only to lengthen the time in which you tensely had to wait for him to come home with whatever was really on his mind?

Predictably, the first folk arriving and peering around for the A2B were white and heading for the university. Going to see my fiancée, said one; considering the medical school, said two more. I nodded and tried to judge from their clothes what parts of the country they were from. Next, a dapper coffee-colored man strode up, decked out in sport clothes and soft leather shoes. He saw me smoking—I had to get that done before meeting my father—and asked me for a light. As his left hand motored in spiraling circles, he put one foot out in front of the other and told me he was a judge. (I much wanted to believe him.) Told me that sometimes he just had to get out of town.

Told me how he would slip into his chambers, change clothes, grab his overnight bag, go down the service elevator to the street, and then high-step over to the El train that went out to O'Hare and, you know, be Gone. He asked if I had ever taken that El train; told me to try it sometime.

The A2B came and we all clambered aboard, the last-minute arrivals including a wizened black couple wearing church clothes—I couldn't help placing them however unfairly as the couple in the eviction scene in Ellison's *Invisible Man*—and a heavy-set brown woman, exquisitely dressed, who I instantly knew would be the van's "other driver." She squeezed in next to me, humming, and dabbing her faint perspiration in an elegant manner worthy of Ella or Sarah.

We weren't too far into Hillary Clinton's neighborhood of Park Ridge before everybody heard from the lady next to me. "Mister Driver? Mister Driver? Do you think you could turn up the air conditioning?" Now, it was a cool day and the air conditioning wasn't even on. But the driver, even though he was too young to have been of the old school of waiter's waiters or porter's porters, was accommodating. After blues-lining out something about how he hadn't turned on no air conditioner on the thirty-goddamn-first of March in all his born days, he mellowed and told some lie about how A2B Coach always wants to please. The chill hit the elderly couple instantly. Their skin ashened as they hunched into their winter coats.

Pretty soon we all were cold to the bone. I looked over at the clutch of white folks, shuddering like they were back in North Dakota, and could see in their eyes that they were just going to shut their mouths and ride this one out. Clearly, they feared that one little word would bring an NAACP lawsuit, or worse, the signifying wrath of the lady next to me. No, white folks weren't going to bail us out this time. I looked for the judge; thought I might see him righteously agitated, and cold, too. But the judge was dozing—or pretending to doze. I understood: if the brother had been telling the truth all along, he didn't need to get in a fracas on the A2B while sneaking back to his courtroom. So, it was up to me.

Before I opened my mouth, my whole history in Chicago flew by me. I asked myself for the umpteenth time why I had left and why I always came back. I asked myself what I loved and what I dreaded. Then I asked myself why I was pondering these things when all I had to do was to say, "Excuse me, I'm cold, all these people are cold, please turn the cooling down." But it came out another way: "Mr. Driver, sir," I said, echoing the lady but adding my own flourish, "could we please have some heat?"

The white folks were grateful; the elderly black couple murmured, "Amen." You couldn't tell about the dozing judge, but I thought I saw a smile. We waited for the lady next to me to explode, but she surprised us by saying, "You know, I thought it was cold. This bus is cold." And she started humming again. All was peaceful for a jot until the driver likely lost his mind. "Y'all want air conditioning," he said. "Y'all want heat. Y'all don't know what you want, don't never know what you want." So it was coming, not from the lady next to me but from the driver, and it was coming. I thought we were going to hear about Mississippi next, as he began to careen the van down the expressway. But I was wrong: the tune was in the key of Arkansas. "Been up to this city for thirty years," he began. The old couple whispered, "O Lord." "Been here driving every kind of car, cab, truck, van, what have you." "Please," I said. "But this job a motherfucka," he swore. "'Bout time I got back to Arkansas."

From Roosevelt Road to Oakwood Boulevard, we heard about Arkansas. The landscape the driver painted—each tug at the steering wheel another swipe of his brush—had nothing to do with civil rights and troops and Little Rock and Governor Faubus and what trouble must have been at his door thirty, forty years ago. It was more like that Archibald Motley painting, *Landscape-Arkansas,* a pretty scene from a dream. I couldn't hear all he said, the big lady next to me kept whispering non-sense at me, but I heard something about fishing and butter-milk. And there was the part about growing turnip greens and collards out in the garden. The driver's voice got louder and gruff when he told us about how in Arkansas, "Black folks *knows* when they wants hot, and *knows* when they wants cold." Then he half-turned his head and said, "And the white folks are *comprehensible!*" Comprehensible? Com-pre-hensible?? That fifty-dollar word made me wonder if the driver were a preacher on the side.

I got off the van at Hyde Park's Ramada Inn, curious about what else was in store for the rest of the passengers, maybe espe-cially the white folks, as they rode deeper into the South Side. After brushing off the cabbies eager for a fare, I shouldered my bags and started walking the two long blocks to my fa-ther's apartment building. I was walking through an area called Indian Village, so-called because the high-rise buildings had names like Blackhawk and Mohican. As a boy, I used to be in-vited to birthday parties by white classmates living in the Black-hawk or some such apartment house and have a heck of a time getting past the white doorman until my friend's mother or fa-ther came down in the elevator, all flushed and sorry, to get me. I was walking and thinking about all that, and realizing that I didn't care about that anymore. Or rather, I didn't care about it half as much as I cared about the trepidations of walking a block further and entering the building in which my mother and her mother had lived their last days, leaving my father behind, much to his astonishment, confusion, and anger, too. Of enter-ing that building, of struggling through the revolving door with my bags jostling me, there was but one verity: the people manning the door, and even those vacuuming the lobby and su-pervising with their clipboards, were going to hail me and maybe hug me, too. And I would hug them back. After that, I was on my own, seeking the elevator to the twenty-eighth floor, settling into the apartment in which I had never really lived but which had been the family's home for almost twenty years. Then came the wait for my father, who was a long time coming.

Even after putting up with the A2B Coach and its meandering path to the South Side, I still got out to my father's place a full hour before we were supposed to meet there. Borrowing the keys left for me with the doorman, I let myself into the apartment, my head bobbing from side to side, not because I expected to find someone waiting for me, but because I was already curious about what might have changed and what had been left untouched in the three years since my mother had died. Nothing much caught my eye until I went into the bathroom my mother had come to use more and more instead of the one off her bedroom. The cosmetics were gone, the pills were gone; the myriad items for doing hair and painting nails and all the rest were gone. I said to myself, "Maybe he's gotten around to doing something about her clothes, too." But I didn't look to see.

What I did do was look for the family photo albums that had been on my mind ever since I had planned this trip. I wanted to find the photo of my grandfather astride a camel in Egypt with the Sphinx in the background; it was taken in 1905, back when he must have thought that life had more in store for him than endless shifts at the post office. I was looking, too, for my mother's wedding picture, so beautiful yet so contrived since there had never been a wedding with a flowing gown and a groom handsome in a cutaway but instead a rushed, almost secret ceremony, to be confessed to later.

There were two other photos I was burning to find. One documented my father's initiation into his college fraternity. Clipped from the pages of the Chicago *Defender*, it offered a youthful image of my father I did not wish to forget, and it provided proof of something very interesting to me even though it had never been talked about in the family: my father was initiated in the same group with the novelist Frank Yerby—and so my father must have known Yerby, and maybe my mother did too.

The other photo was one of me at three years old. Frankly, I liked it as an adorable toddler photo—an adorable toddler who, I was pleased to admit, was me. But something else was also part of the attraction: women, then and now, look at the photo and say, "Mmm, is that a little Peter Pan collar shirt you have on there? Now, look how the straps of those little houndstooth trousers are going through the nice little loops in that Peter Pan collar shirt. Mmm, your momma was sure dressing you." Of course, I like all that. Of course, right now, there is a whole side of me that yearns to say, "Sweetheart, I'm dressing right for being with a woman like you, and I was dressed right for being with you ever since I was three. I've been Anticipating you." With fantasies such as these, I searched for the toddler photo, and for the others, too. The hour I had to kill before my father was supposed to arrive went by as quickly as the ore boat on the Lake out the window met the horizon, then disappeared.

Another hour shot by, still no sign of my dad. I thought about running down to the bookstore I liked on Fifty-third Street—the one with the fantastic fiction section that was the only one I knew of that made a point of displaying hard-to-find books from the tiniest of presses. I thought as well—and now I was starting to get pissed about being stood up—about going out and having lunch on my own. Yes, the deal had been that my father and I would meet at the apartment and then go to lunch somewhere in the neighborhood. But now I was thinking: "No deal now. I had just half a bagel and a glass of juice at break of day, and that was break of day, eastern time. I'm going out." Thinking that way gave me a rush but no momentum, no push out the door. I had never played casual with meeting my father or with any of the small measures of filial piety in all my life. And so, after I woofed and barked and stomped around the apartment, and after I even gazed longingly down from the twenty-eighth floor upon the roofs of the bookstore and a half-dozen restaurants on Fifty-third Street, I settled into waiting some more.

My father arrived close to 3 P.M., hidden behind an array of parcels much like a child hidden behind a cluster of balloons. I thought he had been at work but obviously he had been shopping. "Needed a few things for the trip to St. Louis tomorrow," he said, as he heaped the bags on a corner of the dining room table. The bags were from some of the choicer North Michigan Avenue men's furnishing shops. That got me to thinking about what he possibly could have needed that he didn't have (every closet brimmed with his finery), and more, what—or who—he was dressing up for in St. Louis. In his postcard, he had told me that he might have to go out of town right in the middle of my visit; that's why he suggested that I not come. I had immediately called to say that I couldn't cancel my business appointments and that we should just make the best of the couple of days we could visit together, should he really have to go out of town. Well, here it was: he was going and he was going the next day. "So, what's in St. Louis?" I asked, aware of the edge in my voice and aware, too, that we had not yet even said hello. "I'll tell you over lunch," he said, gesturing toward the door and rebuttoning his coat. And so we went out, walking stiffly together, silent with the thought that we had to get some things said.

We headed west on Fifty-third Street, passing under the IC tracks and arriving at the corner of Fifty-third and Lake Park. A glance at the Hyde Park Bank building reminded me of my business appointments in the morning; the window display at the bookstore with the great fiction section promised that I'd have at least one pleasant thing to do after my father left town. We strolled up to a restaurant, Valois', a neighborhood institution now even more on the map because a young sociologist had just published a book, *Slim's Table*, about the middle-aged black men who gathered there for meals. Since my father had read the book and had sent me a copy of it, I thought we might be heading in there. But we weren't and one look in the window told me why: my father might have been seventy-three, but he wasn't about to resign himself to the company of frumpled old men picking at meat loaf and staring at their glasses of water. No, we were going down the street a little further to Mellow Yellow, a place brighter and younger and hipper, surprisingly so when you thought about how it was hopelessly stuck with its corny sixties name.

We settled at a table by the window onto the street. On another day, I would have pointed out to the storefronts across the street where there were once stores like Kiddie Kicks where my sister and I would get our school shoes. But the day that lay before me and my father, or rather, what was left of it, did not seem the occasion for getting lost in simple memories. We didn't need to get lost; we needed to get on with it. "You first," I said to myself, and, as if he heard me, my father said, "Tell me again why you're here in Chicago."

It would have been grand, as they say in the novels, if I could have said, "I'm here to see you—we need to make a point of seeing each other now that Mom has died." But those phrases and the feelings behind them, while so paramount when I had planned this trip, were now lost in the pockets of a present misery. When I reached for words, what came out was, "I've been living in Connecticut for twenty years. There's no point to my still having a bank account here. I'm going to close the account in the morning. I am going to take my savings. . . . " *Home* was the last word of that sentence; I knew it and he did too.

The waiter came and took our orders. We both ordered something sensible like salads with strips of grilled chicken breast. My father tried to take advantage of this interruption and turn the subject of what I planned to do with my savings into a discussion of pension plans. "Are you still putting everything into TIAA, or do you put something in CREF?" he asked, while forking around in his salad. We'd been there before, and before, all my life it seemed, I'd given in to what seemed his plea to make a side issue the real issue until it piddled down to nothing. Ignoring his question, I fired my own: "So, what's in St. Louis?" I held him to his promise to tell me over lunch.

"I'm going to St. Louis to go to a dance," he began. "An old friend, an acquaintance of mine" (I marveled at the backtracking: "Old friend" had already become "acquaintance") "has asked me to escort her to a dance, and so I'm going." He continued, "She is the widow of a doctor we knew. When your mother and I would go to party weekends in St. Louis, they were one of the couples hosting and entertaining us. I've been seeing her for about a year. I've been meaning to tell you." He then told me her name.

I didn't respond right away and that worried him. "I've been meaning to tell you," he repeated, "but I didn't know what you'd think about my starting to see other women." He meant women other than my mother, and he sought my appreciation for his appreciation for my feelings. But this I sadly knew was another deflection, another attempt at escape from frank exchange. Aiming at straight-talk, I said, had to say, "So what you are telling me now, but couldn't tell me weeks ago, or even a week ago when you sent me that postcard, is that you are going to spend the weekend with a ladyfriend, someone you've known a long time and liked, someone you have introduced to my sister but have not even mentioned to me."

As I awaited his answer, it occurred to me that while I was trying to say, "Why haven't you talked to me, why haven't you told me this before?" what he was hearing, with ears tuned only to particular frequencies, was that even his daughter might not be able to keep something to herself. That the problem with families, he surmised, was that they were composed of family members; and that no matter whether they were mammy-made by your mother or by your wife, these family members, near and far, might write or call to ask permission to drive or fly or even walk into your life. When my sister moved from Boston to Kalamazoo, she once said to him, "I'm so close now." He said, "But I need my privacy."

And yet, once, when the woman from St. Louis was visiting, my sister visited, too. Ignoring the awkward, absurd introduction in which the ladyfriend was told of my sister that she was meeting the Supreme Court, the two women retired to a back room, genuinely made friends of each other, exchanged phone numbers, and began the then hopeful process of trying to figure out how to moderate my father's lifestyle and save him. In the months to come, when their concern offered the fragrance of adoration, he was attentive, gallant. But when it took on for him the stench of intrusion, he backed away and sought the company of a new—and to us, strange—group of friends.

Right now, over a lunch I was almost too angry to eat, I was intruding, too. That, and the fact that we had never been able to go beyond opening salvos, meant that the lunch was over. (We both would have made very poor boxers for, at least with each other, we were prone to lunge and exhaust ourselves before the first bell.) "I have to get back and start packing," he said, as we both threw money on the check. The full import of that didn't dawn on me until we were actually back in the apartment and he left me alone in the living room while he retired to his bedroom and began to bustle about.

I wandered in circles, unable to settle into a chair, to distract myself with the newspaper, to pick up a book. My eye fell on the neat row of family publications, including a rather complete assembly of my own stuff, and I thought again of how artfully someone had managed to plant books and offprints in a living room without exactly displaying them. When my mother was alive, this was her classy way of expressing family pride in subtle, tailored terms. But what was being expressed now? In that room, now, each book might as well have been a lamp, a coaster.

I was peering out at the Lake, retracing the step-by-step descent of the airplane I had been on that morning, knowing that it had flown from my right to my left, a glint in the sky first above the steel mills then above the Lake then above the Loop, when my father reappeared. Something was in his hand, I soon saw it was a pair of socks. "I have to take these back," he said. "Look, they're defective." I half looked. "I'm going to take these back," he emphasized. But I never dreamt that he meant right then until I heard the jingle of his car keys. "Mother in heaven," I thought, "he's actually going down to the car and going downtown."

I should have stopped him, or at least tried to do so. But what was I going to say? Telling him he already had fifty billion pair of perfectly good socks seemed no more persuasive than pointing out I had just traveled a thousand miles to spend time with him and he ought not to go. And so he disappeared into the elevator and the garage and the teeming rush-hour traffic, determined to return his socks but really to buy another two hours of time away from me and our prickly conversation. I just waved him on, said nothing, just waved him on. It wasn't a wave of good-bye or a wave of dismissal. It was a cross between a blotting out and a benediction. I wished him well on his completely absurd journey. But also, after all the bullshit, I wanted a smoke, and with him gone that was now a possibility.

Sometime after I had furtively puffed two cigarettes while out on the balcony, too scared to enjoy them since I am deathly scared of heights, I realized that my father and I were due for dinner at the house of old, old friends in less than an hour, and he was not yet back. When it got down to twenty-five minutes before dinner, I started into one of those shake-of-your-head unbelieving laughs that you learn when your children become teenagers, and you can't believe that right when the whole family needs to go out the door to get somewhere, they suddenly want to take a shower. Right then, my father arrived, and his first words were, "I need to take my nap; missed it earlier." Why he had missed his nap and everything else that was supposed to have happened that afternoon begged to be addressed, but what I said was, "You know, we're due at the Runners in twenty minutes." "Call them," he yawned, and I did.

We were a good hour late getting to the Runners, but they were as gracious as I knew they would be and just wanted us to get in the door and be at home. Drinks were served and soon came salads, too soon, but that happens when you are late and you throw your hosts off schedule. This should have been a little party of the sort that comes naturally to people who have known each other for over forty years; I certainly was with three of the people who had raised me from birth. But there were funny awkwardnesses, lapses in conversation that were hard to fathom. I was struck by how the Runners and my dad talked as if they hadn't seen each other in a long time, which didn't seem possible to me. Then I remembered a telephone conversation I'd had with Dorothy weeks before, when I'd called to tell her I'd be coming to town. "Of course, we're going to see you, we'll be here," she began. "But you know, you're going to have to talk to your father and check his schedule. Step's so busy. I try to get him over here. I tell him he's welcome anytime, anytime, like every Wednesday when Runner's home early. But I don't know. And I don't want to impose. . . . "

I had scoffed when I heard this. After all, Dorothy had been my mother's best friend and is my sister's godmother, and Charlie once told me that my dad was like a brother to him. I'd thought maybe Dorothy was misinterpreting something, but here, now, as I watched my father glance at his watch or glimpse into space, I knew things were askew. Was it about my mother, was it about how the Runners and the Steptos had been young together, a foursome together, had bought a two-family building together, and lived together for years? Could it be something that sentimental yet monumentally heartfelt—or could it be something else?

My mother may have been in the glimpses into space but not in those at the watch. The watch: minutes were passing but not in the time zone of savoring memories or friendships. My father was determined not to spend his last days in the sinkhole of memories, and he was carefully measuring the time he spent with old friends. And even though he was about to fly off to St. Louis the next day, he was becoming increasingly certain that he wasn't going to spend his last days with a woman who was the friend of old friends. It smacked of prearrangement, of inevitability. Your wife dies, and your friends descend from far and near to legislate who your new mate will be. Even your children are colluding: your daughter makes friends with one of the designated desirables; your son thinks someone, even someone he doesn't know, might be good in your life.

Toward the end of dinner, I observed again how obviously my father wanted to be elsewhere, and thought about an exchange we'd had a year or two before. I was in Chicago, and we were driving to a bar in South Shore that also served Chinese food. He asked, "Do you have a bar?" "What do you mean?" "I mean," he said, "is there a place you go to meet your friends?" I had to confess I had no such bar. I thought about mentioning that at my age I was still picking up kids from school, that I still needed my evenings to prepare for classes, but I let that go. So, too, did I not comment, once we were at the bar, that the crew that crowded around him and hailed him seemed hardly friends. From the snips of conversation I heard, they struck me as sycophants and bloodsuckers, parasites eager to press on to an older man who might be able to do them some favor in the city since he had been, briefly, head of the board of health.

So, was that where Dad wanted to be? Did he want to be out at his bar? Was that why he was glancing at his watch? All I know is that as soon as dinner was over, he was out the door, saying brightly, "Going away tomorrow, have to pack." Dorothy and Charlie urged me to stay another hour, promising me a ride home. "Yes, stay," my father said. At that point, I didn't need any convincing, and I settled back into my chair.

When I got back to the apartment, later than I thought I would, my father was asleep. Whether or not he had gone to his bar, he was asleep now; the door cracked, the room dark. I lingered at the door, listening to the rise and fall of his breath, not labored but distinct in the utter quiet of the apartment. I wanted to hear him sound like he was at peace, though I doubted that he was, and yes, he sounded peaceful.

Not quite ready for bed, I went and poured myself a nightcap, then retreated back to the room I usually stay in with one of the family photo albums in tow. "This one is an old one," I said to myself as I turned the pages. "This is one from when my parents were my age." I soon came upon a photo I hadn't planned to borrow, but later did.

It's a photo of my father holding my sister, then an infant, with the blanket around her for that moment being generously open, so that the photographer can see her, but maybe too because it seems to be a warm day. My usually tall and erect father is curiously hunching down, scrunched over. My thought about this before has always been, "You can't really tell, but he's hunched like that to be closer to Jan, to have his face close to hers." But now I am wondering if his posture might also have something to do with who is next to him on his right. On my father's right is his father, as well dressed as my father is as both men are in good suits. No matter how much my father hunches and scrunches, he can't erase the fact that he is distinctly taller than his father. But maybe he wants, in this one rare moment, to minimalize the difference; maybe he wants his face closer not only to Jan's but to his father's as well. Well below the two men, Robert Louis and Robert Charles, stands a seven-year-old boy,

Robert Burns. He's not in a suit like his father and grandfather, but he's dressed nicely—sport shirt, pleated slacks, a little cap on his head—his mother wouldn't have it otherwise. But he's not exactly standing. He's doing something funny with his body; it's in an odd S-curve, swerving first toward the grandfather and then at the top of the S toward his father and sister. The gymnastics of it all has put a contorted smile on his face, like what you see on the face of a high jumper, whose grimace all through the process of leaping has suddenly become something else the moment he knows he's high enough in the air to make it all happen. Then you look again and note: the boy snaking his way up into the atmosphere of his menfolk, as they pose with his months-old sister, is standing on his tiptoes. That's how much I wanted to be in the picture.

In the background is brick, nothing but brick wall. It is the brickface of my grandfather's apartment building, and that alone should make it seem something other than brick, something softer. But it's brick. We in the picture are up against the wall.

Rising in the morning, I drape on my bathrobe and make my way to the front of the apartment. Immediately, I spy my father, awash in the morning light streaming in the lakefront windows, intent with the morning newspaper. Though his back is to me, I can tell he is already dressed for the day; his packed bags are near beside him, angled toward the door. "Have you already had breakfast?" I ask, moving closer. "There's cereal in the cupboard and English muffins in the fridge," he replies. "Juice and milk are in the fridge. Sorry, the milk is skim milk; that's all I use these days." From that I gather he's had breakfast.

Sensing how soon he plans to depart, I say, "Look, I don't have to be anywhere before eleven. Let me drive you to the airport. I can throw on some clothes in a minute." But as I move down the hall to dress, he replies, "Don't trouble yourself. I've called my driver. He should be here any minute." "Your driver?"

I say. Having a driver was news to me. "Well," he began, "he's not my driver exclusively. Henri drives a Yellow Cab. But he has a beeper or something, and I can arrange for him to drive me without going through the dispatcher. He's very punctual and courteous. He should be here soon."

As if my father had snapped his fingers, the phone rang, and it was the doorman from the lobby announcing that Dr. Stepto's cab—Henri—had arrived. My father rose and leaned toward his bags, but I swept forward and grabbed them before he could. We went out the apartment door and down to the elevator. We must have been quite a sight: an older gentleman in a fine grey suit, striding with purpose, with a balding man behind him, disheveled in his bathrobe, struggling along with a couple of suitcases.

At the elevator we stopped and my father turned to me, handing me something. "This is Henri's card," he said. "You might like to have him take you to the airport when you go back on Sunday." I glanced down at the card in my hand. On the left appeared the logo of the Yellow Cab Company. On the right, in the same shade of yellow, was a smiley, have-a-good-day happy face. In between, was Henri's full name, "Henri Pouissant." As the elevator arrived and clunked open, it occurred to me that Henri was one of the new guys, one of the new American dreamers. Even in this detail, my father was making certain he wasn't going to be driven into the past.

From the back of the elevator, my father spoke his last words to me. "Henri drives a nice car," he said, "very clean. He's very attentive to me." Like a good son, I thought. Then the blue doors of the elevator—blue as the Lake—shut, and my father was gone. The cables behind the doors rumbled and mumbled, dropping my father down to the earth.

THOMAS LYNCH

Poet and essayist Thomas Lynch (1948–) is the only undertaker in Milford, Michigan, where, he says, "Each year I bury a couple hundred of my townspeople." Following two books of poetry, Lynch published his first book of prose in 1997. A loosely connected collection of personal essays, The Undertaking: Life Studies from the Dismal Trade, *became a finalist for the National Book Award in nonfiction.*

Lynch's father, Edward, was also an undertaker, and it was from his father that Thomas learned his trade. One Saturday when he was ten or twelve Thomas was invited by his father to go to work with him; he followed his father to his office and from there to the embalming room, where a man was laid out on the porcelain table with a sheet over his head. "Who was he?" asked the boy. "How old was he?" and "How did he die?" Answers to which the father provided.

And so began an education. When Thomas was fifteen his father's father died, and "Because my father owned a funeral home, it fell to my brother Dan and me to dress Pop Lynch and casket him—the first of my people I ever tended to professionally."

In an essay from The Undertaking *called "The Right Hand of the Father," Lynch recalls how familiarity with the capriciousness of death made his father ever fearful for the safety of his nine children. From that fearfulness grew overprotectiveness and the impulse always to give negative answers to childhood requests for liberties and excursions. "My father," he writes, "had seen in the dead bodies of infants and children and young men and women, evidence that God lived by the Laws of Nature, and obeyed its statutes, however brutal. . . . For my father, what we did, who we became, were incidental to the tenuous fact of our being: That We Were seemed sufficient for the poor worried man. The rest, he would say, was gravy." Now, says Lynch, his fears for his own children are similar.*

The following selection reveals that not only did Lynch learn his trade from his father, but he practiced it upon him as well. Titled "Gladstone" in his book, the essay appears here with its original title as published in the London Review of Books.

Embalming Father

The undertakers are over on the other island. They are there for what is called their Midwinter Conference: the name they give to the week in February every year when funeral directors from Michigan find some warm place in the Lesser Antilles to discuss the pressing issues of their trade. The names for the workshops and seminars are borderline: "The Future of Funeral Service," "What Folks Want in a Casket," "Coping with the Cremation Crowd"—things like that. The resorts must have room service, hot tubs, good beaches, and shopping on-site or nearby. No doubt it is the same for orthodontists and trial lawyers.

And I'm here on the neighboring island—a smaller place with a harbor too shallow for cruise ships and no airport. I'm a ferryboat ride from the undertakers from my home state. But I've timed my relief from the Michigan winter with theirs in case I want to register for a meeting and write off my travel. It is legal and sensible and would reduce the ultimate cost of funerals in my town where I am the funeral director and have been for twenty-five years now.

But I just can't work up any enthusiasm for spending any

portion of the fortnight discussing business. It's not that they aren't a great bunch, chatty and amiable as stockbrokers or insurance types; and, out of their hometowns, incognito, hell-bent on a good time, they can be downright fun, if a little bingy. It's just that it seems I've been on a Midwinter Conference of my own for a long time. Enough is enough. I need to walk on the beach now and contemplate my next move.

My father was a funeral director and three of my five brothers are funeral directors; two of my three sisters work pre-need and bookkeeping in one of the four funeral homes around the metro area that bear our name, our father's name. It is an odd arithmetic—a kind of family farm, working the back forty of the emotional register, our livelihood depending on the deaths of others in the way that medicos depend on sickness, lawyers on crime, the clergy on the fear of God.

I can remember my mother and father going off on these Midwinter Conferences and coming back all sunburned and full of ideas and gossip about what my father insisted we call our "colleagues" rather than the "competition." He said it made us sound like doctors and lawyers, you know, professionals—people you could call in the middle of the night if there was trouble, people whose being had begun to meld with their doing, who were what they did.

Our thing—who we are, what we do—has always been about death and dying and grief and bereavement: the vulnerable underbelly of the hardier nouns: life, liberty, the pursuit of . . . well, you know. We traffic in leavetakings, good-byes, final respects. "The last ones to let you down," my father would joke with the friends he most trusted. "Dignified Service" is what he put on the giveaway matchbooks and plastic combs and rain bonnets. And he loved to quote Gladstone, the great Victorian Liberal who sounded like a New Age Republican when he wrote that he could measure with mathematical precision a people's respect for the laws of the land by the way they cared for their dead. Of course, Gladstone inhabited a century and an England in which funerals were public and sex was private and, though the British were robbing the graves of infidels all over the world for the British Museum, they did so, by all accounts, in a mannerly fashion. I think my father first heard about Gladstone at one of these Midwinter Conferences and lately I've been thinking how right they were—Gladstone, my father.

My father died three years ago tomorrow on an island off the Gulf Coast of Florida. He wasn't exactly on a Midwinter Conference. He'd quit going to those years before, after my mother had died. But he was sharing a condo with a woman friend who always overestimated the remedial powers of sexual aerobics. Or maybe she only underestimated the progress of his heart disease. We all knew it was coming. In the first year of his widowhood, he sat in his chair, heartsore, waiting for the other shoe to drop. Then he started going out with women. The brothers were glad for him. The sisters rolled their eyes a lot. I think they call these "gender issues." In the two years of consortium that followed, he'd had a major—which is to say a chest ripping, down for the count—heart attack every six months like clockwork. He survived all but one. "Three out of four," I can hear him saying. "You're still dead when it's over." He'd had enough. Even now I think of that final scene in David Lean's old film when Zhivago's heart is described as "paper thin." He thinks he sees Lara turning a corner in Moscow. He struggles to get off the bus, loosens his tie, finally makes it to the sidewalk where, after two steps, he drops dead. Dead chasing love, the thing we would die for. That was my father—stepping not off a bus but out of a shower in his timeshare condo, not in Moscow but on Boca Grande, but chasing, just as certainly, love. Chasing it to death.

When we got the call from his woman friend, we knew what to do. My brother and I had done the drill in our heads before.

We had a traveling kit of embalming supplies: gloves, fluids, needles, odds and ends. We had to explain to the security people at the airlines who scrutinized the contents of the bag, wondering how we might make a bomb out of Dodge Permaglo or overtake the cabin crew with a box marked "Slaughter Surgical Supplies" full of stainless steel oddities they'd never seen before. When we got to the funeral home they had taken him to, taken his body to, the undertaker there asked if we were sure we wanted to do this—our own father, after all?—he'd be happy to call in one of his own embalmers. We assured him it would be OK. He showed us into the prep room, that familiar decor of porcelain and tile and fluorescent light—a tidy scientific venue for the witless horror of mortality, for how easily we slip from is to isn't.

It was something we had always promised him, though I can't now, for the life of me, remember the context in which it was made—the promise that when he died his sons would embalm him, dress him, pick out a casket, lay him out, prepare the obits, contact the priests, manage the flowers, the casseroles, the wake and procession, the Mass and burial. Maybe it was just understood. His was a funeral he would not have to direct. It was ours to do; and though he'd directed thousands of them, he had never made mention of his own preferences. Whenever he was pressed on the matter he would only say, "You'll know what to do." We did.

There's this "just a shell" theory of how we ought to relate to dead bodies. You hear a lot of it from young clergy, old family friends, well-intentioned in-laws—folks who are unsettled by the fresh grief of others. You hear it when you bring a mother and a father in for the first sight of their dead daughter, killed in a car wreck or left out to rot by some mannish violence. It is proffered as comfort in the teeth of what is a comfortless situation, consolation to the inconsolable. Right between the inhale and exhale of the bone-wracking sob such hurts produce, some frightened and well-meaning ignoramus is bound to give out with "It's OK, that's not her, it's just a shell." I once saw an Episcopalian deacon nearly decked by the swift slap of the mother of a teenager, dead of leukemia, to whom he'd tendered this counsel. "I'll tell you when *it's* 'just a shell,'" the woman said. "For now and until I tell you otherwise, *she's* my daughter." She was asserting the longstanding right of the living to declare the dead dead. Just as we declare the living alive through baptisms, lovers in love by nuptials, funerals are the way we close the gap between the death that happens and the death that matters. It's how we assign meaning to our little remarkable histories.

And the rituals we devise to conduct the living and beloved and the dead from one status to another have less to do with *performance* than with *meaning*. In a world where "dysfunctional" has become the operative adjective, a body that has ceased to work has, it would seem, few useful applications—its dysfunction more manifest than the sexual and familial forms that fill our tabloids and talk shows. But a body that doesn't work is, in the early going, the evidence we have of a person who has ceased to be. And a person who has ceased to be is as compelling a prospect as it was when the Neanderthal first dug holes for his dead, shaping the questions we still shape in the face of death: "Is that all there is?" "What does it mean?" "Why is it cold?" "Can it happen to me?"

So to suggest in the early going of grief that the dead body is "just" anything rings as tinny in its attempt to minimalize as it would if we were to say it was "just" a bad hair day when the girl went bald from her chemotherapy. Or that our hope for heaven on her behalf was based on the belief that Christ raised "just" a body from dead. What if, rather than crucifixion, he'd opted for suffering low self-esteem for the remission of sins? What if, rather than "just a shell," he'd raised his personality, say, or The

Idea of Himself? Do you think they'd have changed the calendar for that? Done the Crusades? Burned witches? Easter was a body and blood thing, no symbols, no euphemisms, no half measures. If he'd raised anything less, of course, as Paul points out, the deacon and several others of us would be out of business or back to Saturday Sabbaths, a sensible diet, and no more Christmases.

The bodies of the newly dead are not debris nor remnant, nor are they entirely icon or essence. They are, rather, changelings, incubates, hatchlings of a new reality that bear our names and dates, our image and likenesses, as surely in the eyes and ears of our children and grandchildren as did word of our birth in the ears of our parents and their parents. It is wise to treat such new things tenderly, carefully, with honor.

I had seen my father horizontal before. At the end it had been ICUs mostly, after his coronaries and bypasses. He'd been helpless, done unto. But before that there had been the man stretched out on the living room floor tossing one or the other of my younger siblings in the air; or napping in his office at the first funeral home in full uniform, black three-piece suit, striped tie, wing tips, clean shave; or in the bathtub singing "from the halls of Montezuma to the shores of Tripoli." He had outbreaks of the malaria he'd gotten in the South Pacific. In my childhood he was, like every father on the block, invincible. That he would die had been a fiction in my teens, a fear in my twenties, a specter in my thirties and, in my forties, a fact.

But seeing him, outstretched on the embalming table of the Anderson Mortuary in Ft. Myers with the cardiac blue in his ears and fingertips and along his distal regions, shoulders and lower ribs and buttocks and heels, I thought, *this is what my father will look like when he's dead*. And then, like a door slammed shut behind you, the tense of it all shifted into the inescapable present of *this is my father, dead*. My brother and I hugged each other, wept with each other and for each other and for our sisters and brothers home in Michigan. Then I kissed my father's forehead, not yet a shell. Then we went to work in the way our father had trained us.

He was a cooperative body. Despite the arteriosclerosis, his circulatory system made the embalming easy. And having just stepped from the shower into his doom, he was clean and cleanly shaven. He hadn't been sick, in the hospice or intensive care sense of the word. So there were none of the bruises on him or tubes in him that medical science can inflict and install. He'd gotten the death he wanted, caught in full stride, quick and cleanly after a day strolling the beach picking seashells for the grandchildren and maybe after a little bone bouncing with his condo-mate, though she never said and we never asked and can only hope. And massaging his legs, his hands, his arms, to effect the proper distribution of fluid and drainage, watching the blue clear from his fingertips and heels as the fluid that would preserve him long enough for us to take our leave of him worked its way around his body, I had the sense that I was doing something for him even though, now dead, he was beyond my kindnesses or anyone's. Likewise, his body bore a kind of history: the tattoo with my mother's name on it he'd had done as an eighteen-year-old marine during World War II, the perfectly trimmed mustache I used to watch him darken with my mother's mascara when he was younger than I am and I was younger than my children are. The scars from his quintuple bypass surgery, the A. A. medallion he never removed, and the signet ring my mother gave him for his fortieth birthday, all of us saving money in a jar until fifty dollars was accumulated. Also there were the graying chest hairs, the hairless ankles, the male pattern baldness I see on the heads of men in the first-class section of airplanes and in the double mirrors in the barber's shop. Embalming my father I was reminded of how we bury our dead and then become them. In the end I had to say that maybe *this is what I'm going to look like dead.*

Maybe it was at a Midwinter Conference my father first thought about what he did and why he did it. He always told us that embalming got to be, forgive me, *de rigueur* during the Civil War when, for the first time in our history, lots of people—mostly men, mostly soldiers—were dying far from home and the families that grieved for them. Dismal traders worked in tents on the edge of the battlefields charging, one reckons, what the traffic would bear to disinfect, preserve, and "restore" dead bodies—which is to say they closed mouths, sutured bullet holes, stitched limbs or parts of limbs back on, and sent the dead back home to wives and mothers, fathers and sons. All of this bother and expense was predicated on the notion that the dead need to be at their obsequies, or, more correctly, that the living need the dead to be there, so that the living can consign them to the field or fire after commending them to God or the gods or Whatever Is Out There. The presence and participation of the dead human body at its funeral is, as my father told it, every bit as important as the bride's being at her wedding, the baby at its baptism.

And so we brought our dead man home. Flew his body back, faxed the obits to the local papers, called the priests, the sexton, the florists and stonecutter. We act out things we cannot put in words.

Back in 1963, I can remember my father saying that the reason we have funerals and open caskets was so that we might confront what he called "the reality of death." I think he'd heard that at one of these conferences. Jessica Mitford had just sold a million copies of *The American Way of Death,* Evelyn Waugh had already weighed in with *The Loved One,* and talk had turned at cocktail parties to "barbaric rituals" and "morbid curiosities." The mortuary associations were scrambling for some cover. Clergy and educators and psychologists—the new clergy—were assembled to say it served some purpose after all, was emotionally efficient, psychologically correct, to do what we'd been doing all along. The track record was pretty good on this. We'd been doing—the species, not the undertakers—more or less the same thing for millennia: looking up while digging down, trying to make some sense of all of it, disposing of our dead with sufficient pause to say they'd lived in ways different from rocks and rhododendrons and even orangutans and that those lives were worth mentioning and remembering.

Then Kennedy was shot dead and then Lee Harvey Oswald and we spent the end of November that year burying them—the first deaths in our lives that took for most of us boomers. All the other TV types got shot on *Gunsmoke* on a Friday and turned up on *Bonanza,* looking fit by Sunday night. But Kennedy was one of those realities of death my father must have been talking about and though we saw his casket and cortege and little John John saluting and the widow in her sunglasses, we never saw Kennedy dead, most of us, until years later when pictures of the autopsy were released and we all went off to the movies to see what really happened. In the interim, rumors circulated about Kennedy not being dead at all but hooked to some secret and expensive hardware, brainless but breathing. And when the Zapruder film convinced us that he must have died, still we lionized the man beyond belief. Of course, once we saw him dead in the pictures, his face, his body, he became human again: loveable and imperfect, memorable and dead.

And as I watch my generation labor to give their teenagers and young adults some "family values" between courses of pizza and Big Macs, I think maybe Gladstone had it right. I think my father did. They understood that the meaning of life is connected, inextricably, to the meaning of death; that mourning is a romance in reverse, and if you love, you grieve and there are no exceptions—only those who do it well and those who don't. And if death is regarded as an embarrassment or an inconvenience, if the dead are regarded as a nuisance from whom we seek a hurried riddance, then life and the living are in for like treatment. McFunerals, McFamilies, McMarriage, McValues. This is the mathematical precision the old Britisher was talking about and what my father was talking about when he said we'd know what to do.

Thus tending to his death, his dead body, had for me the same importance as being present for the births of my sons, my daughter. Some expert on *Oprah* might call this "healing." Another on *Donahue* might say "cathartic." Over on *Geraldo* it might have "scarred him for life." And Sally Jesse Whatshername might mention "making good choices." As if they were talking about men who cut umbilical cords and change diapers or women who confront their self-esteem issues or their date rapists.

It is not about choices or functions or psychological correctness. A dead body has had its options limited, its choices narrowed. It is an old thing in the teeth of which we do what has been done because it is the thing to do. We needn't reinvent the wheel or make the case for it, though my generation always seems determined to.

And they are at it over on the other island. Trying to reinvent the funeral as "a vehicle for the healthy expression of grief," which, of course, it is; or as "a brief therapy for the acutely bereaved," which, of course, it is. There will be talk of "stages," "steps," "recovery." Someone will mention "aftercare," "post-funeral service follow-up," Widow to Widow programs, Mourners Anonymous? And in the afternoons they'll play nine holes, or go snorkeling or start cocktails too early and after dinner they'll go dancing then call home to check in with their offices just before they go to bed, to check on the gross sales, to see who among their townspeople has died.

Maybe I'll take the boat over tomorrow. Maybe some of the old-timers are there—men of my father's generation, men you could call in the middle of the night if there was trouble. They remind me of my father and of Gladstone. Maybe they'll say I remind them of him.

HENRY LOUIS GATES, JR.

Henry Louis Gates, Jr. (1950–), has written or edited more than two dozen scholarly works and is the author of numerous essays, articles, and reviews for such publications as The New Yorker, *the* New Republic, *and the* New York Times Book Review. *Gates, who is the recipient of a MacArthur Foundation "genius" award, is professor of English and Chair of Afro-American Studies at Harvard University, where he has been a faculty member since 1991.*

Gates grew up in Piedmont, West Virginia, whose then-population of twenty-five hundred included most of Mineral County's 381 blacks. His youth took place during the beginning of the civil rights movement and encompassed a period when, as Gates puts it, Americans of his race went from being "colored to Negro to black to Afro-American." In addition to its strife between white and black, the era spurred deep tensions within black families and communities—for many of the most cherished black institutions were challenged or brought to an end by integration, says Gates.

The summer after Gates's freshman year at college, he and a group of friends tried to force the integration of a local nightclub, with the result that one member of the group was assaulted and injured and the club's owner closed his business rather than comply with an ensuing legal order. In contrast, Gates says his father "was not a race man." His father was skeptical of the Reverend Dr. Martin Luther King, Jr., and in speaking of him would pronounce all of his names "to drag out his scorn." As a teenager, Gates recalls that he and his friends would argue with his father from sunup till sundown. Argue about "Vietnam, Black Power, Dr. King, Stokely, Afros, the Panthers, the time of day." They'd argue, take a break, then argue some more. When Gates grew the first Afro in Piedmont, his father called it "KKK hair: Knotty, Kinky, and Kan't-comby."

Still, Gates recalls the arguing as an improvement over an even earlier strain that had driven them to silence. Here, in this passage from his 1994 memoir, Colored People, Gates shows too that his father strove always to instruct his son in the ways of the world as he understood them. Big Mom is Gates's maternal grandmother, matriarch of the Coleman family and mother of twelve; Nemo was her oldest son. Skippy is Gates's childhood nickname.

Playing Hardball

Daddy worked all the time, every day but Sunday. Two jobs—twice a day, in and out, eat and work, work and eat. Evenings, we watched television together, all of us, after I'd done my homework and Daddy had devoured the newspaper or a book. He was always reading, it seemed, especially detective stories. He was a charter subscriber to *Alfred Hitchcock's Magazine* and loved detective movies on TV.

My brother Rocky was the one he was close to. Rocky worshiped sports, while I worshiped Rocky. I chased after him like a lapdog. I wanted to be just like him. But the five years between us loomed like Kilimanjaro. We were always out of phase. And he felt crowded by my adoring gaze.

Rocky and I didn't exactly start off on the right foot. When I was born, my parents moved my brother to Big Mom's house, to live with her and Little Jim, who was our first cousin and Nemo's son and the firstborn male of our generation in the Coleman family. It was not an uncommon arrangement to shift an older child to his or her grandparents', because of crowding. Since we had only three rooms, plus a tiny room with a toilet, my parents thought the move was for the best. And Big Mom's house was only a couple hundred yards straight up the hill. Still, it's difficult to gauge the trauma of that displacement, all these years later. Five years of bliss, ended by my big head popping out.

But Rocky was compensated: he was Daddy's boy. Like the rest of Piedmont, they were baseball fanatics. They knew who had done what and when, how much everyone had hit, in what inning, who had scored the most runs in 1922, who the most rbi's. They could sit in front of a TV for hours at a time, watching inning after tedious inning of baseball, baseball, baseball. Or sit at Forbes Field in Pittsburgh through a doubleheader without getting tired or longing to go home. One night, when I was seven, we saw Sandy Koufax of the Dodgers pitch one game, then his teammate Don Drysdale pitch another. It was the most boring night of my life, though later I came to realize what a feat I had witnessed, two of baseball's greatest pitchers back-to-back.

I enjoyed *going* to the games in Pittsburgh because even then I loved to travel. One of Daddy's friends would drive me. I was fascinated with geography. And since I was even more fascinated with food, a keen and abiding interest of mine, I liked the games for that reason too. We would stop to eat at Howard Johnson's, going and coming. And there'd be hot dogs and sodas at the games, as well as popcorn and candy, to pass the eternity of successive innings in the July heat. Howard Johnson's was a five-star restaurant in Piedmont.

I used to get up early to have breakfast with Daddy, eating from his plate. I'll still spear a heavily peppered fried potato or a bit of egg off his plate today. My food didn't taste as good as his. Still doesn't. I used to drink coffee, too, in order to be just like Daddy. "Coffee will make you black," he'd tell me, with the intention of putting me off. From the beginning, I used a lot of pepper, because he did, and he did because his father did. I remember reading James Agee's *A Death in the Family* and being moved by a description of the extra pepper that the father's wife put on his eggs the very morning that he is killed in a car. Why are you frying eggs *this* time of day, Mama asked me that evening. Have you seen the pepper, Mama? I replied.

An unathletic child with too great an interest in food—no wonder I was fat, and therefore compelled to wear "husky" clothes.

My Skippy's not *fat,* Mama would lie. He's husky.

But I *was* fat, and felt fatter every time Mama repeated her lie. My mama loved me like life itself. Maybe she didn't see me as fat. But I was. And whoever thought of the euphemism "husky" should be shot. I was short and round—not obese, mind you, but *fat.* Still, I was clean and energetic, and most of the time I was cheerful. And I liked to play with other kids, not so much because I enjoyed the things we did together but because I could watch them be happy.

But sports created a bond between Rocky and my father that excluded me, and, though my father had no known athletic talent himself, my own unathletic bearing compounded my problems. For not only was I overweight, I had been born with flat feet and wore "corrective shoes." They were the bane of my existence, those shoes. While Rocky would be wearing long, pointy-toed, cool leather gentlemen, I'd be shod in blunt-ended, round-toed, fat-footed shoes that nobody but your mother could love.

And Mama *did* love those shoes. Elegant, she'd say. They're Stride-Rite. Stride-wrong, I'd think. Mama, I want some nice shoes, I'd beg, like Rocky's.

Still, I guess they did what they were meant to do, because I have good arches now. Even today, I look at the imprint of my wet foot at a swimming pool, just to make certain that my arch is still arched. I don't ever again want to wear those dull brown or black corrective shoes.

What made it all the more poignant was that Rocky—tall, lean, and handsome, blessed with my father's metabolism— was a true athlete. He would be the first Negro captain of the basketball team in high school and receive "the watch" at graduation. (He was the first colored to do that too.)

Maybe Mama thought I was husky, but Daddy knew better, and he made no secret of it. "Two-Ton Tony Galento," he and Rocky would say, or they'd call me Chicken Flinsterwall or Fletcher Bissett, Milton Berle's or Jack Benny's character in a made-for-TV movie about two complete cowards. I hated Daddy for doing that and yielded him as unconquerable terrain to my brother, clinging desperately to my mother for protection.

Ironically, I had Daddy's athletic ability, or lack thereof, just as I have his body. (We wear the same-size ring, gloves, shoes, shirt, suits, and hat.) And like him, I love to hear a good story. But during my first twelve or so years we were alienated from each other. I despised sports because I was overweight and scared to death. Especially of baseball—hardball, we called it. Yet I felt I had no choice but to try out for Little League. Everyone my age did Little League, after all. They made me a Giant, decided I was a catcher because I was "stout, like Roy Campanella," dressed me in a chest protector and a mask, and squatted me behind a batter.

It's hard to catch a baseball with your eyes closed. Each time a ball came over the plate, I thanked the Good Lord that the batter hadn't confused my nappy head with the baseball that had popped its way into my mitt. My one time at bat was an experience in blindness; miraculously, I wasn't hit in the head. With a 3 and 2 count, I got a ball, so I walked. They put in a runner for me. Everybody patted me on the back like I had just won the World Series. And everybody said nice things about my "eye." Yeah, I thought. My tightly closed eye.

Afterward, Pop and I stopped at the Cut-Rate to get a caramel ice-cream cone, then began the long walk up the hill to Pearl Street. I was exhausted, so we walked easy. He was biding his time, taking smaller steps than usual so that I could keep up. "You know that you don't have to play baseball, don't you, boy?" All of a sudden I knew how Moses had felt on Mount Sinai. His voice was a bolt out of the blue. Oh, I want to play, I responded in a squeaky voice. "But you know that you don't *have* to play. I never was a good player. Always afraid of the ball. Uncoordinated too. I can't even run straight." We laughed. "I became the manager of the team," he said. That caramel ice cream sure tasted good. I held Daddy's hand almost all the way home.

In my one time at bat, I had got on base. I had confronted the dragon and he was mine. I had, I had ... been absurdly lucky ... and I couldn't *wait* to give them back their baseball suit. It was about that time that Daddy stopped teasing me about being fat. That day he knew me, and he seemed to care.

Yes, Pop and I had some hard times. He thought that I didn't love him, and I thought he didn't love me. At times, we both were right. I didn't think you wanted me around, he told me much later. I thought that I embarrassed you. He did embarrass me, but not like you might think, not the usual way parents embarrass children in front of their friends, for example. He had a habit of correcting me in front of strangers or white people, especially if they were settling an argument between me and Pop by something they had just said, by a question they had answered. See, I *told* you so, he'd say loudly, embarrassing the hell out of me with a deliberateness that puzzled and vexed me. I hated him when he did that.

And despite my efforts to keep up, he and my brother had somehow made me feel as if I were an android, something not quite a person. I used to dream about going away to military school, and wrote to our congressman, Harley Staggers, for a list of names. I used to devour *McKeever and the Colonel* on Sunday nights and dream about the freedom of starting over, at a high-powered, regimented school away from home. Daddy and Rocky would make heavy-handed jokes about queers and sissies. I wasn't their direct target, but I guess it was another form of masculine camaraderie that marked me as less manly than my brother.

And while I didn't fantasize about boys, I did love the companionship of boys and men, loved hearing them talk and watching their rituals, loved the warmth that their company could bring. I even loved being with the Coleman boys, at one of their shrimp or squirrel feeds, when they would play cards. Generally, though, I just enjoyed being on the edge of the circle, watching and listening and laughing, basking in the warmth, memorizing the stories, trying to strip away illusions, getting at what was really coming down.

I made my peace with sports, by and by, and was comfortable watching Rock and Daddy watch sports. But I could never experience it with the absorption they were capable of, could never live and breathe sports as they did. Oh, I loved to watch all the tournaments, the finals, the Olympics—the ritual events. But my relation to sports was never as visceral and direct as theirs.

After I returned my Little League uniform, I became the team's batboy and then the league's official scorekeeper, publishing our results in a column in the *Piedmont Herald,* our weekly newspaper.

Much more than sports, I had early on developed an avidity for information about The Negro. I'm not sure why, since Daddy was not exactly a race man. Niggers are crabs in a barrel: if he said that once, he said it to us a thousand times. My father was hard on colored people—and funny about it too.

Aside from a brief stint as a student in New Jersey, Daddy's major contact with Negro culture from Elsewhere had been in the army, at Camp Lee, Virginia. He used to tell us all kinds of stories about the colored troops at Camp Lee, especially blacks from the rural South. It was clear that the army in World War II had been a great cauldron, mixing the New Negro culture, which had developed in the cities since the great migration of the twenties and thirties, and the Old Negro culture, the remnants of traditional rural black culture in the South.

Camp Lee was where colored soldiers were sent to learn how to be quartermasters—butlers, chefs, and service people, generally. Because the army replicates the social structure of the larger society it defends, almost all black draftees were taught to cook and clean. Of course, it was usually women who cooked and cleaned outside the army, but *someone* had to do the work, so it would be black men. Gender and race conflate in a crisis. Even educated black people were put in the quartermasters.

Well, Camp Lee was a circus and my daddy its scribe. He told us stories about how he beat the system, or damn well tried to. The first day, he had raised his hand when an officer asked who knew accounting. How hard could it be? he responded when I laughed. Hell, all you had to be able to do was add and subtract. The one thing I knew, he said, was that an accountant had an office and everybody else had to do basic training. Now, which one would *you* have picked? For two years, he stayed at Camp Lee and avoided being shipped to the front. Everybody else would be processed, then shipped out to Europe. But Daddy became a staff sergeant, serving as secretary and accountant to the commanding officer, who liked him a lot. He sent for Mama, who took a room in a colored home in town. Daddy slept there too. Mama got a job in a dry cleaner's. The pictures that I carry of them in my wallet are from this time, 1942.

The war wouldn't take Pop any farther than Camp Lee, but even that was an experience that stayed with him. There he encountered the customs and sayings, the myths and folklore, of all sorts of black people he had never even heard about. The war did more to recement black American culture, which migration had fragmented, than did any other single event or experience. "War? What is it good for? You tell 'em: absolutely nothing." Nothing for the Negro but the transfer of cultures, the merging of the old black cultures with the new. And the transfer of skills. Daddy was no "race man," but for all his sardonicism, he respected race men and women, the people who were articulate and well educated, who comported themselves with dignity and who "achieved." Being at Camp Lee, an all-colored world, he'd say a decade later, was like watching episodes of *Amos and Andy*.

Hard as Daddy could be on colored people, he was Marcus Garvey compared to *his* father. Pop Gates used to claim that the government should lock up all the niggers in a big reservation in Kansas or Oklahoma or somewhere, feed them, clothe them, and give them two names: John or Mary. Nobody would hurt them, he'd add plaintively when his children would either protest or burst into howls of laughter. Pop Gates *hated* to see black people in loud clothes, and he hated just as much our traditional poetic names, such as Arbadella or Ethelretta. Made-up names, he'd say. Shouldn't be allowed, he'd say.

I was more aggressive around white people than Daddy, and it didn't go down well with him—or anybody else. Especially my Coleman uncles. Daddy, as noted, would almost never take my side in front of others. And if he felt I had violated a boundary, he would name it publicly and side with the boundary. He would do so loudly, even with what struck my child's ears as a certain malice. It tore me up.

He was not always this way with me. At a Little League game when I was ten, I told off a white man, Mr. Frank Price, not for anything he'd done to me, but for the rude way he treated Mr. Stanley Fisher, a black man in his sixties, who was maybe twenty years Price's senior. The details are murky, but Price had been rude to the older man in a way that crossed a line, that made the colored people feel he was a racist.

I do remember that I was unable to control myself, unable to contain my anger. I found myself acting without thinking. I felt the blood rushing to my face, and a flood of nasty words poured out of my mouth, just this side of profanity. Everybody on the first-base side of the Little League field over in Westernport looked up and froze in silence as I stood in front of that big-bellied man's fat red face and told him to leave Mr. Stanley alone. Then I turned to Mr. Stanley and told him not to waste his dignity on that trash: "Don't sweat the small stuff," I said. The colored held their breaths, and Daddy looked like a cat caught between two fighting dogs and not knowing which way to turn. Even Mr. Stanley's face showed surprise at this snot-nosed kid talking right up in some redneck's face. Mr. Stanley must have been more embarrassed by me than reassured.

Daddy stepped in finally, put his arm around my shoulder, and started woofing at Frank Price and giving him those dirty glares of his, all the while pushing me gently up the field toward Stanley and the colored men who always sat together on their lawn chairs out in right field. And we then all walked together up the dusty back road that bordered the Little League field like the rim of a crater, passing the new filtration plant, which made the whole place stink worse than the sulfurous chemicals that it had been built to remove, and all the old colored men were saying what an asshole Frank Price was and always had been, and how he had been rude to Stanley, and how nobody liked or respected him (not even white people), and how nobody within earshot should pay that motherfucker no mind.

Now, you know you are supposed to respect your elders, don't you? Daddy said to me much later, after we had bought a caramel ice-cream cone, to go, at the Cut-Rate. And you know you are not supposed to talk back to older people, now don't you? And you know that Stanley Fisher can take care of himself? And you know that you can get in trouble talking back to white people, don't you? Don't you, boy? Boy, you crazy sometimes. That ice cream is dripping down your fingers. Don't let it go to waste.

BERNARD COOPER

A lifelong resident of Los Angeles, Bernard Cooper (1951–) is the author of a novel and two highly regard collections of short memoirs: Maps to Anywhere *and* Truth Serum. *His work has appeared in* Gentleman's Quarterly, Paris Review, *and the* Los Angeles Times Magazine, *and three of his essays have been included in the annual* Best American Essays *collections. Winner of an O'Henry Award, Cooper teaches writing at Antioch University, Los Angeles; in 1999 he received a Guggenheim Fellowship.*

Much of Cooper's best work calls on his childhood memories of an idyllic Southern California in the early 1960s, intertwined with his dawning and reluctant realization that he was attracted to men. In one such incident, with his parents away at an Orange County brunch, he sought to exorcise his desires on the eve of his entry into the eighth grade by burning his collection of Pony Boys! *magazines on the garage floor—only to watch in panic as countless bits of charred male musculature drifted down and about his father's workbench.*

Cooper's father, Edward, was born in 1906 in Philadelphia, the son of Russian Jewish immigrants. In 1940 he passed the Califor-

nia state bar exam and began a long career as a divorce attorney —a career informed by a voracious lust for the opposite sex and his own clandestine encounters; women, recalls Bernard, stirred in his father "an impulse as strong as the will to survive." But it was more the intensity of the impulse than its focus that best characterized Edward S. Cooper; for he was, says Cooper, "a man wracked by an excess of energy." Throughout his childhood, Cooper remembers that his father brought home bales of office work; he gardened till sunset, wore trails in the carpet from nighttime pacings, and when he ate, he "ate in nervous surges, spearing and gulping, his face flushed, the veins in his temples blue." In his essay "Imitation of Life," Cooper says of his father's hunger that it "was edged with desperation; he owned a house, a four-door sedan, his law practice burgeoned year after year, yet despite what he had, it wasn't enough, and nothing, nothing could fill him up."

Edward Cooper lived to the age of ninety-four. He lived well past the death of his first wife, Bernard's mother, through a well-intentioned but short-lived second marriage, and long enough to witness the deaths of his three oldest sons. His troubles tempered him as he aged, and he became talkative and gentle, introspective. The two grew closer, and Bernard allowed himself the observation that he and his father were "starting to look and sound alike." Eventually they even grew close enough to broach topics long unspoken.

"Picking Plums" was first published in Harper's Magazine in 1992. In 1996 Cooper included it in Truth Serum.

Picking Plums

It has been nearly a year since my father fell while picking plums. The bruises on his leg have healed, and except for a vague absence of pigmentation where the calf had blistered, his recovery is complete. Back in the habit of evening constitutionals, he navigates the neighborhood with his usual stride—"Brisk," he says, "for a man of eighty-five"—dressed in a powder blue jogging suit that bears the telltale stains of jelly doughnuts and Lipton's tea, foods which my father, despite doctor's orders, hasn't the will to forsake.

He broke his glasses and his hearing aid in the fall, and when I first stepped into the hospital room for a visit, I was struck by the way my father—head cocked to hear, squinting to see—looked so much older and more remote, a prisoner of his failing senses. "Boychik?" he asked, straining his face in my general direction. He fell back into a stack of pillows, sighed a deep sigh, and without my asking described what had happened:

"There they are, all over the lawn. Purple plums, dozens of them. They look delicious. So what am I supposed to do? Let the birds eat them? Not on your life. It's my tree, right? First I fill a bucket with the ones from the ground. Then I get the ladder out of the garage. I've climbed the thing a hundred times before. I make it to the top, reach out my hand, and . . . who knows what happens. Suddenly I'm an astronaut. Up is down and vice versa. It happened so fast I didn't have time to piss in my pants. I'm flat on my back, not a breath left in me. Couldn't have called for help if I tried. And the pain in my leg—you don't want to know."

"Who found you?"

"What?"

I move closer, speak louder.

"Nobody found me," he says, exasperated. "Had to wait till I could get up on my own. It seemed like hours. I'm telling you, I thought it was all over. But eventually I could breathe normal again and, don't ask me how, God only knows, I got in the car and drove here myself."

"You should have called me."

"You were probably busy."

"It was an emergency, Dad. What if you hadn't been able to drive?"

"You don't have to shout. I made it here, didn't I?" My father shifted his weight and grimaced. The sheet slid off his injured leg, the calf swollen, purple as a plum, what the doctor called "an insult to the tissue."

Throughout my boyhood my father possessed a surplus of energy, or it possessed him. On weekdays he worked hard at the office, and on weekends he gardened in our yard. He was also a man given to unpredictable episodes of anger. These rages were never precipitated by a crisis. In the face of illness or accident my father remained steady, methodical, even optimistic. When the chips were down, he was an incorrigible joker, a sentry at the bedside. But something as simple as a drinking glass left out on the table could send him into a frenzy of invective. Spittle shot from his lips. Blood ruddied his face. He'd hurl the glass against the wall.

His temper rarely intimidated my mother. She'd light a Tareyton, stand aside, and watch my father flail and shout until he was purged of the last sharp word. Winded and limp, he'd flee into the living room, where he would draw the shades, sit in his wing chair, and brood for hours. Mother got out the broom and the dustpan and—presto!—the damage disappeared. Shards of glass slid into the trash can, chimed against the metal sides. And when Mother lifted her foot from the pedal and the lid fell shut with a thud, I knew the ordeal was over.

Even as a boy, I understood how my father's profession had sullied his view of the world, had made him a wary man, prone to explosions. He spent hours taking depositions from jilted wives and cuckolded husbands. He conferred with a miserable clientele: spouses who wept, who spat accusations, who pounded his desk in want of revenge. At this time, California law required that grounds for divorce be proven in court, and toward this end my father carried in his briefcase not only the usual legal tablets and manila files but bills for motel rooms, matchbooks from bars, boxer shorts blooming with lipstick stains. It was his job to exploit every detail of an infidelity, to unearth the most tawdry and incontrovertible evidence of betrayal. Year in and year out, my father met with a steady parade of strangers and itemized insults, blows, deceits.

After one particularly long and vindictive divorce trial, he agreed to a weekend out of town. Mother suggested Palm Springs, rhapsodized about the balmy air, the cacti lit by colored lights, the street named after Bob Hope. When it finally came time to leave, however, my mother kept thinking of things she'd forgotten to pack. No sooner would my father begin to back the car out of the driveway than my mother would shout for him to stop, dash into the house, and retrieve what she needed. A carton of Tareytons. An aerosol can of Solarcaine. A paperback novel to read by the pool. I sat in the back seat, motionless and mute; with each of her excursions back inside, I felt my father's frustration mount. When my mother insisted she get a package of Saltine crackers in case we got hungry along the way, my father glared at her, bolted from the car, wrenched every piece of luggage from the trunk, and slammed it shut with such a vengeance the car rocked on its springs. Through the rear window, my mother and I could see him fling two suitcases, a carryall, and a makeup case yards above his balding head. The sky was a huge and cloudless blue; gray chunks of luggage sailed through it, twisting and spinning and falling to earth like the burnt-out stages of a booster rocket. When a piece of luggage crashed back to the asphalt, he'd pick it up and hurl it again.

Mother and I got out of the car and sat together on a low wall by the side of the driveway, waiting for his tantrum to pass. "Some vacation," she said, lighting a cigarette. Her cheeks imploded from the vigorous draw. In order to watch him, we had to shield our eyes against the sun, a light so stark it made me want to sneeze. Sometimes my father managed to launch two or three pieces of luggage into the air at the same time. With every effort, an involuntary, animal grunt issued from the depths of his chest. Once or twice, a suitcase flew up and eclipsed the sun, and I remember thinking how small and aloof it really was, not like the fat and friendly star my classmates drew in school.

Finally, the largest suitcase came unlatched in midflight. Even my father was astonished when articles of his wife's wardrobe began their descent from the summer sky. A yellow scarf dazzled the air like a tangible strand of sunlight. Fuzzy slippers tumbled down. One diaphanous white slip drifted over the driveway and, as if guided by an invisible hand, draped itself across a hedge. With that, my father barreled by us, veins protruding on his temple and neck, and stomped into the house. "I'm getting tired of this," my mother grumbled. Before she stooped to pick up the mess—a vast and random geography of clothes—she flicked her cigarette onto the asphalt and ground out the ember.

One evening, long after I'd moved away from home, I received a phone call from my father telling me that my mother had died the night before. "But I didn't know it happened," he said.

He'd awakened as usual that morning, ruminating over a case while he showered and shaved. My mother appeared to be sound asleep, one arm draped across her face, eyes sheltered beneath the crook of her elbow. When he sat on the bed to pull up his socks he'd tried not to jar the mattress and wake her. At least he thought he'd tried not to wake her, but he couldn't remember, he couldn't be sure. Things looked normal, he kept protesting—the pillow, the blanket, the way she lay there. He decided to grab a doughnut downtown and left in a hurry. But that night my father returned to a house suspiciously unlived-in. The silence caused him to clench his fists, and he called for his wife, "Lillian, Lillian," as he drifted through quiet, unlit rooms, walking slowly up the stairs.

I once saw a photograph of a woman who had jumped off the Empire State Building and landed on the roof of a parked car. What is amazing is that she appeared merely to have leapt into satin sheets. Deep in a languid and absolute sleep, her eyes are closed, lips slightly parted, hair fanned out on a metal pillow. Nowhere is there a trace of blood, her body caught softly in its own impression.

As my father spoke into the telephone, his voice about to break—"I should have realized, I should have known"—that's the state in which I pictured my mother: a long fall of sixty years, an uncanny landing, a miraculous repose.

My father and I had one thing in common after my mother's heart attack: we each maintained a secret life. Secret, at least, from each other.

I'd fallen for a man named Travis Mask. Travis had recently arrived in Los Angeles from Kentucky, and everything I was accustomed to—the billboards lining the Sunset Strip, the 7-Elevens open all night—stirred in him a strong allegiance. "I love this town," he'd say every day. Travis's job was to collect change from vending machines throughout the city. During dinner he would tell me about the office lobbies and college cafeterias he had visited, the trick to opening different machines, the noisy cascade of nickels and dimes. Travis Mask was enthusiastic. Travis Mask was easy to please. In bed I called him by his full name because I found the sound of it exciting.

And my father had fallen for a woman whose identity he meant to keep secret. I knew of her existence only because of a dramatic change in his behavior: he would grow mysterious as quickly and inexplicably as he had once grown angry. Ordinary conversations would take confusing turns. One night I phoned him at home and tried to make a date for dinner.

"Sounds good," he said. "How about next . . . " A voice in the background interrupted. "As I was saying," he continued, "I'll have the papers for you by Friday."

"OK," I said stupidly. "What papers?"

"It's no problem at all."

"Dad, what's going on?"

"We'll have to have them countersigned, of course."

"Let me guess. You have company."

"No," he said. "Thank *you*."

After he hung up, I began to wonder why my father couldn't simply admit that he had a girlfriend. I'd told him on several occasions that I hoped he could find companionship, that I knew he must be lonely without my mother. What did he have to gain by keeping his relationship a secret? Or was it *my* existence he was trying to hide from her? I'd gone back to watching the evening news with Travis when an awful thought occurred to me. Suppose a robber had forced his way into my father's house, pointed a gun at his head, and ordered him to continue talking as if nothing had happened. What if our officious conversation had really been a signal for help? I tried to remember every word, every inflection. Hadn't there been an unnatural tension in his voice, a strain I'd never heard before? I dismissed this thought as preposterous, only to have it boomerang back. Nearly an hour passed before I decided to call him again. Six rings. Seven. His voice was dreamy, expansive, when he answered, his hello as round and buoyant as a bubble. I hung up without speaking, and when I told Travis I was upset because my father refused to be frank, he said, "Honey, you're a hypocrite."

Travis was right, of course. I resented being barred from this central fact of my father's life but had no intention of telling him I was gay. It had taken me thirty years to achieve even a modicum of intimacy with the man, and I didn't want to risk a setback. It wasn't as if I was keeping my sexual orientation a secret from everyone; I'd told relatives, coworkers, friends. But my father was a man who whistled at waitresses, flirted with bank tellers, his head swiveling like a radar dish toward the nearest pair of breasts and hips. Ever since I was a child my father reminded me of the cartoon wolf whose ears shoot steam, whose eyes pop out on springs, whose tongue unfurls like a party favor whenever he sees a curvaceous dame. As far as my father was concerned, desire for women fueled the world, compelled every man without exception (his occupation testified to that), was a force as essential as gravity. I didn't want to disappoint him.

Eventually, Travis Mask's company transferred him to Long Beach. In his absence, my nights grew long and ponderous, and I tried to spend more time with my father in the belief that

sooner or later an opportunity for disclosure would present itself. We met for dinner once a month in a restaurant whose interior was dim and crimson, our interaction friendly but formal, both of us cautiously skirting the topic of our private lives;
we'd become expert at the ambiguous answer, the changed subject, the half-truth. Should my father ask if I was dating, I'd tell
him yes, I had been seeing someone. I'd liked them very much, I
said, but they were transferred to another city. Them. They. My
attempt to neuter the pronouns made it sound as if I were
courting people en masse. Just when I thought this subterfuge
was becoming obvious, my father began to respond in kind.
"Too bad I didn't get a chance to meet them. Where did you say
they went?"

Avoidance also worked in reverse: "And how about you,
Dad? Are you seeing anybody?"

"Seeing? I don't know if you'd call it *seeing*. What did you order, chicken or fish?"

It may seem as if this phase of our relationship was in some
way an unhappy accommodation, but I enjoyed visiting with
my father during that period and even found it challenging to
find things to talk about. During one dinner we discovered that
we shared a fondness for nature programs on television, and
from that night on, when we'd exhausted our comments about
the meal or the weather, we'd ask if the other had seen the show
about the blind albino fish that live in underwater caves, or the
one about the North American moose, whose antlers, coated
with green moss, provide camouflage in the underbrush. My father and I had adapted like those creatures to the strictures of
our shared world.

And then I met her.

I looked up from a rack of stationery at the local Thrifty one
afternoon and there stood my father with a willowy black
woman in her early forties. As she waited for a prescription to
be filled, he drew a finger through her hair, nuzzled the nape of

her neck, the refracted light of his lenses causing his cheeks to glow. I felt like a child who was witness to something forbidden: his father's helpless, unguarded ardor for an unfamiliar woman. I didn't know whether to run or stay. Had he always been attracted to young black women? Had I ever known him well? Somehow I managed to move myself toward them and mumble hello. They turned around in unison. My father's eyes widened. He reached out and cupped my shoulder, struggled to say my name. Before he could think to introduce us, I shook the woman's hand, startled by its softness. "So you're the son. Where've you been hiding?" She was kind and cordial, though too preoccupied to engage in much conversation, her handsome features furrowed by a hint of melancholy, a sadness that I sensed had little to do with my surprise appearance. Anna excused herself when the pharmacist called her name.

Hours after our encounter, I could still feel the softness of Anna's hand, the softness that stirred my father's yearning. He was seventy-five years old, myopic and hard of hearing, his skin loose and liver-spotted, but one glimpse of his impulsive public affection led me to the conclusion that my father possessed, despite his age, a restless sexual energy. The meeting left me elated, expectant. My father and I had something new in common: the pursuit of our unorthodox passions. We were, perhaps, more alike than I'd realized. After years of relative estrangement, I'd been given grounds for a fresh start, a chance to establish a stronger connection. The final hurdle, however, involved telling my father I was gay, and now there was Anna's reaction to consider. But none of my expectations mattered. Later that week, they left the country.

The prescription, it turned out, was for a psychotropic drug. Anna had battled bouts of depression since childhood. Her propensity for unhappiness gave my father a vital mission: to make her laugh, to wrest her from despair. Anna worked as an elementary school substitute teacher and managed a few rental properties in South Central Los Angeles, but after weeks of functioning normally, she would take to my father's bed for days on end, blank and immobile beneath the quilt she had bought to brighten up the room, unaffected by his jokes, his kisses and cajoling. These spells of depression came without warning and ended just as unexpectedly. Though they both did their best to enjoy each other during the periods of relative calm, they lived, my father lamented later, like people in a thunderstorm, never knowing when lightning would strike. Thinking that a drastic change might help Anna shed a recent depression, they pooled their money and flew to Europe.

They returned with snapshots showing the two of them against innumerable backdrops. The Tower of London, the Vatican, Versailles. Monuments, obelisks, statuary. In every pose their faces were unchanged, the faces of people who want to be happy, who try to be happy, and somehow can't.

As if in defiance of all the photographic evidence against them, they were married the following month at the Church of the Holy Trinity. I was one of only two guests at the wedding. The other was an uncle of Anna's. Before the ceremony began, he shot me a glance which attested, I was certain, to an incredulity as great as mine. The vaulted chapel rang with prerecorded organ music, an eerie and pious overture. Light filtered through stained-glass windows, chunks of sweet color that reminded me of Jell-O. My old Jewish father and his Episcopalian lover appeared at opposite ends of the dais, walking step by measured step toward a union in the center. The priest, swimming in white vestments, was somber and almost inaudible. Cryptic gestures, odd props; I watched with a powerful, wordless amazement. Afterward, as if the actual wedding hadn't been surreal enough, my father and Anna formed a kind of receiving line (if two people can constitute a line) in the church parking lot, where the four of us, bathed by hazy sunlight, exchanged pleasantries before the newlyweds returned home for a nap; their honeymoon in Europe, my father joked, had put the cart before the horse.

During the months after the wedding, when I called my father, he answered as though the ringing of the phone had been an affront. When I asked him what was the matter, he'd bark, "What makes you think there's something the matter?" I began to suspect that my father's frustration had given rise to those ancient rages. But my father had grown too old and frail to sustain his anger for long. When we saw each other—Anna was always visiting relatives or too busy or tired to join us—he looked worn, embattled, and the pride I had in him for attempting an interracial marriage, for risking condemnation in the eyes of the world, was overwhelmed now by concern. He had lost weight. His hands began to shake. I would sit across from him in the dim red restaurant and marvel that this bewildered man had once hurled glasses against a wall and launched Samsonite into the sky.

Between courses, I'd try to distract my father from his problems by pressing him to unearth tidbits of his past, as many as memory would allow. He'd often talk about Atlantic City, where his parents had owned a small grocery. Sometimes my mother turned up in the midst of his sketchy regressions. He would smooth wrinkles from the tablecloth and tell me no one could take her place. He eulogized her loyalty and patience, and I wondered whether he could see her clearly—her auburn hair and freckled hands—wondered whether he wished she were here to sweep up after his current mess. "Remember," he once asked me, without a hint of irony or regret, "what fun we had in Palm Springs?" Then he snapped back into the present and asked what was taking so long with our steaks.

The final rift between my father and Anna must have come abruptly; she left behind several of her possessions, including the picture of Jesus that sat on the sideboard in the dining room next to my father's brass menorah. And along with Anna's possessions were stacks of leather-bound books, *Law of Torts,* *California Jurisprudence,* and *Forms of Pleading and Practice* embossed on their spines. Too weak and distracted to practice law, my father had retired, and the house became a repository for the contents of his former office. I worried about him being alone, wandering through rooms freighted with history, crowded with the evidence of two marriages, fatherhood, and a long and harrowing career; he had nothing to do but pace and sigh and stir up dust. I encouraged him to find a therapist, but as far as my father was concerned, psychiatrists were all conniving witch doctors who fed off the misery of people like Anna.

Brian, the psychotherapist I'd been living with for three years, was not at all fazed by my father's aversion to his profession. They'd met only rarely (once we ran into my father at a local supermarket, and twice Brian accompanied us to the restaurant), but when they were together, Brian would draw my father out, compliment him on his plaid pants, ask questions regarding the fine points of law. And when my father spoke, Brian listened intently, embraced him with his cool blue gaze. If the subject of Brian's occupation arose, my father seemed secretly delighted to learn that there were so many people in the world burdened with grim and persistent problems, people worse off than either he or Anna. My father relished my lover's attention; Brian's cheerfulness and steady disposition must have been refreshing in those troubled, lonely days. "How's that interesting friend of yours?" he sometimes asked. If he suspected that Brian and I shared the same house, he never pursued it. Over the years my father and I had come to the tacit understanding that I would never marry, and instead of expressing alarm or asking why, I'm afraid he simply assumed that the problematic examples of his own marriages had made me a skeptic when it came to romance and therefore a confirmed bachelor. And if my father did understand, consciously or subconsciously, that Brian and I were in love, I liked to believe he was happy I ended up with someone sane and solvent—a witch doctor, yes, but a doctor nevertheless. My father, in short, never seemed compelled to inquire about the particulars of my life (it was enough to know I was healthy and happy) until he took his fall from the plum tree.

I drove my father home from the hospital, tried to keep his big unwieldy car, bobbing like a boat, within the lane. I bought my father a pair of seersucker shorts because long pants were too painful and constricting. I brought over groceries and my wok, and while I cooked dinner he sat at the dinette table, leg propped on a vinyl chair, and listened to the hissing oil, happy, abstracted. I helped him up the stairs to his bedroom, where we watched *Wheel of Fortune* and *Jeopardy!* on television and where, for the first time since I was a boy, I sat at his feet and he rubbed my head. It felt so good that I grazed his good leg, as contented as a cat. He welcomed my visits with an eagerness bordering on glee, and didn't seem to mind being dependent on me for physical assistance; he leaned his bulk on my shoulder wholly, and I felt protective, necessary, inhaling the scents of salve and Old Spice, and the base, familiar odor that was all my father's own.

"You know those hostages?" asked my father. He was sitting at the dinette, dressed in the seersucker shorts, his leg propped on the chair. The bruises had faded to lavender, his calf back to its normal size.

I could barely hear him over the broccoli sizzling in the wok. "What about them?" I shouted.

"I heard on the news that some of them are seeing a psychiatrist now that they're back."

"So?"

"Why a psychiatrist?"

I stopped tossing the broccoli. "Dad," I said, "if you'd been held hostage in the Middle East, you might want to see a therapist, too."

The sky dimmed in the kitchen windows. My father's face was a silhouette, his lenses catching the last of the light. "They got their food taken care of, right? And a place to sleep. What's the big deal?"

"You're at gunpoint, for God's sake. A prisoner. I don't think it's like spending a weekend at the Hilton."

"Living alone," he said matter-of-factly, "is like being a prisoner."

I let it stand. I added the pea pods.

"Let me ask you something," said my father. "I get this feeling—I'm not sure how to say it—that something isn't right. That you're keeping something from me. We don't talk much, I grant you that. But maybe now's the time."

My heart was pounding. I'd been thoroughly disarmed by his interpretation of world events, his minefield of non sequiturs, and I wasn't prepared for a serious discussion. I switched off the gas. The red jet sputtered. When I turned around, my father was staring at his outstretched leg. "So?" he said.

"You mean Brian?"

"Whatever you want to tell me, tell me."

"You like him, don't you?"

"What's not to like."

"He's been my lover for a long time. He makes me happy. We have a home." Each declaration was a stone in my throat. "I hope you understand. I hope this doesn't come between us."

"Look," said my father without skipping a beat, "you're lucky to have someone. And he's lucky to have you, too. It's no one's business anyway. What the hell else am I going to say?"

But my father thought of something else before I could speak and express my relief. "You know," he said, "when I was a boy, maybe sixteen, my father asked me to hold a ladder while he trimmed the tree in our backyard. So I did, see, when I suddenly remember I have a date with this bee-yoo-tiful girl, and I'm late, and I run out of the yard. I don't know what got into me. I'm halfway down the street when I remember my father, and I think, Oh, boy. I'm in trouble now. But when I get back I can hear him laughing way up in the tree. I'd never heard him laugh like that. 'You must like her a lot,' he says when I help him down. Funny thing was, I hadn't told him where I was going."

I pictured my father's father teetering above the earth, a man hugging the trunk of a tree and watching his son run down the street in pursuit of sweet, ineffable pleasure. While my father reminisced, night obscured the branches of the plum tree, the driveway where my mother's clothes once floated down like enormous leaves. When my father finished telling the story, he looked at me, then looked away. A moment of silence lodged between us, an old and obstinate silence. I wondered whether nothing or everything would change. I spooned our food onto separate plates. My father carefully pressed his leg to test the healing flesh.

ROLAND MERULLO

Essays and articles by Roland Merullo (1953–) have appeared in Newsweek, Yankee, *the* Boston Globe Sunday Magazine, *and the* Philadelphia Inquirer, *among other places. He is the author of four books, including three novels, and his work has been translated into both German and Spanish. In the 1990s Merullo spent six years on the faculty at Vermont's Bennington College, and he now teaches at Amherst, not far from his home in Williamsburg, Massachusetts.*

Merullo is perhaps best known for his novel Revere Beach Boulevard, *which tells the story of an Italian-American family in Revere, Massachusetts, a small, working-class city across the harbor from Boston. Merullo himself grew up in Revere, as did his father, Roland Sr. Both Rolands attended public schools in Revere, but in junior high school the path of the younger Roland's life began diverging from that of his father's when a woman his parents did not know suggested that they should consider a more rigorous academic future for their boy. Merullo says his mother took the lead in this, but his father's "ambition for me was as great if not greater than hers." With the help of a scholarship, and after two years at a Catholic prep school, he finished high school at Phillips Exeter Academy, in New Hampshire; from there he went to Brown University, where he studied Russian and received both under-graduate and graduate degrees. There was no precedent, says Merullo, for such schooling in his family.*

All the more puzzling, then, to the father were the early uses to which his son put this education. After a brief go as a civil servant living abroad, Merullo fell into a life of Bohemian poverty and work with his hands. For the latter, there was plenty of prece-dent—in 1971 Merullo himself, after his graduation from Exeter, had worked for a summer at the construction site of the John Han-cock Tower in Boston's Back Bay, a job his father got him through connections. But wasn't it the point of education that it let you es-cape such a life?

Years later Merullo wrote about his summer at the Hancock in an essay for Forbes. *Though he appreciated his father's help in landing him the job (an attitude that would later change with changing circumstances), Merullo says nothing of it in the* Forbes *essay, writing only that he "knew somebody who knew somebody." Nor are there characters in his fiction based on his father.*

In 1998, however, Merullo published "What a Father Leaves." Appearing in a special issue of Witness *magazine on American families, Merullo says that of all he has written, this is the piece that is "closest to my heart." He didn't begin work on it until nearly a decade after his father had died. And even then, he says, it took him "years" to write.*

What a Father Leaves

On a June day when the world was at war, my father came into this life in a simple wooden house on Tapley Avenue, in Revere, Massachusetts. He died, without providing any advance notice, in a slightly fancier home on Essex Street. A little more than sixty-six years separated that birth and that death, a little more than a mile separated those two houses. Though he was an ordinary man in many respects, he knew extraordinary sorrow at an early age, and, later, extraordinary triumph, and among the tempers and memories he bequeathed me was the conviction that it is possible to find a solid bottom beneath those tidal sweeps of good and bad fortune.

His childhood was typical of the childhood of millions of first-generation European immigrants in the first quarter of this century: a small piece of a large family that was caught between the strictures of the old world and the promises and possibilities of the new. His parents—Giuseppe Merullo, a tailor, and Eleonora DeMarco Merullo, a housewife—had come to America from poor hilltop villages in southern Italy, settled briefly in Boston's North End, then married and moved a few miles north to the city of Revere—the countryside then—where they bought a house and began to fill it with children. My father was born in 1916, after Philomena and Carmen, and before Gloria, Violet, Anthony, Joseph, and Robert, but no tangible proof of his existence has come down to me from those years, no snapshots of him as a boy, no school papers or early artwork, only scraps of anecdote passed along by his brothers and sisters, who remain close to each other and to me.

His family was, by turns, relatively wealthy and relatively poor. Giuseppe—Joe, as he came to be called—owned his own tailor shop and lost it in a fire, owned one of the first automobiles in the neighborhood and lost it to medical bills after a fall, owned the house on Tapley Avenue, lost it in the Depression, then bought it back again in 1938. At one point in the 1930s, Eleonora had to sell her wedding ring to buy food, and the nearest tailoring work Joe could find was in Rockland, Maine, a twelve-hour drive to the north.

The streets were dirt, street lamps shone beneath crimped metal hats the color of poorly cared-for teeth. The Merullo children slept two to a bed, kept warm in winter by bricks that were heated in the coal stove, then wrapped in a towel and placed beneath the blankets at their feet. The family put up their own vegetables and made their own wine and root beer. The boys tilled the garden, shoveled snow, smoked cigarette butts they found on the sidewalk; and the girls listened to opera with their father on Sunday afternoons, cared for the babies, learned to cook at their mother's shoulder, were courted by boys from similar families on chaperoned outings.

The Revere of those days consisted of clusters of plain wooden houses set among rolling fields, its politics controlled by men of English and then Irish descent, its underworld run mainly by Jews, its three-mile crescent shoreline (America's first public beach) fronted by amusement rides, food stands, and dance halls that drew tourists from as far away as the West

Coast, its social life revolving around a synagogue and a dozen churches, men's clubs, the Revere Theater on Broadway. Six square miles of salt marsh and low hills a stone's throw from the metropolis, home to Italians, Poles, Russians, French Canadians, Irish, English, Jews, Scots, Germans, and a handful of blacks, the city was—unfortunately and perhaps unfairly—known primarily for political scandal, underworld dens, and racetracks. In fact, though, it was not much different from places like Brooklyn, Jersey City, and South Philadelphia: a certain rough humility, an emphasis on family loyalty and the vibrant, sometimes violent, life of the street, a brew of American ambition and European tradition that would, in future generations, bubble over into something more sedate and suburban, leaving room for different immigrants, new dramas.

It was in that hothouse of hope and defeat that the seed of my father's life sprouted. I know that he was a good, perhaps even a brilliant student, that as a young boy he cared so much about his clothes that he would take out his handkerchief and spread it carefully beneath him before sitting down on a neighbor's concrete wall, that he was baptized Orlando and went to school Roland, that he spoke Italian before speaking English but carried no trace of accent into adulthood. Those are the few puzzle pieces that survive. The remainder of his first eighteen years is a wash of American history almost identical to the history of twenty million other Orlandos, Patricks, and Sauls.

My father belonged to the generation of Americans we are now in the process of forgetting, a generation that had the misfortune to make the leap from high school into adulthood with the chasm of a world Depression yawning beneath their boots. In 1934, he graduated from Revere High School with honors, but there was no tradition of college in his family (his older brother and sister had dropped out of school to help bolster the family income), no money for tuition, no clearly marked route along which his ambition might travel.

In the farms that spread across western Revere then, he found work with a produce company called Suffolk Farms, picking carrots and cucumbers for twelve dollars a week. Over the course of the next few years, he moved up to a public relations position, studied civil engineering in night school, and when he'd earned his certificate, left Suffolk Farms for a job on a surveying crew. "On hot days," he would tell me forty years later, "I couldn't stand to be out there in my clean clothes while the other guys were sweating with their picks and shovels. Some days I took off my shirt and climbed down in the ditches with them and helped them out for a few hours."

That remark speaks volumes about him, about the confusion of longing for better and loyalty to his roots that runs like a refrain through his life. Even after he'd abandoned pick and shovel and surveyor's transit and climbed up into the high, fragile branches of Massachusetts State Government, he could not bring himself to leave Revere. He still met his childhood friends at Wonderland Dog Track one or two nights a week for an evening of modest losing, still seemed to feel as comfortable lunching with judges and senators at Dini's in Boston, as he did with city workers, plumbers, and bookmakers at Louie's corner coffee shop a few blocks from where he'd been born.

The remark speaks to something else, as well. My father was a gregarious man, and cared—sometimes to a fault—what impression he made in society. Like many Italian-American men, many men of all ethnic groups and races, he was shadowed by a societal definition of masculinity that has more to do with being brawny and tough than with any of the finer attributes. He worried that his arms and hands did not look strong enough, he worried about how he had dealt with and would deal with pain. Surrounded by war veterans, star athletes, and street fighters, he was pricked by a nagging devil of doubt because he was none of those things.

I am taking liberties here. He never said any of this to me.

Such tender introspection would have been as alien to him as corned beef to his mother's kitchen. And yet, I have a storehouse of small clues that stand in for his words. I see the footprints of that same devil on the carpet of my own home, I see the strength to be taken from traditional masculine stereotypes, as well as the wreckage they wreak in me, in brothers and cousins, in friends' marriages. Once in a while, in the midst of a discussion of the roles women have been made to play in our society, I hear an echo of my father's voice: "Sometimes on hot days—"

In 1941, he married, and began working as a draftsman for a Boston firm called Stone and Webster, his first real office job. The work consisted of designing power stations and submarine periscopes, and he liked it well enough. That December, when America was pulled into the war, he tried three times to enlist, but was turned down because of a punctured eardrum, forced to watch as the world convulsed and bled and the men of his generation went off to face their appointed sufferings.

For someone who felt embarrassed about working in a shirt and shoes next to bare-chested men with shovels, the idea of being left behind while neighbors went to war must have been next to unbearable for him. But, other than to state the facts of his case—the punctured eardrum, the three rejections—he did not speak to me about it.

As fate would have it, his own sufferings found him soon enough: on March 26, 1942, his wife of thirteen months died in childbirth. Again, only small pieces of this woman's life have drifted down to me through the shifting seas of familial memory. In the few snapshots I have seen, she is a happy girlfriend and then a happy newlywed, thin, dark-haired, pretty. I know that she was waked in her wedding gown, that, in the weeks and months after her death, my father's suffering seemed bottomless. "We would just be sitting down to dinner," one of my uncles told me only a year ago, "and the phone would ring. It would be the caretaker at the cemetery in West Roxbury, where Vi was buried, asking us to send someone over there right away because Roland was sitting next to the grave, weeping, and the caretaker wanted to close up and go home."

But the sense of this grief has reached me only third-hand, and only years after my father's death. Though I often wish it had been otherwise, he did not talk about grief and tragedy with me and my brothers. Every once in a while, during some poignant pause in the busyness of his life, he would be alone with one of us and make a comment like: "Someday I'll tell you everything. Someday we'll sit down and I'll tell you things." But what these things were we had little idea, and the promised "someday" never arrived.

Perhaps in deference to his second wife, my mother, he never spoke about his first marriage in our presence. I learned of it by a chance remark. Playing in the backyard one summer afternoon, I was summoned to the fence by our elderly neighbor, Rafaelo Losco, who handed over an armful of greens for me to pass on to my grandmother. Rafaelo had another man with him, a visiting brother or friend, and the man was running his eyes over my face with such intensity I felt as though a blind person were fingering my eye sockets and lips. "What is your name?" he demanded.

"Roland."

"Roland's son?"

"Yes."

"I've known your father forty years. I knew his wife when she was growing up. His first wife, I mean."

I only nodded, and turned away with my armful of escarole, but the words claimed a place in my memory. His *first* wife. I was old enough by then—seven or eight—to know something about secrets, to sense that this piece of information had been kept out of my reach for a reason, and I did not mention it, not to my parents or grandparents or brothers or friends, for close to two decades.

It seems peculiar now, that in all the times I must have been alone with my father during those years, I never asked about his first wife, or even let him know that I knew of her existence. It seems strange that he and my mother, and their parents and brothers and sisters, conspired in such a silence when it would have been so much easier all around to tell the story, once, answer the questions, and be done with it.

But ours was a Catholic world in which marriage was supposed to last for all eternity, and this was the 1950s and 1960s, when the ethos of emotional confession had not yet broken the polished shell in which we lived. And I believe there was an element of superstition involved as well, remnant vapors of an ancient stew of belief and mystery: to speak of tragedy would be to invite it. The closest any relative ever came to raising the subject was when one of my father's sisters asked me, in private, what I thought happened when people who'd been married more than once died and went to heaven. Which spouse were they in heaven with, did I have an opinion? Had I heard anything about this at Sunday school?

Whatever the reason or combination of reasons, the fact of my father's first marriage lay in the deep, undisturbed shadows of our family consciousness until the winter of 1978. In that year, I began knocking down, piece by piece and without spite, the edifice of expectations my parents had been erecting since my birth. I'd taken my college degrees a few years earlier, and, after a stint with USIA in the Soviet Union, I'd turned away from both an academic and a diplomatic career. With much fanfare, I joined the Peace Corps, went off to a primitive island in the Pacific, then quit after less than six months. Penniless, long-haired, hosting a menagerie of tropical bacteria, I returned to America and found work driving a cab in Boston, a job which seemed to crush the last of my parents' hope for me like crystal beneath a greasy work boot. In the space of eighteen months, I had gone from being a source of pride to a source of embarrassment, and in December I put the finishing touches on that swan dive into dishonor by announcing that I was moving in with my Protestant girlfriend.

As a boy, I'd seen a neighbor burst into tears at her daughter's engagement to *il protestante,* but it was 1978 now, and such "mixed" marriages no longer shocked Revere's papists. My parents had met Amanda before my Peace Corps venture, and approved of her from the start. The problem was not Amanda's religion or nationality (my mother, though Catholic, was of English ancestry, so that could hardly be an issue) or even the fact that we were having unblessed sex. The problem was that, by moving in together, we were openly confessing to this unblessed union, making it public, running up the flag of *disgrazia* for everyone in the family, in Revere, to see.

There were harsh words that night in the house on Essex Street, hurt feelings on both sides. My father, mother, and I shouted at each other across a widening chasm, tore at the sticky filaments that bound us, took turns pacing the kitchen, accusing. It had a different feeling than other arguments, the words were sharper, the consequences heavier. I was trying to embarrass them, smudge their good name. They were trying to meddle with my happiness. After that night, my mother did not speak to Amanda or me for several weeks.

My father was quicker to rebound. After we'd simmered for an hour in separate rooms, I said I was going to take the subway into Boston and spend the night with Amanda, but he offered to drive me instead.

We left the house in silence, drove along Revere's dark streets, acting out our epic of stubbornness. It did not occur to me that he might have offered the ride out of anything other than his reflexive generosity, a trait I took almost completely for granted at that point. In our culture, stinginess—with money, time, or assistance—was second only to disloyalty on the tablet of cardinal sins: why wouldn't he offer to drive into Boston and back at ten o'clock on a Sunday night?

Somewhere in Chelsea he said: "I guess things don't stand still. I changed my mind on Vietnam. I guess I'll end up changing my mind on this."

I said nothing, determined to win, for once, as I had seen him win so many times. We were climbing the flat arc of the Mystic River Bridge, a cold darkness beyond the windshield, harsh words still echoing behind us.

"You know this will lead to marriage," he went on, and I told him that if this led to marriage, it would be fine with me. He gave one of his short, tight-lipped nods. "She's a nice girl, a family girl."

This high compliment changed the air between us, and it began to seem to me that something positive had come of our fight. We had somehow knocked a hole in the too-respectful shield I'd put up around him, in the notion of father-as-king that brings so much stability to Italian families even as it nourishes the seeds of inadequacy in some sons and grandiose imitation in others. The trick was to thrust aside that notion without trampling on the man behind it, and we had somehow managed that. So I ventured a step into uncharted territory.

"You were married before, weren't you, Pa?"

"That's right."

"What happened?"

"She died."

"How?"

"In childbirth."

For a moment I turned my eyes away, touched, embarrassed, by the grief in his words, thirty-six years after the fact. It seemed to me then that, in two short sentences, I had an explanation for everything: his temper and frustrations, his fear that any telephone call might bring the worst imaginable news, his penchant—almost an obsession—for attending wakes and soothing the bereaved, his armor and distance and pride and stoicism, his superb, sometimes dark, sense of humor, his faith that the universe was ordered beyond any human understanding.

I had a key to him, at last. In love myself, the idea of losing a beloved struck me in a deeper place than it would have on some other night.

I was watching him now across the front seat, but he would not look at me.

"What happened to the baby?"

"The baby died, too."

"And then what was your life like?"

"Bitter," he said. "Until I met your mother. Bitter."

With that word, we buried the subject and never raised it again. In time, relatives would help me fill in some of the details: After Vi's death, my father withdrew almost totally from the social whirl on which he'd thrived. For years and years he did not date. His easygoing personality hardened a bit. He sought solace in his church, his brothers and sisters, a small group of family friends. His parents sold the house on Tapley Avenue (he and Vi had lived in the upstairs apartment) and moved a mile west to Essex Street, and my father passed most of the 1940s that way, enveloped in a womb of sorrow, loneliness, and defeat, while around him the world was again at war.

Very, very gradually he emerged. With the assistance of my mother (a lovely physical therapist who had volunteered to work with polio victims at the height of the epidemic, and then spent two years at Walter Reed Hospital, rehabilitating men who'd lost arms and legs in the war—in short, a woman who'd had some experience bringing a bit of light back into the lives of the wounded and lonely) his bitterness faded enough for him to want to make another try at building a family.

In 1948, he and my mother were engaged. He went into local politics and was elected to the city council, ran for state representative two years later and was narrowly defeated. On Veterans Day weekend in 1951, Roland Alfred Merullo and Eileen Frances Haydock were wed, and, after a brief honeymoon in Washington, D.C., they moved into the four-room apartment above my father's parents.

In 1952, my mother suffered a miscarriage in her fourth month of pregnancy. In 1953, she bore Roland, Jr., the first of three sons. In 1954, with my mother and me waiting in the car, my father, who had been out of work for the past several weeks, walked into the offices of the Volpe Construction Company in Malden, without an appointment, and asked the boss for a job. The boss, John Volpe (future governor and U.S. Secretary of Transportation), gave him a job, not as an engineer but as a worker in the gubernatorial campaign of a man named Christian Herter.

There began an unlikely association that would radically change the course of my father's life. Herter was tall, lanky, and wealthy, and displayed in his speech, clothing, and posture all the entitlements and credentials of what would later come to be known as the White Anglo-Saxon Male Power Establishment. And my father was a big-chested, six-foot Italian who had never spent a week outside his neighborhood, who had not been to college, or to Europe, or even to Vermont, for that matter; a Republican in a nest of Democrats; white and male but entitled to nothing and wanting everything.

They became fast friends, and their friendship endured until Herter's death in 1964. A strong orator, very careful about his clothes and manners, my father was a natural on the campaign trail, a great asset in the predominantly Italian-American precincts north of Boston. When Herter was elected Governor of Massachusetts in 1954, he chose as his personnel secretary a working-class Republican from a provincial neighborhood on Boston's tattered northern cuff.

In any government, but especially in one as patronage-fueled as the State Government of Massachusetts, personnel secretary is a position of vastly underestimated power. Acting by the rules on which he had been raised, my father found work for a long list of relatives and friends, filling the agencies of state with men and women he knew and trusted, or simply men and women who needed a boost in their lives, a steady paycheck, a safe niche they could cling to until retirement age. In so doing, he accumulated a huge bank account of favors, an account he would draw on unashamedly later in life, finding summer work for nieces and nephews and sons, interceding with judges, lawyers, cops, making a phone call here, pulling a string there, tweaking and twisting and cajoling and sometimes shoving the many-limbed beast of state power.

At some point in my early twenties, I turned my back on that side of him, refused similar assistance for myself, cast a harsh eye on what seemed to me then little more than nepotism. We used to argue about it from time to time. When I interviewed for my first government job in the USSR, he half-seriously offered to pull some strings for me in Washington. "You do that," I said, "and I'll refuse the job if I get it."

"You don't think other people will be doing that for their own?"

"I don't care," I said, and I didn't. But how easy it was for me, with my fancy education, to cast a righteous and condescending eye upon his string-pulling, the survival- by-connection ethos in which and by which the people of his time and place lived. And how clear it is to me now that solitary achievement is not the only measure of worth, that all of us are constantly engaged in a give-and-take of affection and advantage, doing favors and having favors done for us. But I was young then, and full of myself, and, like many other twenty-four-year-olds, planning to remake the world according to my pure vision.

In 1956, Chris Herter went to Washington as Undersecretary of State (in 1958, when Dulles resigned, he advanced to the Secretary's job) in the Eisenhower administration, and offered to bring his personnel secretary along for the ride. But, for my father, Washington was too far from Revere, from his brothers and sisters and parents, from the faces and corridors he knew. He respectfully declined the offer and seemed, in later years, untroubled by regret. In 1958, the *Boston Globe* printed a picture of Secretary Herter above a story suggesting he would be the party's nominee for president. My father is standing beside him, gearing up, perhaps, for another campaign, revving up old ambitions, ready to give Washington a shot this time. But Herter was already in a wheelchair by then, stricken with polio and about to cede his front-runner status to Richard Nixon. The rest, as they say, is history.

Before Herter left Massachusetts, he offered my father his choice of several high-level, if low-paying, jobs in the state bureaucracy, among them, head of the Metropolitan District Commission and Director of the Industrial Accident Board. My mother talked him out of the MDC job, a prestigious, but high-profile position that came under regular attack from one camp or another: press, politicians, populace; he settled in as Director of the IAB.

It was a good job, and another man would have been content there, with a corner office overlooking Boston Common, weekly trips to the western part of Massachusetts to inspect safety conditions at state-insured factories, S. S. Pierce food baskets at Christmas time from the managers of those factories, extended lunch hours during which he'd prowl downtown Boston's bargain clothing stores and buy suits and shirts for his friends and brothers, whether they'd asked him to or not.

For a while, in fact, he was happy at the Industrial Accident Board, and from the late fifties until the mid-sixties his life settled into a tame pattern it had not known before and would not know again. He was president of St. Anthony's Holy Name, a member of the Knights of Columbus, the ITAM club, the Children's Hospital Association. On summer weekends, he golfed at public courses with friends he'd known for forty years. He bowled and bet the greyhounds and played whist for nickels with his brothers, made the rounds of his sisters' homes for coffee and pastry on Sunday mornings after church. In the vacant lot next door to his parents' house, he and my mother built an eight-room, Colonial-style home, a grand structure by the standards of our street. They took my brothers and me on modest summer vacations—three days at Lake Winnipesaukee, a week at a friend's house near the Cape Cod canal; they drove us to church on Sunday mornings, to Little League games.

There were smudges on this idyllic tableau, the ordinary frustrations and dissatisfactions of family life. His temper, short of fuse and short of duration, could be triggered by something as small as a spilt glass of milk, and our Sunday dinners were sometimes broken up by needless argument. He was not as careful with money as he might have been: I remember him hunkered down over a table covered with bills, puffing his pipe, unapproachable. And he might have traded a few hours of his social life for a few more hours at home.

But he paid his bills, and visited the sick, and came home sober every night. And he tried, without ever actually apologizing, to make up for his outbursts by taking us with him when he made the rounds of his sisters' and brothers' houses, or by slipping us a dollar or two when we left the house with friends.

My father protected himself with a kind of fake-gruff exterior which could be funny or intimidating, depending on the context, and which completely broke apart when his own father died on a June night in 1965. He summoned us to the table the next morning as we were about to leave for school. I was twelve, my brothers nine and seven, and, while we knew our grandfather was ill, we'd had no prior experience with death. My father had had no prior experience bringing news of death to his children, and when he sat in one of the kitchen chairs and gathered us around him, there were tears in his eyes and a sad twitch to his face that we had never seen.

"God called Grandpa last night," he said, after a struggle.

We had no idea what this meant, why God should be calling Grandpa up on the phone, and why it should upset our father so much. Washed, combed, and lit with the anticipation of one of the year's final school-day mornings, the last thing we expected was that we would never again see the man who had lived beneath or beside us every day of our lives.

"God called Grandpa last night," my father repeated. Now there was more trouble in his face, and my mother was wringing her hands as if to urge the words out of him, and his grief was so enormous and so pent-up, that even without any understanding of death we had a sense of something new and terrible invading our house.

"What do you mean, Pa?" I said, but by this point I was close to knowing.

"Grandpa died last night," he managed, finally. The fake-gruff exterior collapsed, the five of us huddled in its ruins, and wept.

Not long after that, the prestige and comfort of the Director's job began to lose some of its appeal for him. Perhaps it was the fresh sense of mortality he felt after his father's passing. Or perhaps there was some regret there, after all, at not having gone to Washington. My father had had a taste of the high life, a bit of fame and power, and perhaps, after a decade, the Industrial Accident Board had begun to look like just another sinecure.

Since his carrot-picking days, he'd cherished the dream of

becoming a lawyer, and in the course of his duties at the Board, he'd rubbed shoulders with lawyers and judges day after day. And so, in 1966, at the age of fifty, he met with the Dean of Admissions of Suffolk Law School and convinced her to admit him without an undergraduate degree.

For the next four years he rose at six o'clock on weekdays, left the house at seven-thirty, made the forty-minute subway commute to downtown Boston, worked at the Board until five or five-thirty, attended classes at Suffolk from seven to ten, then rode the subway back to Revere. My mother met him at Beachmont station and drove him home, set the table again, cooked a second supper. At eleven o'clock, she went upstairs to bed, and he went down into the basement room he'd refinished, and hit the law books there until one or two A.M.

At Suffolk, an average grade of seventy was required to pass. My father's average in his first year was sixty-nine. Suffolk gave him the choice of repeating the year or failing out of school. He repeated the year, moved his average up ten points, and made steady, unspectacular progress through the rest of his law school career. By the time of his graduation in 1970, he stood in the middle of his class, a B student, age fifty-four, with a family and a full-time day job as his extracurricular interests.

What a deep and resonant triumph it was for him, that graduation. What a party we threw. His mother, siblings, and in-laws came to our house for the event, all forty of our cousins, old family friends, new friends from law school, monsignors and mayors, bricklayers and hairdressers, neighbors who'd lived within shouting distance of us for thirty years on Essex Street without having any idea of my father's secret ambition. He rarely drank, but he drank that night. For the only time in my life I saw him slightly tipsy, dancing with my mother in the cellar room where he had spent so many studious hours.

When the celebration ended, he took a week off to putter around the house, then returned to work at the board, studying at night and on weekends for the Bar Examination, which he took for the first time that fall. A score of one hundred out of a possible two hundred was required to pass; the examiners told him he had scored "in the high nineties."

Still working full-time, still maintaining the house and showing up at our baseball games, he took the bar a second time, and failed again. He failed a third time and a fourth, at six-month intervals, and by then even his closest friends were counseling surrender. You've made your point, they told him. You did something almost nobody else could have done at your age. Let it rest. But, for better or worse, he was not the type to let something rest. Not even close to the type. His customary response to those who advised him to give up the chase was a not very facetious: "Go to hell."

The twice-yearly notice from the Board of Massachusetts Bar Examiners had come to be a terrible ritual in our home: the buildup of fear and hope, the arrival of the letter, the bad news, which my father took stoically, clamping his teeth down on the stem of his pipe, staring out the kitchen window in a gray-headed, 220-pound silence, ashamed beyond any speaking of it.

The fifth such letter was delivered in March of 1975, on a dreary Saturday morning. My father had just taken the curtains from the living-room windows, my mother was in the kitchen washing the floor. Steve, Ken, and I were doing a fair imitation of dusting when we heard the mailman's tread on the front step. I retrieved the mail, saw the letter from the Bar Examiners, handed it over to him, and retreated. He stood at the window in the cold spring light and turned the envelope over twice in his hands, preparing himself, stretching out those last minutes of hope. My mother waited in absolute silence in the kitchen. My brothers hovered near the top of the stairs; I stayed in the front hall, spying.

With an engineer's precision, he slid his letter-opener beneath the flap and drew out a single sheet. He unfolded it with one hand, scanned it, then looked up and out at Essex Street with an expression I could not read. Defiance? Anger? Reluctant surrender? For half a minute he stared out at the cars at the curb, the tilting telephone poles and rusting TV antennas, and then he pushed three words up through his throat in the general direction of my mother: "El, I passed." My mother shrieked, we ran to embrace him, we wept, we shook his hand, kissed him. For the rest of that day my brothers and I floated around the neighborhood in an ecstasy of pride and relief.

For several more years the sun of good fortune shone upon him. His many local friends sent him what law business they had, wills mostly, small troubles. One or two of the companies he'd worked with put him on retainer. He resigned from the Industrial Accident Board and accepted a part-time job as a Workers' Compensation Specialist at Revere City Hall, trying to sort out the truly injured from the professional fakers, wrangling with the city council on which he had once served, then, at home, earning more money in an evening than he'd previously earned in a week.

During the six years of my father's law career, I was building up my own small business, a one-man painting and carpentry operation in northwestern Massachusetts and southern Vermont, three and a half hours from Revere. Too poor, at first, to afford a vehicle, I kept my tools in a knapsack and rode to jobs on a ten-speed bicycle with my handsaw twanging and bouncing over the back wheel.

For six dollars an hour I replaced panes of glass, scraped and painted the soffits of old garages, patched ceilings, peeled up tile from rotted bathroom floors. Nothing puzzled him more than this lifestyle of mine, this freedom and indigence. Here was a son who had earned both a Bachelor's and a Master's degree from an Ivy League school, who had worked for the State Department behind the Iron Curtain, who, in his late twenties, held credentials admitting him to the choicest precincts of the non-Revere world. And what was he doing? Living in the woods rebuilding porches for old Vermonters, reading at night in the Williams College library because he and his wife could not afford to heat their apartment, nailing up clapboards in the freezing cold.

My claim that it was all temporary, that I was pursuing a writing career, made little impression on him. "When," he said to me during his one visit to the country, "are you going to take responsibility?" I thought of reminding him of his days climbing down into ditches, his pursuit—stubborn, illogical—of a life that suited him, in spite of the odds . . . but I made a joke instead, biding time it turned out I did not have.

The last time I saw him was in Revere in the summer of 1982. We'd bought a vehicle by then, an old repainted Sears van which he'd found for me at auction. Amanda and I had driven down to celebrate his sixty-sixth birthday, and I'd spent part of the weekend scraping and painting the front entrance of the house so that it would be more presentable to his clients. On the morning we were to head back home, I came down into the kitchen and found a hundred-dollar bill on the table and a note. Tender phrases were never a specialty of my father's. He was not a rough man by any means, but neither was he comfortable with the more delicate aspects of human relationship, not, in any case, where his sons were concerned. (When I was going out on dates in my college years, he would watch me combing my hair and spraying deodorant, would hand me the keys to his Pontiac, slip me ten bucks, and say: "Be careful"—the closest we ever came to a father-son talk on sexuality.)

Tender expressions were not his specialty, but that note was filled with tenderness. How glad he and my mother were that we visited, how grateful for the work I'd done, how much they loved Amanda, and so on. All of this folded around a hundred dollars, the equivalent, in those lean years, of my weekly income. Amanda came downstairs and I said to her, "Look at this, will you? My father, huh?"

I did not realize that he had not yet left for his job at City Hall, and was standing a few feet away at the back door, staring out into the yard. He made a small coughing sound, and I saw him, and we went through the usual ritual of me refusing the money and him refusing to take it back three or four times before I finally folded the note into my wallet, thanked him, and kissed him good-bye.

For two months the note remained there. One day in July I decided I was being sentimental or superstitious—unmanly traits—and threw it into a trash barrel on a beach on Long Island.

Two weeks later I was painting a house in Williamstown, up on a ladder in the bright morning sun, when I heard a car pull to the curb and saw my wife get out. Amanda crossed the lawn and stopped at the foot of the ladder. "Be down in a minute," I said. "Just let me finish this piece of trim before the sun comes around."

"Come down now," she said.

"One second, I just—"

"Come down now, Rol."

I climbed down and stood facing her. "Bad news," she said.

He died in his sleep, with no sign of the struggle that had marked so much of his life, and for months and months after his death I dreamt of him regularly—straightforward, extremely vivid dreams that did not require the assistance of an analyst to interpret. In one, he was sitting in the back seat of a white limousine, at the passenger side window, and I saw the limo pull out of a driveway and sprinted after it, waving and waving, calling out, "Good-bye, Pa. Good-bye. Good-bye!" But he was looking straight ahead, smiling, and didn't see me.

Now, close to the age when my father decided to attend law school, I occasionally dream of him still. Sometimes we argue, sometimes I tease him about not visiting us. He often smiles in these dreams, but rarely speaks. Each year that passes, each incremental diminution of my own powers, brings a sharper understanding of the force of his will, the effort and self-belief and self-sacrifice and pure stubbornness that can be read between the lines of his resume. I have, it turns out, inherited a portion of his discipline, but what matters more to me is his gift of a sense of perspective, what he would have called his "faith," a certain spiritual or psychological ballast that holds a person close to some center line, even amidst the greatest victories and the deepest bitterness. I keep a framed photo of him on the wall in the room where I write, and say a word to it from time to time, when things are going very badly, or very well.

GREG JALBERT

A lifelong resident of Maine, Greg Jalbert (1954–) has published in
Yankee and Down East *magazines and is currently at work on a
pair of novels and a collection of personal essays—all set in the
Maine woods. He has worked as a registered Maine Guide (a title
he no longer holds), as a copywriter for the L. L. Bean catalog
company, and in advertising.*

*Fort Kent is a small border town on the St. John River at the
extreme northern tip of Maine, across the shore from New Bruns-
wick. Greg's father, Robert, was born here in 1922; he grew up here,
and when he came home from World War II he chose law as his
profession so that he'd be able to earn a living in Fort Kent. He
was, says his son, "a traditional country lawyer" who handled
most every kind of case that came his way—corporate, civil, and
criminal; most important, though, he was self-employed, which
allowed him to spend whatever time he saw fit on the waters of the
Allagash River.*

*The Allagash empties into the St. John fifteen miles upriver
from Fort Kent. Its waters form one of the premier destinations for
canoeists in the lower forty-eight states, and its drainage basin,*

says one field guide, remains "one of the most remote, expansive, and undeveloped regions in the United States." Here did Robert Jalbert's heart and soul make their home.

Like his father, Greg Jalbert was born and raised in Fort Kent. Like his father, he too spent a great deal of his youth on the Allagash. And like his father, he first went away to college at the University of Maine, in Orono. But unlike his father, Greg Jalbert eventually left Fort Kent and the Allagash, moving in 1986 with his wife and family to southern Maine.

He gives the reasons for this departure from the land of his father in the selection presented here. "In the Kingdom of the Jalberts" was first published in 1990 in Yankee.

In the Kingdom of the Jalberts

I grew up among river men. My father was dependent on the wilderness for his life, and I was dependent on him.

Although he was an influential Fort Kent lawyer, hosting senators and advising governors on key issues, the thought of living an ordinary life terrified him. In the Allagash wilderness he became part child, part wild man in search of adventure.

As soon as the ice cleared, we began our expeditions on the Allagash. Ten miles up the river from Allagash Village, we were often stopped early in the year by a wall of jammed ice. It looked like the blunt face of a glacier and cut us off from the portage trail around Allagash Falls. Using a ladder he had tied to the top of our duffle, we portaged the gear and hauled the canoe up and over the jam. Then he took one last look downriver and, like a hunted man, pulled the ladder up after himself. Only once, arriving at the falls in the dark, when the ice wall was leaning, threatening to fall on us, do I remember his turning back.

He roared his outboard down through the rapids above the falls, guiding the canoe towards the lip before cutting it hard into shore and up into the brush. Every time he motored down to the lower landing, part of me shot over the falls and drowned. Terror was often the price I had to pay to be with Robert Jalbert on the Allagash River.

But while my school friends waited for the latest western to appear on the colossal screen of the Savoy Theater in Fort Kent, I sat in his lap while his hand, square and broad as the mitt of a bear, covered my own on the throttle. Together we gunned our twenty-foot, broad-beamed canvas canoe up against the north-flowing river, following a secret channel known only to river men.

It was there, just beyond the falls, that we entered a rich, mystical landscape, the kingdom of the Jalberts. When the log drives ended along the Allagash around 1940, the lumber camps and depots were closed. Other than a handful of men from Allagash Village, my family was alone in the woods. There was no one else to look for them if they got lost, to rescue them if they got hurt.

They crossed Round Pond in November and swamped the canoe with ice and water. They pole-vaulted over sluices at Long Lake Dam. When the pole snapped, they were carried away in the flume. They got Jeeps stuck in the middle of icy rivers; they were snowbound in out camps and had to walk miles through deep snow without snowshoes; but they never got hurt. They never got a hook caught in their ear. They never bled.

On an island just upriver from the falls, my great-grandfather leased land from the paper company in the 1800s and raised cattle and produce to feed the men in the lumber camps and depots. My grandfather Willard was born on that farm. As boys, he and his brothers captured a moose and harnessed it to the sleigh. Later his mother died in childbirth. Even though we did not own a single acre of land, we Jalberts felt a certain right to a territory earned through our struggle to survive and the losses we endured.

Summers, when the river was so low and there seemed no hope of passage, my father poled the canoe over gravel bars and we fished the cool-water pools at Rosie's Rock and Jalbert Brook, where my grandfather and Uncle Willard had lived in a camp and cut logs, piled them at the landing still visible today, and then knocked out the key log in the spring to launch the log drive and return home from the winter woods.

Justice William O. Douglas was guided by my grandfather. There were many old guides in the North Woods, but only my grandfather was called simply, "The Ole Guide." It was Justice Douglas, after one expedition, who popularized the expression, "There's three kinds of bears along the Allagash: the black bear, the brown-nosed bear, and the *Jal-bear*."

Often I think the Jalberts were the wildest. Ours was the only family to haul upriver and over a portage trail refrigerators, stoves, furniture, and building supplies. One of the camps was logged in just three days from the time the trees were felled to the time the peak-o-gee was rolled into the notches at the top of the roof. Without time to cut trails, the men dragged thirty-foot logs through the brush, the butts cradled in the spiked cant hooks of two peaveys as the men bulled against the handles. Their skin was stained black with spruce pitch.

One day in the mid-1940s an enraged paper company representative landed in a float plane. He marched up to my father, my uncle Willard, and the Ole Guide and demanded to know what right they had to build camps without a lease the company refused to give them. The Jalberts backed the little man—who had just threatened to burn them out—into the clothesline, which held him like a snare. "Burn these camps," my father growled and swept his arm to include the timber along the surrounding ridges, "and you'll never put out the fire." A few days later the lease appeared. People who asked politely were turned down.

These were the stories of my childhood. And sitting in the

bow of my father's canoe, I searched for a way to become as worthy as the men who gave me their name. But I could not even cast a fly.

For luck, my father spat cigar juice on his fly. He cast so delicately it fell without dimpling the water. He twitched it once, twice. "Watch!" he hissed, the cigar squeezed tight between his teeth. As if commanded, the trout leaped from the water. My father's lips curved up into a cocky smile.

But in the fall, he abandoned me. All I knew of his hunting adventures I learned in my father's home movies. Sitting beside him in the dark, I watched as a bear leaped on my father's back. In that moment, even with him sitting so close, I felt the terror of his loss from me. My father plunged his skinning knife into the heart of the animal, but the bear continued to fight. They rolled through the snow, neither one in command of the other. Finally my father rolled on top and again he stabbed the bear. As the bear struggled to rise one last time, it collapsed. On the screen my father is worn but victorious.

Sports came great distances to be guided by Jalbert men. But now that I am the age of my father in those movies, I can see how the myth of an inviolate wilderness and of my invincible family began to unravel when I was four years old on a sultry afternoon on the twenty-second day of August in the year 1958. It is the day that I will always believe changed the river and our lives forever.

The sky was the dull yellow shade of overripe wheat. I sat quietly beside my sister in the middle of our Old Town canoe and stared over my mother's hands in the bow. At the landing below Allagash Falls, my mother remarked how silent the birds were. They, along with the other animals, seemed to have disappeared.

Within half an hour the gear had been portaged a quarter of a mile. As my father flipped the canoe onto his back, the rain began to fall. At a fork in the trail, he perched the bow in the branches of a tree. We scurried under the canoe and hunkered down as he dashed up the trail for the food.

"It's just a clearing-off shower," he told us cheerfully as he dove under beside us. The rain began to sizzle along the canvas. My mother cut slices of homemade bread, spread them thick with mayonnaise, and layered on slices of bologna.

Then hail, the size of a boy's fist, hurled from the sky. The air grew cold. As night fell, bolts of lightning slivered the air. Thunder cracked. My mother offered us soda and Whoopie Pies, and my sister stopped crying. For a while we licked the luxurious cream from between the two chocolate moons of cake. My father told us about angels bowling in heaven. He sang cowboy songs as the water eddied around our red and yellow rain boots. For a while the terror left me. But after we had eaten, after the songs and the stories, I saw, for the first time, the expression of fear as the lightning flashed against his face. Something had entered the woods he could not wrestle to the ground.

During a break in the storm he loaded us into the canoe. As thunder once again began to close in, we could see in the distance a light hovering above the river, which seemed to fly away the faster we approached it. Finally we idled up to a steep bank, and I saw faces pressed flat against rain-smeared glass. Against my will, my father picked me up and carried me inside.

Bobcat skins hung from the walls and their pungent, steamy smell assaulted me. In the glow of kerosene lanterns they came shimmering back to life. Outside, the storm circled and pounced, hissing and spitting through the chinking. My mother pulled off our wet clothes while a woman as wide as a door offered meat as strong and sour as the smell of her skin. I refused it. I clung to my mother. Desperate, I would not let them leave me there alone.

In the morning we motored up the river. I saw steam rising from scars that ribboned the hillsides. The air was pungent with the aroma of sapwood and overturned earth. Among the cross-piled timber stood twenty-foot spires of cedar, spruce, and rock maple, their tops twisted off and flung away. The landscape seemed to have been ravaged by a giant bear. As brush collected around the canoe, we became the center of a small drifting island. We waited for my father to ease our shock by telling a story. He stood up and mumbled but a single word: "Tornado." For me it would come to mean an eerie, haunted place where two rivers meet along the water of the dead, until the word came to mean simply, "the end."

At the center of the storm my father called a clearing-off shower, the tornado had hopped, skipped, and jumped through five townships, an area of more than 150 square miles. During its rampage, it knocked down twenty-five hundred acres of timber with a loss of twenty-one thousand cords of high-quality spruce and fir. The swaths stretched from one hundred feet to a quarter of a mile wide.

To salvage the timber, woodcutters came into the Allagash with chain saws. Instead of driving logs down river, they bulldozed roads for trucks to haul the logs to the mills. But just as they had for over a hundred years, horses twitched the logs from the cuttings to the yard beside the road.

From our camps at Windy Point there on Round Pond, we could hear for the first time the whine of chain saws. The cutters came from the west, from St. Pamphile, Quebec. Midway down through the Round Pond Rips, they built a bridge to continue swamping out a road east to Musquacook.

The roads, rough and rutted in the spring and summer, made our camps more accessible. First we could drive within twenty miles of Round Pond, then fifteen, and then only a few years after the tornado, within five. When the Canadian contractors put up gates to preserve the country for themselves, my father cut them down or shot off the locks.

By the early 1960s the horses were replaced by all-wheel-drive diesel skidders, which churned through the woods on wide tractor tires as tall as a man. In a little over two hours they twitched as much timber as a horse could twitch in a day. Then huge tree harvesters came plodding through the woods on tires eight feet tall and over three feet wide. In one hour one man could cut one hundred trees. At some point we stopped listening for the woodcutters.

After the woods around Round Pond were cut and opened to a flood of Canadian hunters, we found an isolated pocket of timber up along Musquacook Stream where no one could reach us. In the late 1960s we guided sports from a base camp that was only a teepee, and then we built a rustic out camp. They came from New Jersey and depended on us to escort them into the deep woods, an area so far beyond their wildest dreams that it really terrified some of them.

We continued to prove ourselves by snubbing a canoe down through white water, using a pole to suddenly stop over a fishing hole. Even in rain we could bake reflector-oven biscuits as light and flaky as any gourmet restaurant. And our stories still connected sports to the frontier past. But I was beginning to lose track of what was real and what was not.

Along with the new machines, the spruce budworm caterpillar began devastating the forest. Threatened with a vast loss of inventory all through the 1970s, the paper companies bull-dozed year-round logging roads into areas they proceeded to clear-cut.

In the midst of the clear-cutting epidemic, my uncle Willard and his son, Billy, were killed in a car accident. My father found his way out of grief in the woods, renovating my uncle's worn-out camps at Round Pond. But even his relationship to the camps had changed. Since the creation of the Allagash Wilderness Waterway in 1968 the camps were no longer ours.

I remember the shock in my father's face, the quiver of uncertainty in his voice, when he gathered us around the table to announce that he might not be able to save the camps. He was forced to sell them and accept a lease from the State of Maine.

In tin canoes, park supervisors blindly banged into every river rock. Flustered, they claimed the channel was a fiction designed to humiliate and embarrass them. My father roared past them, in honor of the river men who dug it, spray arcing like wings, even in low water, even in the dark.

Something in him began to fade, though he still plotted hunting strategies. According to those plans, we would extend our network of hunting trails from our camp at Burntland Brook into areas where he had dreamed of stag bucks. But he rarely hunted there. He left the camp with us at dawn, only to return by nine or ten o'clock. I would come back for lunch and find him reading or sleeping.

In the fall of 1977 my father and I returned to the out camp for the last time. We drove nearly fifty miles an hour down a wide gravel road where we had once slogged four miles through snow over our knees after a surprise blizzard. The road had been cut past the door. In the coming darkness of that day, we could see ahead of us a machine more alien than skidders and timber harvesters—a Winnebago. New Jersey plates. My father would not look at the vehicle as he turned the Jeep around, as if by ignoring it he could make it disappear. The wilderness as a landscape for possibilities was truly and forever gone.

In the early evening of May 21, 1980, father stepped into a bush plane overloaded with gasoline. A canoe was strapped to the pontoons. The winds were severe. The plane was flown by a pilot who had very little experience with that kind of load under those conditions. Anchored in a fishing hole in Round Pond, I waited for him. Like my grandfather and my father, I told the old stories to the fishermen I was guiding. Driven by wind, the lake swells were humped and twisted as haystacks. If we'd had a radio, I would have called him not to come, though he probably would not have listened to me. When a plane circled my boat and dipped its wing, I changed my bait, hoping to catch a string of trout that would impress even my father and gain his approval, applause, and praise. The plane landed across the lake at the camp. A motor sputtered to life, and a friend aimed the bow of the canoe straight at us.

My father's plane had been struck by a gust of wind, spiraling out of the sky soon after takeoff. On impact it had burst into flames. In the funeral parlor river men gathered in the back of the room. The organist played "The Red River Valley," a haunting song he often sang to himself. As the casket was slipped into the hearse, a wail, like the shriek of a child, rose from the throat of a woman who spoke for us all; only this wail was not intended to reach into another room, but beyond the edge of the world to pull my father back.

I continued to guide sports, continued to tell stories in an attempt to rekindle the passion of the past. But I never told them that when I watched the old home movies after my father's death, I realized that the bear he killed with a knife was already dead and he was only acting for the camera.

I protected the myth of my father far too long. The wild man in him frequently lost control. I never told them how he once flew at me screeching because I had forgotten to open the stove damper and the camp had filled with smoke. That afternoon, when he stalked among paper birches, I raised my rifle and zeroed in on his chest. Staring at each other, we both knew I had not mistaken him for a buck. He turned away and never said a word.

After struggling for five years to maintain not only the camps but the family legend, I too gave up—gave up the lease and moved away. The Allagash had become a place where I needed a permission slip to build or renovate a camp, cut a trail, or cut firewood. I was not permitted to cut brush so the breeze could blow through the campsite and carry away the blackflies. When I left, the Allagash forest was, at some points, a five-hundred-foot strip of standing timber, like the false front of a Hollywood movie set, hiding clear-cuts that stretched from one horizon to the other. Even in the islands of standing timber, the trees were diseased and rotting. The blowdowns were so cross-piled that I could not hunt through them. I don't go back to the camps anymore.

Still, as I watch the home movies, I see river men remarkable beyond anyone I could ever hope to meet. I see myself in my father's lap and for a moment know no greater joy, contentment, or security.

Now when I go back to the Allagash, I tent along the river. Along the trail to the fire tower, my daughter, Alaina, stops beside a chipmunk hole and in the awkward language of a three-year-old builds the story of Mrs. Chipmunk inviting the Field Mouse for tea. Micaela stops us abruptly and points under the mossy belly of a cedar. Cupping her hand against my ear, she whispers, "Lady Slipper." I am astonished and embarrassed; I have never noticed one before. There is still a place along this river for enchantment. At eight years old, my son, Zachery, sits confidently in the stern of our canoe and begins the education of a river man by hitting rocks. And remembering.

In late autumn, when the tourists and even the rangers have disappeared, I canoe the Allagash alone. The water and spruces are black. The canoe becomes heavy with ice rime. Floes of slush rattle like marbles along the hull. I manage to dip the paddle as silently and rhythmically as my father, as though I have entered his body.

I hunker down along the riverbank and tinder a fire, brew a pot of tea, roast my half-frozen sandwich. The weight of my uncle's rawhide coat is a comfort against the cold. Over the river valley, the clouds are pleated and heavy with snow. Through the hollow impending air, I hear a haunting cry calling my name. Though I know it is only a coyote, I listen for my father, my uncle, and the Ole Guide, whose voices enter me, as if to say, "Tell this story," as if it is their last hope of reckoning anything.

DAVID BEERS

Born in Ohio, raised in California, David Beers (1957–) now lives in Vancouver, British Columbia, where he works as a freelance writer. His work has appeared in The Nation, Vogue, *and* Mother Jones; *his 1993 essay, "The Crash of Blue Sky California," helped win a National Magazine Award for* Harper's Magazine.

"Blue Sky" traced the rise and fall of the California aerospace industry through its telling of the story of Beers's father, who retired in 1992 after thirty-two years with Lockheed Missiles and Space Company. Hal Beers earned a degree in aeronautical engineering from Purdue University (along with classmate Neil Armstrong), after which he joined the navy; by the age of twenty-two he was flying jets off an aircraft carrier. Surely the future seemed promising: in the spring of 1956 Beers married David's future mother after a six-week courtship and later that fall he was chosen to participate in a mission to set a new speed record for a flight from San Diego to New York to San Diego.

But things did not go as they might have. His companions set the record, but Beers had to quit the flight early because of mechanical problems; thirteen months later, finding he didn't like life aboard ship, he left the navy. Later still, when Neil Armstrong set first foot on the moon, Hal Beers was at home fixing a broken toilet.

In 1960 Beers accepted a job offer from Lockheed. The Cold War and the space race were funneling huge sums of money into the company and prospects again seemed bright, especially as Beers gained ever-greater access to work on secret projects. But life in Lockheed's "Black World" proved less glamorous than advertised. Beers was never able to tell his family what he did, but in general, writes his son, his job "was to make numbers slide off his slide rule." This in a vast, windowless room. Nor was the expression of social conscience tolerated; when he once wore a black armband to work to protest the Vietnam War, he was counseled by a supervisor to remove the item if he wanted to keep his job—the job he needed to support his wife and four children.

Such constraints ground at the spirit of Hal Beers. They fueled an anger he was not always able to contain, and by the time David was as young as twelve the father had taken to telling the son that working for a big corporation meant a life of compromise and that he should avoid taking on too many obligations too soon—advice the grown son has heeded well: as a freelancer, David is his own employer and not until he was in his late thirties did he himself become a father.

After his Harper's *essay, David Beers expanded his material and in 1996 he published* Blue Sky Dream: A Memoir of America's Fall from Grace. *The following adaptation from Beers's book first appeared in the* New York Times Magazine.

Blue Sky, California

My father and I are together in the sky. I am eight and he has taken me up in the Piper Cherokee, a four-seat, single-prop, family sedan of an airplane he rents once in a while. My father's idea is that we will fly over our house and get a look at it from a new vantage point, from high above the Santa Clara Valley on a clear summer morning. We will fly over at an agreed-upon time and my mother will stand in our backyard and wave.

"Won't be long till we get there. Five, ten minutes. Have a look." My father's voice in my headphones cuts through the vibrating thrum of the airplane's engine. He smiles and traces a circle on the window with the tip of his index finger, as if marking an intersection on a road map. I follow his finger, look down and suddenly, vaguely, I am terrified.

My fear has nothing to do with any lack of faith in my father's piloting. I know, from snapshots and dinner-table stories, that my father was once a special sort of pilot who flew a navy jet fighter. And this morning—one of his happy, whistling days—I have been reassured by his exchanges with the man in the control tower. *Cherokee victor bravo niner over.* That is the way men must speak to each other when they know exactly what they are doing.

No, the queasy doubt rushing over me comes from what is there below, staring up—a labyrinth of freshly scraped earth and cedar-shingled roofs and severe little lawns and blacktop ribbons bent with such precise consideration that I feel I'm looking at some immense, far-too-complicated board game. Down there, we could be *anywhere.*

I search out the familiar shape of our cul-de-sac, but what I see, like berries growing on trellised vines, are many, many cul-de-sacs. How could one of these tiny, repeated shapes be our very own? From up here one could never see the brand-new lemon yellow Naugahyde couch just installed with such momentous pleasure in front of our television set. From here one could not see my sister, Marybeth, four years old, or my baby brother, Dan, or the melon stomach of my mother, pregnant with my sister-to-be, Maggie. From here one could not see the baby food jars filled with nuts and bolts on my father's workbench, or, hanging above it by a nylon thread, the dusty model of his navy jet fighter. From here there is no way to see the sky blue walls of my bedroom.

"Got your bearings yet?" My father is helping me orient myself as we fly on toward our neighborhood, our house, my mother who will be down there waving. "Those big structures there, recognize them? They're the hangars at Moffett Field. And in there somewhere is your dad's place of work. That's Lockheed."

This holds great interest for me, given that I have never been inside Lockheed Missiles and Space Company. I have only seen, once from the company parking lot, the barbed wire and chain-link and sentry kiosks that my father passes through each day. As I follow my father's eyes down, I see a large, white radar dish pointed toward the heavens, and around it many tight-lidded shoe boxes, windowless, gray, some with smaller dishes and antennae twisting off their roofs. *In there, somewhere.* "See the freeway? Going in over there," he says, pointing to a great trench of flattened dirt. I know there is a great trench of flattened dirt not far from our house, but I also know it is but one of many. Wherever my family drives I see the yellow graders and dump trucks and bulldozers making their endless gouges in the ground. And so I wonder, is that great trench down there ours?

"Eighty-five, and over there two-eighty."

Yes, those sound like the ones the adults talk about eagerly as they stand in front of their new tract homes on these warm summer evenings, their cigarettes glowing, their laughter drifting over to us kids as we chase each other yard to yard. Eighty-five will connect to two-eighty, with its signs naming it "The World's Most Beautiful Freeway." They are the freeways that will connect to the expressways that connect to our cul-de-sac and house and yard, where—*there, I see her now*—my mother is waving to us, in the sky.

My mother taught us words for getting the attention of St. Anthony, who, she said, would guide us to whatever we were looking for but had not yet found:

> *Tony, Tony, listen, listen.*
> *Hurry, hurry, something's missin'.*

Hers was a perfect prayer for a blue-sky family in the early 1960s, as colorfully casual as a tiki lantern, resistant to any doubt that we in our suburban frontier held the interest of heaven.

A crisis would develop. Mutterings, hard soles stepping hard in the back of the house, my father moving with those quickened, long strides that sent us children edging into corners, onto chairs, anywhere that might have been, as he would say to us, "out of the WAY!" His keys were missing again. He was yanking open drawers and shoving hands between seat cushions. He was muttering: "For cripes' sake." He was late for Lockheed.

> Tony, Tony, look around.
> Something's lost and must be found.

"It's worked before," my mother would say, upbeat. "You just have to believe." She would move her lips in prayer just beyond my father's vortex.

Someone would be drawn to some unlikely spot, and there would be the keys, waiting for my father's exasperated swipe at them. After he and his keys had disappeared in a puff of exhaust around the corner, headed for Lockheed, we children would move out of the corners of the house, reclaim the empty spaces, and the best possibilities for the day would be there for us, as if by some small miracle.

Some evenings my father would bring me publicity photographs of Lockheed products to hang in my bedroom. There were stubby-winged jets and fire-swathed rockets, satellites that hung in space like tinfoil dragonflies. And my favorite, the submarine-launched, nuclear-tipped Polaris missile. To a boy who thumbtacked its picture on his wall, the Polaris was a perfectly pure and universal shape, white and smooth, frozen above the convulsed ocean surface through which it had just burst. Lockheed photographed its missiles headed up, never killing end down. As a child, I didn't wonder what the Polaris was for. Perhaps once launched it just stuck there in the firmament like a dart in the ceiling. That the Polaris was so obviously the future exploding out of the sea seemed reason enough to create it.

"We never looked at a used house," my father remembers of those days in the early 1960s when he and my mother went shopping for a home of their own in the Santa Clara Valley. "A used house simply did not interest us." Instead they roved in search of the many billboards advertising Low Interest! No Money Down! to military veterans like my father. "We shopped for a new house," my father says, "the way you shopped for a car."

On warm evenings in the spring of 1962, after dinner, my parents would place my baby sister in her stroller and the four of us would set out from the too small, used house they were renting in a subdivision named Strawberry Park, walk six blocks and pick up a wide trail cut into the adobe ground, a winding roadbed awaiting asphalt. We would make our way across muddy clay that was crosshatched by tractor treads, riven by pipe trenches. We would breathe in the sap scent of two-by-fours stacked around us, the smell of plans ready to go forward. Finally we would arrive at Lot 242 of Unit 6 of Tract 3113, 14,500 square feet of emptiness that now belonged to us. All around the outline were piles of cherry and plum and apricot trees, their roots ripped from the ground, the spring blossoms still clinging to their tangled-up branches.

My father would go from stake to yellow-ribboned stake, telling us where the kitchen would be, which windows would be getting the most sun. Later, after the skeletons of walls were up, we would wander through the materializing form of our home, already inhabiting with our imaginations its perfect potentiality.

I learned early to study my father's face as he came through the door after his Lockheed workday. If his eyebrows were where they should be—at rest on a line-free forehead—there was every chance of the usual Dad, the loving and fun Dad who would want to know all about "life around here" that day. If he gathered up my pretty, dark-haired mother in a languorous kiss and called her one of his nicknames, if he said, "What's new, Scrappy?" as he pulled from the cupboard the glass bubble for mixing martinis, if he filled it with ice and liquor and stirred with the glass wand, if he lifted a child into one arm while he loosened his tie with the other and then took a lip-smacking sip of his drink, if he did such things, then prospects for the night ahead were excellent. He might even be coaxed after dinner to transform himself into the Hairy Umgawa, the monster who wrestled all comers on the shag carpet of the living room until, inevitably, he lay panting and defeated under a pile of children.

But what if, when my father came through the door, the eyebrows were not where they should be? What if a critical mass of lines had gathered on his forehead and pressed the eyebrows together and down? What if he stepped through the door to the everyday sound of a pot clattering or a baby crying and those eyebrows darted low even as the eyes widened and showed too much white? These were indicators that he was this night, at some point, likely to erupt in rage. I remember many dinners that went from happy chatter to grim conflagration in the instant it took a child to knock over a small glass of milk.

Whenever his impatient anger would find a target in me my day would disintegrate. The touch-off might be the skid mark I left on the driveway with my bike, or the screwdriver I had forgotten to return to its hook on the wall, some bit of disorder that hadn't much bothered him the day before. But this day I hadn't taken proper precautions and now he was standing over me, his eyes with far too much white in them, his face inches from my own. *Useless ninny!* he was shouting. *Giiiyaaad!*—a yell that trailed off into a gagging sound. *You're useless! Useless! Have you a brain in your skull?* I would find it impossible not to cower, not to cry, so I would cry and that only redoubled the onslaught—*Stop your pathetic blubbering!*—until my head ached and the world was red-tinged by tears and everyone within range was utterly miserable.

To prevent any such scene, I fine-tuned my powers of surveillance. I studied the forehead, the eyes, the corners of the mouth that might tighten and dip. If his legs were all I could see, sticking out from beneath an automobile in the garage, I listened to the tone of his grunts as he grappled with the repair job. Some grunts, the favorable ones, were rounded, open uhhhs resonating with satisfaction at progress made. As often, though, they were bitten-off growls of frustration, the surest sign that I should not say whatever I had come to say, that I should not let my father know I had ever been there.

Sometimes, that option was denied me. "Dave! I need your help here!" my father would call out. Perhaps he had fearlessly winched the car's guts straight out of its engine compartment, or, having opened the back of a television set, was probing that inscrutable landscape with yet another strange new tool. My father who could do anything would tell me to stand by him and hold a flashlight beam on the exact spot where he was performing his mysterious manipulations. "Dammit Dave, put the light right here," he would say as my attention inevitably atrophied and my aim relaxed. I could have learned by asking questions, but I knew that if I asked one too many his impatience might jump like electricity from the task that frustrated him over to me. And so I asked little, my father offering little, father and son collaborating on the day's project, operating strictly on a need-to-know basis.

The system of compartmentalized secrecy at Lockheed was self-regulating. Workers were expected to turn in any colleague who spoke too freely or handled secret documents improperly. "If you found yourself flunking polygraph tests your clearances were rescinded," my father explains. "Your ticket was pulled, which made you an unemployable engineer at Lockheed. You'd go to NASA, where the work was completely unclassified and deadly dull. The money and promotions were in the highly classified jobs. Security clearances were merit badges that opened all kinds of doors for you."

My father, naturally, would submit willingly to polygraph tests, having nothing to hide and everything to gain. Had he revealed details of his work to anyone outside the proper compartments? No, he could always answer truthfully.

At the dinner table, his young son would also ask him questions.

"What are you working on, Dad?"

"Welllll . . ." A question like that always invited a long pause. "Let's just say that I'm helping to troubleshoot a very complicated piece of equipment for the government."

"Is it something that goes into space, Dad?"

He would chuckle and cock an eye at the ceiling, weighing just what he could tell his nine-year-old son that might not show up later as a damning twitch of the polygraph's needle. At our dinner table, Lockheed was always listening in.

I soon learned to stop asking.

In the late sixties, when Vietnam and Neil Armstrong came to inhabit our living room via the television, my father's work for Lockheed in all likelihood had more connection with war-making than with moon-walking. Those were years when he grew more pensive and grouchy, as if shaken from a dream he could never get back to. As his volatility increased he required all the more surveillance. One afternoon, during an argument with my mother, my father did an uncharacteristic thing. He punched the wall in the entryway of our home, making a hole in the dry wall. The next morning, he came to it with his tool box and carefully made a patch, but there was a faint outline if you knew where to look.

My father tried to solve his gloom by building in our garage a Thorpe T-18, a "home-built" airplane. When that project proved too expensive and time-consuming, he turned, in the quiet hours of evenings, to reading. A Lockheed friend had piqued his interest in books that tried to make sense of society, human nature and where the country was headed. My father became a student of John Kenneth Galbraith's critique of corporate culture as the misplaced pursuit of money over life's more fulfilling rewards. He soaked up Eric Hoffer's ideas about adults gripped by "juvenile" restlessness, which, in turn, is produced by economic dislocation due to technology. He read Desmond Morris's theories about humans as "naked apes" gone neurotic in the too-crowded cages of the cities. This was a brooder's bibliography, books by thinkers suspicious of groupthink and the pronouncements of officialdom. The serious grown-up, these books seemed to say, questions every premise of blue-sky optimism.

If I was beside him holding the flashlight for a fix-it job, he might lay out a book's thesis, making connections to his own experience. He would speak of an insight he'd gleaned about Lockheed: "The primary purpose of any bureaucratic institution is to continually justify its own existence." He would be excited by a semanticist's version of why a husband and wife talk past each other: "Words are useless unless two people agree on their meanings. The map must agree with the territory!" I grasped little of this, but found it exhilarating that he seemed to be asking me, as a potential equal, to accompany him on an intellectual journey just begun.

In his books my father found schematic diagrams that might offer solutions to a malfunctioning America or, perhaps, to the uneasiness in his soul. He was the troubled troubleshooter, a systems engineer in search of systems underlying the human condition.

In the summer of 1972, as I turned fifteen, Nixon operatives were caught bugging the Democratic headquarters in the Watergate complex. In August, on the day after the U.S. withdrew its last combat unit from Vietnam, B-52s pounded that land with the most intensive twenty-four-hour bombing raid of the war. I floated through that summer on glints of sunlight and whiffs of chlorine, an impossibly skinny kid yearning for sex with the beautiful girls on my swim team. My father bought a Ping-Pong table for our backyard deck, where my brother and I slapped the plastic ball back and forth endlessly. At the beginning of the summer my father had been able to defeat me handily, but as the season wore on I improved.

There came a hot evening late in August, with a sky still light and grasshoppers chirping madly, when my mother was off at a church function and my father was doing the dinner dishes. I cajoled him into coming outside for a game that turned out to be the first I'd ever won against him. It started with my father's cheers for me when my putaways skittered off the corners of the table or bounced against his chest. By the end, when I beat him with a backhanded slam, my father had withdrawn into one of his sulks. He went back into the kitchen and muttered as he loaded the dishwasher.

I felt responsible for his sulk, so when my brother took his place at the other end of the Ping-Pong table I loudly said to him, "You know, if Dad got to practice as much as we do, I never would have won against him."

My father's shout came from the kitchen, through the sliding screen door. "The last thing I need, Dave, is for you to patronize me!"

He was onto me. He would not, after all, be fooled by my methods of emotional management. He was turning my words against me as evidence of something even worse, bad faith. That panicked me some, angered me, too. "You may think I was patronizing you, Dad," I shouted back, "but I wasn't!"

I saw him then striding quickly from the kitchen, his face red and hard, one of his arms (the arm of a six-foot-two man who was not skinny) throwing open the sliding screen door as I backed away. I saw his clenched fist before my eyes and then blackness and sparks on the backs of my eyelids as another fist and then another crashed into my cheeks and eyes. I tumbled back and found myself sitting, ridiculously it seemed, on the soft plastic cushion of a chaise lounge. Through hands I'd thrown over my face too late, I watched the back of my father as he disappeared without a word through the screen door, into the house. I heard my brother whimpering from beneath the picnic table. I felt my face not hurting so much as pulsating. Except for the whimpering of my brother and the running of my father's dishwater and the singing of the grasshoppers, all in our backyard was quiet and warm and removed from the world as usual.

I walked then, barefoot, in cut-off jeans and a T-shirt, out of our yard, our cul-de-sac, past Queen of Apostles church and school, past the softball field by the freeway, under the overpass where Interstate 280 intersected Lawrence Expressway, down a strip of burger stands and car dealerships to the Futurama bowling lanes. I went into the bathroom to examine my throbbing face, and in the mirror were blackened eyes and blood-rimmed nostrils. I knew it would only look worse tomorrow, when the blue-sky summer was expected to resume as normal.

When the Futurama closed down at midnight, there was nothing to do but to return home, to open the front door my father had left unlocked, to move through the dark house to my bedroom, to ease myself under the sheets. I lay there a few minutes and my father came into my room without turning on the light. He sat on the edge of my bed and whispered an apology. There was "no excuse" for what he had done, he said. I was silent. He whispered a theory about the rivalry that occurs between two males in confined space, a theory I knew he'd drawn from one of his books. I was in no mood to accept his apology, much less to theorize with him. I remained silent as he said again, "But for all that, there's no excuse for my actions," and left the room.

The next morning my mother cried: "Oh no! What did he

do?" when she saw my face. When next they were alone together, I would guess that he told her what he told me, and that she forgave him, having reached an understanding that he would never do it again. My father never did hit me again. I told the kids on my swim team that I had lunged for a Ping-Pong shot and run my face into the pole that held up the bamboo roof over our deck. My father once heard me telling this story, took me aside and told me never to lie on his behalf. "What I did was wrong. You go ahead and tell anyone you like exactly what I did. Just tell the truth and let me suffer the consequences." I listened silently, staring away without forgiveness as my father said this in a voice that was tired, even gentle.

My father maneuvers the Cessna 172 out of a slow, banking turn, the silver blue of the Monterey Bay slipping behind the mountains at our backs, Silicon Valley's labyrinth of lanes and cul-de-sacs presenting itself before us. He is sixty-two and retired, and has time to fly again. I am thirty-seven and visiting, happy to be sharing stories through our headsets.

He tells me that when he was a young aviator just out of the navy, he had expectations of joining the exciting and select society of engineering test pilots. But certain events overtook him: marriage, me, the job offer from Lockheed, three more children. He confides that there was one instance when claustrophobia finally drove him to leave his desk and make inquiries outside of Lockheed about how a man like him might become a working aviator again. But by then neither the world of test-flying nor airline piloting had any use for my father because somehow, without his marking the time closely enough, he had become thirty-seven years old.

This story of a foiled, last-ditch escape attempt is surprising to me, and it prompts me later, as we drive along the World's Most Beautiful Freeway in my father's brand-new silver and streamlined Camry, to ask him for another revelation. I have never, in the twenty years after my father beat my face black and blue on a summer evening, summoned that memory from him. I have long since forgiven him for it; we are old friends now, he and I. His edgy impatience has softened over the years; he seems to carry more peace within himself. But I am wanting to know the answer to this remaining mystery in my father. So cataclysmic an episode must hold a key to the puzzle he was then. The car is quiet and warm and my father and I have had a good day in the sky and so I ask him, "Do you remember it?"

"Yes," he says. "I hit you, didn't I?" He wears the expression of one asked to recall the plot of an obscure movie. By the look on his face, I presume he would prefer to forget. I feel bad for bringing it up, and I do not expect any more revelations today. Then my father says: "I have been abusive to every one of you in the family. There are so many bad times I've lived to regret."

My father tells me then about how, after raging at his wife or child, he would arrive at Lockheed sick with a remorse that ached like an alcoholic's hangover. He would sit, then, at his desk writing what coworkers assumed was documentation related to the latest secret technology project. In truth, he spent hour upon hour writing long essays to himself, recording feelings observed within, working his way painstakingly toward some diagnosis of the irrational at his core. Whatever came to mind he wrote down, blame heaped not only on himself for becoming a "paper pusher," but also on his wife and children for blocking his way out. What he wrote was often raw and ugly and he never meant it for other eyes, my father tells me. But he kept every page in a folder by his desk, a folder that grew thick over the course of fifteen years, and at times when the hangover of contrition had lifted, he would pull old essays from his file to see where he had been and whether he might now know enough to troubleshoot the problem.

What my father concluded is this. "Puzzling over why I was such a bizarre personality, I resolved it was the difference between myself as reality displayed itself to me, and the inflated self-image I carried around." My father's task, the task that Lockheed Missiles and Space Company had in a sense assigned him, was to sit at his desk and write memos to himself until the expectations of a hot young fighter pilot had been reduced to fit the space that America's Cold War economy had in fact allotted him. He wrote his last letter to himself when his career was about two-thirds over. Just before retiring a few years ago, he passed the entire file through the shredding machine Lockheed provides for classified documents of no further use.

TOM JUNOD

After graduating with a degree in English from the State University of New York, at Albany, Tom Junod (1958–) tried first to find a decent paying job in the world of New York publishing. Repeated failures in this attempt led him finally to an interview his father helped arrange for a job as a traveling salesman; he got the job, but during a sales trip to Los Angeles soon after he was robbed and forced into a hotel bathtub with a gun at his neck. "It was," he told an interviewer years later, "bad."

Nonetheless, the experience proved pivotal. Junod had been trying in his off-hours to write fiction—so-so stuff about "murderous prairie dog colonies" and the like—but after the holdup he wrote a nonfiction account of the event and in so doing found a voice and a gift of which he'd not previously been aware. "At that moment," he says, "I became a different writer."

It took time, though, to capitalize on the change. After losing the salesman position he entered a six-year string of "miserable jobs"—waiter, public relations flack, shipping dock laborer. But the jobs did have the advantage of allowing him to work on his new nonfiction voice, and in 1987 he landed a staff position at Atlanta *magazine*.

In 1991, Junod began placing stories in Life and Sports Illustrated. *A few years later he became writer-at-large for GQ, and in 1997 he took the title with him when he moved to* Esquire. *Featuring what one admiring critic has called "jaw-dropping prose," Junod's work has achieved widespread acclaim, including seven nominations for National Magazine Awards; in 1995 he went beyond nomination when GQ received the prize in feature writing for a Junod piece about a physician (later murdered) who performed abortions, and in 1996 Junod and GQ repeated the feat with an article about a self-professed repentant child rapist. The following year GQ received yet another nomination for another work by Junod—a piece this time about his father.*

Louis Junod was born in 1919 and grew up in Brooklyn. *Lacking a high school diploma, the course he took through life, says his son, was to "create himself" using the materials to which he had greatest access—ego and charisma. As a young man, Lou Junod enlisted in the army and was wounded by shrapnel and concussion at Normandy; after the war he began a career as a traveling salesman for a handbag company and proceeded to raise a family in Wantagh, Long Island. Years later, it was Lou Junod's connections that led to his son's getting his first job—which led in turn to that Los Angeles hotel room where his life as a writer so profoundly changed.*

"My Father's Fashion Tips" was published in GQ in 1996. *The immediate impulse for the piece was a pair of profiles Junod had written earlier involving "fathers not unlike my father"—Tony Curtis and Frank Sinatra. But these aside, he concedes that he'd been wanting to do the story on his father "forever."*

My Father's Fashion Tips

First it was Lubriderm, what my father rubbed briskly between his palms and extended in glistening offering. "How about a bit of the *Lube?*" he'd say when I walked into his bathroom. I was, like, eight years old, or something, so I had no choice but to put my face in his shiny hands. Then, for a long time, it was Nivea. "How would you like a little ... *Nivea?*" he'd ask, with his brown hands singing. Now it was baby oil. Now he was seventy-seven, and I was thirty-eight, and we were sharing a room in a hotel near the ocean. He was sitting in bed, and I was sitting on the floor. He poured the oil into his hands and whisked them together, with a sigh of friction, and applied the oil to his face. Then he said, "Here—rub a little baby oil into your kisser. If you want to stay young, you have to keep well lubricated."

"Baby oil? What happened to Nivea?"

"Too greasy. Baby oil soaks right in. It's the best thing for a man's face."

"Isn't baby oil just as greasy?"

My father raised a thick eyebrow. "Listen to me," he said. *"Learn my secrets."*

He held out the bottle. I held out my palm. "Good, good," he said. "Rub it right in—right in . . . "

There were always secrets. You could not walk into my father's bathroom and not know there were secrets. Secrets of grooming, secrets of hygiene, secrets of preparation, secrets of the body itself—secrets, and knowledge. First of all, he had a bathroom all to himself—his bathroom, Dad's bathroom. And he made it his, by virtue of what he put in it—his lotions, his sprays, his unguents, his astringents, his cleansers, his emollients, his creams, his gels, his deodorants, his perfume (yes, he used perfume, my father did, as his scent—Jean Naté eau de cologne—for he was, and is, as he will be the first to tell you, a *pioneer,* as well as a fine-smelling man), his soaps, his shampoos and his collection of black fine-tooth Ace combs, which for years I thought were custom-made, since that was his, Lou Junod's, nickname in the army: Ace. He called these things, this mysterious array of applications, his "toiletries" and took them with him wherever he went, in a clanking case of soft beige leather made by the Koret handbag company of New York, and wherever he went he used them to colonize *that* bathroom, to make *that* bathroom his own, whether it was in a hotel or someone's house—because "I need a place to put my toiletries." He has always been zealous in his hygiene, joyous in his ablutions, and if you want to know what I learned from him, what he taught me, we might as well start there, with what he never had to say: that fashion begins with the body, and has as much to do with your nakedness as it does with your clothes; that style is the public face you put together in private, in secret, behind a door all your own.

I have a sense of style, I guess, but it is not like my father's—it is not earned, and consequently it is not unwavering, nor inerrant, nor overbearing, nor constructed of equal parts maxim and stricture; it is not *certain.* It does not start in the morning, when I wake up, and end only at night, when I go to sleep. It is not my creation, nor does it create me; it is ancillary rather than central. I don't absolutely f'ing *live* it, is what I'm trying to say. I don't *put it on* every time I anoint myself with toilet water or stretch a sock to my knee or squeeze into a pair of black bikini underwear. Which is what my father did. Of course, when I was growing up, he tried as best he could to teach me what he knew, to *indoctrinate* me—hell, he couldn't resist, for no man can be as sure as my father is without being also relentlessly and re- flexively prescriptive. He tried to pass on to me knowledge that had the whiff of secrets, secrets at once intimate and arcane, such as the time he taught me how to clean my navel with witch hazel. I was eighteen and about to go off to college, and so one day he summoned me into his bathroom. "Close the door," he said. "I have to ask you something."

"What, Dad?"

"Do you . . . clean your navel?"

"Uh, no."

"Well, you should. You're a man now, and you sweat, and sweat can collect in your navel and produce an odor that is very . . . offensive." Then: "This is witch hazel. It eliminates odors. This is a Q-Tip. To clean your navel, just dip the Q-Tip into the witch hazel and then swab the Q-Tip around your navel. For about thirty seconds. You don't have to do it every *day;* just once a week or so." He demonstrated the technique on himself, then handed me my own Q-Tip.

"But, Dad, who is going to smell my navel?"

"You're going off to college, son. You're going to meet women. You never want to risk turning them off with an offen- sive odor."

I never did it—or, rather, I did it that one time and never again. I am a son who has squandered his inheritance, you see; I am incomplete in my knowledge and practice of matters hy- gienic and sartorial. And yet . . . I want to know, and that is why one weekend late last summer I wound up staying with my father in a hotel room that smelled of salt water and mildew, with his bag of toiletries spilling out on the bed and a puddle of baby oil shimmering in my palm: for the blessing of his instruction, for the privilege of his secrets. He had always told me that a man is at the peak of his powers from his late thirties to his early fifties, when he has forced the world to hear his footsteps—that a man comes into the peak of his powers when he *has* power and the world at last bends to *him*. He never told me, however, that that power can be measured by the number of secrets a man knows and keeps, and that when it became *my* time to make the world heed my step, I would want to know *his* secrets, for the paradoxical purpose of safekeeping and promulgation. My father's fashion tips: I'd listened to them all my life, and now that I was finding myself living by them, I wanted to tell them to the world, if only to understand where in hell he got them; if only to understand how someone like my father can come to *know,* without a moment of hesitation or a speck of doubt, that the turtleneck is the most flattering thing a man can wear.

1. THE TURTLENECK IS THE MOST FLATTERING THING A MAN CAN WEAR

This is axiomatic, inflexible and enduring. This is an article of faith and, as we shall see, the underpinning of a whole system of belief. Mention the word *turtleneck* to any of my college roommates and they will say "the most flattering thing a man can wear." Mouth the phrase "the most flattering thing a man can wear" and they will say "the turtleneck." This is because my father was born to proselytize, and when he and my mother visited my college and took me and my friends out to dinner, he sought to convert to his cause not only me—as he has as long as I've been alive—but them as well. Those who wore turtlenecks that evening were commended; those who did not were instructed and cajoled. My father was declamatory in the cause of turtlenecks, and as often as possible he wore them himself. Indeed, this is my wife Janet's first glimpse of Lou Junod: We have sat next to each other, Janet and I, for five hours, as our bus bucked a snowstorm and made its way from a college town in upstate New York to a mall parking lot on Long Island. We have kissed, for the very first time, the night before. We have held hands covertly the entire trip, although she has not yet smelled my neglected navel. Our seats are in the back of the bus, and so we have to wait a long time before we can get out. When we finally reach the front, there is a man standing at the door. He is impatient. He is not standing in the polite semicircle that the other parents have formed outside the bus; indeed, he is trying to stick his face *inside* the bus, and he is impeding the exit of the students ahead of us. He is, however, oblivious to whatever confusion he causes, and his chin is held at an imperious tilt. Although snow falls heavily behind him, he has a very dark tan, and his face shines with steadfast lubrication. He is, by his own description, "not a handsome man, but a very attractive one." He has a strong face: a large nose with a slight hook; thick eyebrows, nearly black; and eyes of pale, fiery green. He is about five-ten and a half or, in his words, "six foot in shoes." He is wearing a leather windbreaker, unzipped, and a pair of beige pants, which he calls "camel," and a ribbed turtleneck, tight to his body and pale yellow. Over his heart dangles a set of gold dog tags—his name is on them—and on his left pinkie is a gold ring of diamond and black onyx. He does not wear a wedding band. "Where is he?" he is saying, theatrically, with a habit of elaborate enunciation that lingers lovingly upon every consonant. "Where is . . . my *son?*" Janet looks at him and then at me and says, "That's not . . . ?" I look at him and say, "Hi, Dad."

Now, the turtleneck in this scene may seem incidental—just another detail, in an accumulation of detail—rather than an organizing principle. Don't be fooled. Anytime my father wears a turtleneck, he is advancing a cause, and the cause is himself. That is what he means when he says that an article of clothing is "flattering." That is where his maxim extolling the turtleneck acquires its Euclidean certainty. The turtleneck is the most flattering thing a man can wear because it strips a man down to himself—because it forces a man to *project* himself. The turtleneck does not *decorate*, like a tie, or *augment*, like a sport coat, or in any way distract from what my father calls a man's "presentation"; rather, it fixes a man in sharp relief and puts his face on a pedestal—first literally, then figuratively. It is about isolation, the turtleneck is; it is about essences and first causes; it is about the body and the face, and that's *all* it's about; and when worn by Lou Junod, it is about Lou Junod. The turtleneck is the most flattering thing a man can wear, then, because it establishes the very *standard* for flattery in fashion, which is that nothing you wear should ever hide what you want to reveal, or reveal what you want to hide. This is the certainty from which all the other certainties proceed; this is why my father, never a religious man—indeed, a true and irrepressible pagan, literal in his worship of the sun—believes in turtlenecks more than he believes in God.

2. THERE IS NOTHING LIKE A FRESH BURN

I do not know exactly what my father looks like, for I do not know what my father looks like without a suntan. I have never seen him pale or even sallow. He does not often use the word *suntan*, however, because he has been going out in the sun for so long that he has as many words for suntan as Eskimos have for snow. There is, for instance, "color," which he usually modifies with a diminutive and uses almost exclusively to entice and encourage his three children—my brother, my sister, and me—to "go outside, stick your face in the sun and get a little color." There is also "glow," which seems to mean the same thing as "color," but which requires less of a commitment—as in, "Just a half hour! Just a half hour in the sun and you'll get a little glow, and you'll look and feel *terrific*." But neither a little glow

nor a little color can substitute for the nearly mystical properties of "a burn." Indeed, a burn is such a powerful thing that my
father never asks his children to get one. A burn is such a powerful thing that in order to get one for himself my father con-
cocted, in his bathroom, a tanning lotion of his own invention,
composed of baby oil, iodine and peroxide (a few years ago, he
tried to improve upon it by adding a few drops of Jean Naté,
"for the scent," and it exploded). A burn is such a powerful
thing that my father went to great lengths to make sure the sun
shined on *him*, all year round, and turned the world into his
personal solarium. In November and December, when he went
out on the road for weeks at a time to make a living selling
handbags, he always ended his trip in Miami and stayed for a
few extra days at the Fontainebleau or the Jockey Club, so that
when he finally came home he would come home—and this is
another of his Eskimo words—"black." In January and February, he would dress in ski pants and a winter coat, cover himself
with a blanket and sit for hours on the white marble steps that
led to the front door of our house on Long Island—steps that
were built with their reflective qualities in mind—with a foil
reflector in his gloved hands and his oiled face ablaze with winter light. (Me, freezing: "How's the sun, Dad?" He, with tanning
goggles over his eyes: "Like *fire*.") In March or April, there was
Florida again, or California, and in the summer there was our
house in Westhampton Beach, where my father indulged his
paganism to its fullest extent; where the ocean was "nectar of
the gods"; where the black bikinis he usually wore under his
trousers he now wore to the beach; where the reflector now on
occasion surrounded his entire body, like some incandescent
coffin; where the sound track was my father singing "Summer
Wind" and tinkling the ice in his cocktails; where he wore straw
fedoras and V-necked angora sweaters; where his sense of style
seemed to stretch all the way to the sunset and his burn was forever fresh. . . .

3. ALWAYS WEAR WHITE TO THE FACE

It's gone now, that house—it's a goner. The ocean took it away, years ago, and now wind and sand blow through where it used to be, straight to the sea. I mean, there's *nothing* left—not even a spike of foundation, nor a snake of plumbing, nor a hank of wiring . . . not even ruins, to mark, in shadow, my father's empire of the sun. That's what we saw, when we drove out there last summer, my father and I, to Westhampton Beach, to 879 Dune Road—that there was nothing at all left to see. Still, we had to see it . . . and then we had to stay at a hotel called the Dune Deck because, say what you will about the Dune Deck, it's still standing. You have to give it that. Its paint is faded, and the planks of its eponymous deck are splintery and mossy, and its rooms smell like old water . . . but at least it is extant and ongoing, this place where my father went to practice the art of swank; where he took my beautiful mother, Fran, for dinner; where he always sported drinks for his pals; where the image I remember is him standing at the bar with a gin and tonic, wearing white jeans— which he called "white ducks"—and a sweater over a bare chest, whistling; where, in the summer, the great Teddy Wilson, from the Benny Goodman Trio, played piano; and where, once upon a time, my father stepped up to the mike, to sing . . . at least it is still *around*, this place where Lou Junod was a star.

A star, yes—that's what my father was, because that's what he wanted to be . . . that's *all* he wanted to be. My father's stardom was unusual in that he didn't have to *do* anything to be a star, even though being a star was what he *worked* at, every day. For instance, my father was a singer without being a singer— without being a pro. A crooner, my dad was, steeped in standards, with a voice that—when it was on—could make you cry. He sang his way through World War II, with an army big band, in a revue called "For Men Only," after he was twice wounded. He sang all over Europe. He sang in Paris. He sang in an after-hours club with the great swinging gypsy, Django Reinhardt, as his accompanist. He never really stopped singing, either, even when he came home, to my mother, to Brooklyn and then Long Island, and then to us—he used to sing at clubs in New York, at closing time. The Little Club, the Harwyn Club.... Not for money—as far as I know, my father never made a dime from his voice—but to *put himself across*. And when he went to see Dean Martin and Jerry Lewis one night at the Copa and Dino passed the microphone around to patrons and asked them to sing a verse, my father was *prepared:* He took the microphone in hand and sang to such effect that Dean Martin had to take it back. "*Hey,*" Dino said, his voice whittled down to a point of low warning. "*Hey,*" he said, glaring at my father over his shoulder, with a squint, with a glance of sudden, alarmed appraisal, sparked by his knowledge that there was now another *man* in the room, and to this man attention must be paid.

It was this, more than anything else, that was the true measure of my father's stardom, especially in the absence of other, more reliable measures, such as box-office returns or record sales or public acclaim: the response he elicited from other stars. See, in my father's stories—and my father is a man of many stories—he has many encounters with celebrities, and each of them ends in the exact same way: with the celebrity in some way *recognizing* my father, with the celebrity finally having to take my father *into account*. If the celebrity is a beautiful woman, she will inevitably end up being *unable to take her eyes off* him, as in, "I saw Ava Gardner at Bill Miller's Riviera, with Sinatra, and she couldn't take her eyes off your old man," or, "Elizabeth Taylor was there—she couldn't stop flirting with your father. It started getting embarrassing—*embarrassing!*" (My father, by the way, is swift and aphoristic in judgment of his peers, and also unsentimental, so that Ava Gardner, in addition to being a "big nympho," was "shorter than I expected—nothing much," and Elizabeth Taylor was "short and dumpy, with a little bit of a facial-hair problem.") And if the celebrity is a man . . . well, then, he can't take his eyes off my father, either, but his regard is sharper, much more complicated, especially if he is something of a kinsman to my father—a fellow traveler—and as such a potential *rival*, like Sinatra and Dean Martin. 1952: Sinatra is at the Copa. Sinatra is, in my father's words, "flat on his ass," because of Ava, the nympho. He is drinking, and his voice is gone. My father sits in the front row, with a client. He makes a request. "'All or Nothing at All,'" he says. Sinatra shakes his head. "'All . . . or Nothing . . . at *All*,'" my father says, now commandingly, with his own exaggerated singer's diction. Sinatra touches his throat and looks at my father, imploringly, pitiably. "Too tough," he whispers, softly and hoarsely, before leaving the stage. "Too tough." 1957: My father goes to Vegas for the first time, in the year before my birth. He rents a convertible and drives across the Arizona desert with the top down, and by the time he gets there he is, well, black, of course, and vibrant with the pulse of the elements themselves. He goes to a coffee shop, and Dean is there, and Dean *recognizes* him—a nod. And then the next day, my father goes down to the casino, to play at the blackjack table, and Dean walks over, tan like my father, but not of course *as* tan as my father, and asks the dealer to step aside. "Let me deal to him," Dean says (or maybe, preferably, "Let me deal to *him*"), and for the next twenty minutes that's what he does—Dean Martin deals cards to Lou Junod. It's just the two of them, two men wearing suits and shirts with French cuffs at twelve o'clock noon, in the middle of the freaking desert, and somewhere along the line it must occur to them—well, at the very least, it occurs to my dad—that they are men who very easily could have lived each other's lives . . . which is why my father always told me never to ask for autographs ("They should be asking for *your* autograph") . . . and which, I suppose, is why, thirty-eight years later, when I was about to interview

John Travolta, this was my father's advice: "Where are you staying? Do they have a pool? OK, this is what you do—listen to your *father:* This afternoon you go to the pool, and you get some goggles to cover your eyes, and you put your face in the sun, and tomorrow you wear white to the face and a nice tie and you show John Travolta how good-looking *you* are."

Ah yes, of course—wear white to the face. A white shirt or a shirt with a white collar. Why? Because it's *flattering,* that's why. Because you can't wear a turtleneck all the time, or even a lot of the time—that's the tragedy of turtlenecks—but you can *always* wear white to the face. And because when you wear white to the face, the light is always shining on you. . . . As it is right now, at the Dune Deck—the sun is shining on my father. He is wearing a polo shirt and khaki shorts and Nike sneakers and white socks. He is retired, and has been for nearly ten years. He has two major complaints, each of which is longstanding: one, that he is "shrinking," and two, that he is losing his hair, or rather, losing his hair at a rate in excess of the rate at which he was losing his hair when he first started complaining about losing his hair, which was at the very least thirty-five years ago. We are drinking cocktails, and our faces are in the sun. "OK, Dad," I say, "what are some of the rules a man should remember when he's getting dressed?"

"Well, always try to wear white to the face," my father says automatically, repeating a motto, a chant, a mantra my brother, Michael, and I have heard, say, a thousand times in the course of our lives, usually when we have worn something *other* than white to the face, and have been accused of thereby "disfiguring" ourselves. "Particularly if you're tan. Gray is the worst color you can wear. Don't ever wear a gray shirt. Gray or *brown.*"

"I have a gray shirt," I say.

"You do? Never wear it." Then, after a moment's reflection, during which my father almost winces, in order to set his teeth for the impeccable rendering of his final judgment: "*Burn* it."

4. MAKE SURE TO WEAR PLENTY OF CUFF

I bring a Calvin Klein blazer to the Dune Deck to wear at night, and when I show the jacket to my father, I make a confession: "Dad, I think the sleeves are a little long."

"Get them shortened immediately," my father says. "For chrissake. I can't stand long sleeves. Jesus Christ! Don't waste any time...."

They work, my father's fashion tips. That's what's funny about them, besides the fact that they are ... well, funny in the first place. They work, or they worked, for him, for my father. They were cohesive and complementary; they spoke in a single voice; they were his manifesto. Take a look, for example, at a picture of my father standing in a group of his fellow salesmen at a Bar Mitzvah circa 1962. Take a look at the one man whose jacket sleeves cover his shirt cuffs, like the sleeves of a cassock. He does not look merely glum or sour; he looks defeated, whipped, *scared,* precancerous—a recessive man, with a receding hair-line. Now take a look at my father, holding in one pinkie-ringed hand a drink *and* a cigarette. He is about forty-three years old, and, by God, he is *glistening,* for he is in his prime, and all the elements are in place. He has a fresh burn, and he is wearing a shirt with a high white collar. He is wearing a suit of midnight blue, single-breasted, with a silver tie and a handkerchief in the pocket (I've never heard him call it a "pocket square"), which he does not fold into regimental points but rather simply "throws in there," so that what shows is just "a puff." He is undoubtedly wearing bikini underwear, for anybody who wears boxer shorts is "a square" or "a farmer," as in, "What are you, a farmer?"; and he is undoubtedly wearing socks, or "hose," that go "over the calf, *knee*-high," for if there's anything he hates more than long sleeves on a suit jacket, it's "ankle socks," because "I can't stand to see someone sitting down with their *ankles* showing—their white ankles and their black socks." His shirt has French cuffs, of course, and he's showing plenty of them—"at least an inch"—and he looks *sharp* . . . and by *sharp* I mean avid, by *sharp* I mean almost feral, by *sharp* I mean that if this were not a Bar Mitzvah but rather a meeting of the Five Families, then the *schnorrer* in the long sleeves and the boxer shorts and the ankle socks would be the guy fingered for a rubout, and the guy showing plenty of cuff would be the man commissioned for the kill. 1962: a good time for sharp dressers. 1962: Even the freaking *president* is a sharp dresser, and he's just about the same age as my father, and as for him, as for Lou Junod, well, he's still coming *on,* and if he looks, in this picture, slightly dangerous, in his own proud display, I also have no doubts that on this resplendent day he was one of the most beautiful men in the world.

"I didn't grow up with any of the advantages," my father says at the Dune Deck. "I didn't have any money; I didn't have any brains—all I had was my looks and my charisma." Yes, that's right: His fashion tips worked because they had to work—because he had nothing else. No education to speak of, and no religion worth naming; no father (his father was a briny, bingeing drunk, and whenever any of us mentioned him, whenever any of us used the words "your father," Dad was quick to correct us: "I *had* no father"); not even any history (to this day, I have no idea when my father's forebears came to this country or who they were or where they came from). He came out of nowhere, thirteen pounds at birth, born to a great, kindly, bawdy woman who played piano in the pits of silent-movie houses. So he was big from the start, Big Lou, but that's all he was, and so he had to just keep getting bigger—for my father, it was celebrity or bust. His mentors, his teachers, his influences—they weren't *men;* they were gorgeous silvered shadows, dancing across movie screens . . . and by the time he was sixteen or seventeen, he was singing their songs, blanching the Brooklyn from his voice on the way home from the theater, and he was dressing like them, or trying to, anyway, and so was everybody else.

That's the most amazing thing about listening to my father's stories of his coming of age—the sheer aspiration in them, and how easily it was shared and *passed around;* the way so many of them begin with my father and one of his rivals squaring off for a fight over a girl and end with the two of them *recognizing* each other before they ever come to blows and then going off somewhere to talk about *clothes,* of all things, and about style, and about class, and to argue over who was the better dresser, Fred Astaire or Cary Grant or Walter Pidgeon. My father believed, absolutely, in the old saw, at once terrifying and liberating, that "clothes make the man," and so did his friends, and so everything they wore had to tell a story, and the story had to be about *them,* because otherwise the world was never going to hear it. That's really my father's first fashion tip, come to think of it: that everything you wear has to add up, that everything has to make sense and absolutely f'ing *signify.* He did not come up in the current culture of corporate individualism, so he could not let himself off the hook by wearing some fucking T-shirt that says NIKE on the front or CHICAGO BULLS; he has never been able to understand the utility of dressing, intentionally, like a slob, nor to discern what preference a heterosexual man is advertising when he wears an earring. "What do they *mean?*" he asks, of earrings. "I've asked, and I've never gotten a good answer. Do they mean that you're a *swinger?* Do they mean that you're *free?* Nobody's ever been able to tell me. . . ."

Irony? Irony is no answer, because in my father's view a man is not allowed irony in the wearing of clothes. Irony is for women, because for them clothes are all about *play,* all about tease and preamble—because for them dressing is all about undressing. For a man, though, clothes both determine and mark his place in the world; they are about coming *from* nakedness, rather than going *to* it—and so irony spells diminution, because irony says that you don't mean it . . . and you *have* to mean it. You have to mean what you wear. Hell, my father remembers what he wore at just about every important moment in his life, and even at moments of no importance at all—moments whose only meaning derived from the fact that my father was wearing clothes worth remembering; moments when it might have seemed to my father that the clothes on his back and the sincere force with which he wore them were enough to deliver him where he wanted to go: "You know, I used to walk on a *cloud* when I walked down Fifth Avenue and went to La Grenouille for lunch. Like I *owned* it, you know? I remember one day I met [a fellow salesman, named Joel] with his wife. I was wearing a beige glen-plaid suit—beautiful—and a shirt with a white collar, with a silk grenadine tie and a set of nice cuff links, and Joel's wife said, 'Joel, I never saw anything like it. Look at the way these women are carrying on over Lou. Every place we go. It's unbelievable.' And it was. It really was. And I used to feel so good, I couldn't believe it—and that was enough to satisfy me. I didn't have to go any further with it. And whatever aspirations I had of being theatrical, of being in show business, I *was*—I was."

5. THE BETTER YOU LOOK, THE MORE MONEY YOU MAKE

There is a woman at the Dune Deck with a dark tan and long black hair and a block of brilliant white teeth. "My God," my father says, "what teeth! Those are the most beautiful teeth I've ever seen in the flesh." Now, I must say that I've heard this before, that this is not a particularly *unusual* utterance from the mouth of my father, because my father has a white fetish—as evinced by his white cars, white pants, white collars, white marble steps, etc.—and on top of his white fetish he has a teeth fetish, so white teeth move him greatly, often in the direction of hyperbole, in regard to both women and men. For instance, a couple of years ago, I went to a baseball game in Atlanta with my parents and ran into a friend of mine named Vince. "My God, what teeth he had!" my father said when we got back to our seats. "Those are the most beautiful teeth I've ever seen in a man." He has also been known to ask, flat out, upon first meeting someone, "Are those your teeth? Jesus, if I'd had teeth like yours . . ."

My father does not have great teeth, and neither do I. Oh sure, he has white teeth now, but as he says, "Those are all money; those are all work." Back when he was singing, he was very self-conscious about his dingy choppers, and he often wonders now whether his teeth were what prevented him from going as far as he could have gone in show business. And as for my teeth . . . well, I was sick a lot when I was a kid and ran a lot of fevers and took a lot of medicines, and so now it's like someone lit a Magic Snake in my mouth—my teeth are an efflorescence of sulfur and carbon and ash. My mouth is forever in the shadows, and so it is no surprise to me, when we go back to our room at the hotel, my father and I, and lie together on his bed, staring at a ceiling slovenly with unsealed seams, that my father says, as he has said so many times before, "Do you mind if I ask you a question? You can tell me to mind my own business, but when are you going to get your teeth fixed? What are you waiting for? You're in the entertainment business now, son—the better you look, the more money you make. Will you listen to your old man for once? The *better* you look, the more *money* you make. The better you *look*, the more money you *make*."

I don't tell him what I realize, at precisely this moment, in answer to his aphorism—that I have chosen to make a living out of printed words for the very purpose of *transcending* my dim teeth, my shadowed mouth. And I don't tell him, because, for my father, there is no possibility of transcendence: He is attached to his teeth, and attached to his body, and attached to his clothes, in a way that I have never been attached to mine. He has nothing else now, except his family, which has become everything to him, while I have *this*, this urge not to sing but to somehow speak and *tell* . . . except that of course in the end writing is the same as wearing clothes: You do it to have some *say* over how you look to the world, and you wind up revealing precisely what you've hidden, and more than you will ever know.

"Dad, what's the best you've ever looked?" I ask him that night at dinner. "I mean, the *precise* moment when you looked your very best." I figure that he will know the answer to this one. I figure that he will talk about the Bar Mitzvah in 1962, or walking down Fifth Avenue to La Grenouille, or coming down the stairs at El Morocco and feeling like "a bride at her wedding," or the night he sang to close a club in Dallas and Zsa Zsa Gabor danced in lonely circles in front of the microphone . . . I figure that there will be a single instant when the world opened up to him and that it will be emblazoned upon his memory. But, no—there is no *single* instant, and when my father answers my question it is without hesitation: "The best I ever looked? Every day of my life. People will think I'm crazy, but I mean it. I felt like a celebrity *every day of my life*. I looked so good, I never wanted to go to bed."

We have the best table in the house, at the restaurant located within the Dune Deck, which is named after its chef, Starr Boggs, and which, by the way, is excellent—or, in my father's appraisal, *elegant*. We are sitting at a corner table, by a window through which you can see the black and white of the ocean and hear its yawn and sizzle and splat, and my father is wearing a yellow polo shirt, white ducks, brown loafers and a white zippered windbreaker with epaulets. I am wearing khakis and a white dress shirt, with its collar unbuttoned, and the Calvin Klein blazer, which my father asked me not to wear when we were getting dressed for dinner: "You're not going to wear a jacket, are you? Aw, c'mon, Tommy—I didn't pack one because I didn't think we'd *need* one. You're going to make me *look* bad." Then he went downstairs to get a drink at the bar before dinner, and as soon as he left the room I put the blazer on and didn't take it off. I wasn't trying to make my father look bad or show him up, but, hell, it was my genetic *destiny* to wear that jacket, and I was ready to claim it. And besides, I had a little glow, and I was wearing white to the face, and I left the cuffs of my shirt unbuttoned in order to show them off, and I have to admit that I looked *pretty fucking good.* "Look at you, you son of a bitch," my father said when I walked into the bar. "You look handsome—handsome! You see what a little color can do? But you have to work on it. You should forget that natural stuff and try to get a little sun whenever you can. That *natural* stuff doesn't cut it anymore—it's not very *in.* . . . "

Does my father look handsome on this night, at the best table in the house? He does; he does, indeed. And now, to tell him so, here come the women. Or, I should say, the *woman*—in this case, a woman about my father's age, whose face is etched with lines of runic complexity and who is wearing a visor that says ROYAL VIKING PRINCESS and enormous square eyeglasses and a white-on-blue polka-dotted jacket over a blue-on-white polka-dotted dress: a peppy, strapping old gal who limps over to our table on a four-pronged cane and says, "Tell me, did you two get the best table in the house because you're so good-looking, or do you know the owner?" Then she looks at my father and introduces herself: "Clara. Clara Strauss. As in Johann. . . . You should look me up sometime. I live in Palm Beach. I used to be a buyer for Federated. Clara Strauss. As in Johann. . . . " Then she leaves, to no music, and we order our food, and when I choose our wine, my father—who is watching me, who is always watching—says, "You've got style, kid; you've got style." His eyes draw fire and color from drink, and now they focus, with an intense effrontery, on the table behind me. "There's an actress over there, and I forget her name. Begins with an *l.* Very famous." I turn around for a second and see a tiny, dark-haired woman with an even tinier head, a woman who is at once exquisite and insectoid, and who is so perfectly composed that she seems to turn all movement into a tremble.

"Susan Lucci," I say.

"That's right, that's right," my father says. "Is that her? Your mother doesn't like her, you know. Not a lot of women do. She's the kind of woman that men like and women don't."

Can she keep her eyes off my father? I don't know, because for the remainder of the meal my back stays to her. But he can't keep his eyes off her, that's for sure; and at one point, he dips his chin, and as he scrutinizes her he strikes a pose of suave regard.

"Dad, what are you *doing?*"

"Trying to catch her *eye,*" he says.

"Well, is it working?"

"She's weakening, my son," my father says. "She's weakening."

We stay at the bar after we finish our meal because my father wants to drink grasshoppers ("You've *never* had a grasshopper? They were the *in* drink at one time") but mainly because he doesn't want the night to end. "I don't have to tell you how much this means to me," he says, with his brown, mottled hand around my wrist. "It's been a long time since I've been in a place like this—with a *crowd* like this." Yes, my father is part of the crowd again, part of the crowd of hustlers and jostlers and guys *coming on,* of cigar smokers and martini drinkers and a woman in a silvery blue cocktail dress who is, in my father's estimation, "stacked" . . . and so the lessons never stop. "Dad, what do you think about that guy turning up his collar under his blazer?" "Your father did that *fifty* years ago." "Dad, what do you think of band-collared shirts?" "I'd wear a band-collared shirt—*to bed.* They look like pajamas. The worst is when they're worn with tuxedos. I can't stand that. They look like the dirty undershirt Dean Martin wore in *Rio Bravo.*"

He falls asleep, in his clothes, the moment we get back to the room. He snores, with his fingers folded on top of his navel, and I take off my shoes and walk down to the ocean, in my blazer and khakis, under a black seam that splits the spangled sky and vaults out into the ocean forever. *The only excuse for a man to grow a beard is if he has a weak chin or acne*—that's what I know from my father. *Make sure to splash some cologne on your privates*—that's another thing. *Never wear navy blue and black*—that's what I came to know on the morning of my wedding, when I wore a navy blue suit and black shoes, and my father said, "What are you—a *policeman?*" ("But Dad, what kind of shoes *should* you wear?" "With a navy blue suit? Navy blue shoes.") As for the rest . . . as for everything else . . . not what I know *from* him, but rather what I know *of* him—that's harder, of course, because, well, why do you wear clothes in the first place, if not to *cover up?* I mean, Adam and Eve found *that* out quick enough—that clothes are totems of simultaneous confession and disguise. They are the masks that unmask you, and what I knew of my father, through his clothes, was this: that he was going out. That he was going away. That he was heading for Miami or Atlanta or Dallas . . . that he was dressing for *other people,* an audience somewhere; that he was dressing for Frank and Ava and Dino and Liz and Zsa Zsa; that he was dressing for the *world;* that he *belonged* to the world as much as he belonged to us, and we had to let him go. *Let him go*—that's what my mother always said when my father was going out, and a few months ago, when I visited one of our old next-door neighbors, this is what she told me: "I remember one day your father was flying south, and he had a *black* tan, and he was wearing a white Bill Blass jumpsuit with a *zipper,* and I said to myself, 'This is the most gorgeous creature I've ever seen.' And I said to your mother, 'Fran, are you going to let this man *out* like this?' And your mother said, 'Ah, let him go. Let him go.'"

And then he came back. He always came back, to tell us what

he had seen and what he had *found out*. He always had news, my father did—he always had the scoop, about who had the smile, who had the handshake, who had the toup. He always told me *what I needed to know* about the world ... and the world told me what I needed to know about him—that, yes, indeed, he owned it. He was a *terror,* my father, when I was young—he was hell-bent on mastery, and for years I was afraid of him ... the sheer, booming size of him. Then, for a long time, I idolized him, until I realized, not very long ago, that I have spent my entire life moving toward him. See, my father doesn't belong to the world anymore—he's given it up, or it's given him up, or it's just flat gone, like our beach house down the road. His world is no bigger now than his family, and he doesn't even have to dress for it. But certain things still belong to *him,* and now, here I am, standing on the beach in the dark, with a seven-hundred-dollar jacket on my back and my trousers rolled and my father snoring back in the room, and I'm stepping into the things my father owns as surely as I'm stepping into the ink of the ocean—because just as the ocean in Westhampton will always be *his,* his secrets will always be his secrets. Lou Junod: He was determined to make his mark, and, by God, he *did,* and now, as I walk into my life I walk into his, into the gift he gave me, his first and final fashion tip: the knowledge that a man doesn't belong to *anyone.* That he belongs to his secrets. That his secrets belong to him.

Acknowledgments

The editor and publisher thank the following for their permission to reprint previously published material.

"Notes of a Native Son" by James Baldwin. Originally published under the title "Me and My House . . ." in *Harper's Magazine*, November 1955. Copyright © 1955 by James Baldwin. The essay was revised and included with its current title in the author's book *Notes of a Native Son*. Copyright © 1955 by James Baldwin. Reprinted by permission of Beacon Press.

"Heavy Lifting" by Geoffrey Wolff. First published under the title "La Jolla, 1962" in the *San Diego Reader*, May 9, 1996. Copyright © 1996 by Geoffrey Wolff. The essay was published with the current title in the 1996 anthology *Family: American Writers Remember Their Own*, Sharon Sloan Fiffer and Steve Fiffer, eds. Reprinted by permission of the author.

"Civilian" by Tobias Wolff. First published in the *Threepenny Review*, Fall 1994. Copyright © 1994 by Tobias Wolff. The essay also appears in the author's book *In Pharaoh's Army: Memories of the Lost War,* copyright © 1994 by Tobias Wolff. Reprinted by permission of Alfred A. Knopf, a Division of Random House, Inc.

"Rising to the Light" by Robert Benson. First published in the *Sewanee Review,* vol. 103, no. 4, Fall 1995. Copyright © 1995 by Robert Benson. Reprinted by permission of the author and the *Sewanee Review.*

"Son and Father" by Sam Pickering. First published in the *Virginia Quarterly Review,* Autumn 1986. Copyright © 1986 by Samuel Pickering, Jr. The essay also appears in the author's book *The Right Distance,* copyright © 1987 by Samuel F. Pickering, Jr. Reprinted by permission of the author and the University of Georgia Press.

"Under the Influence" by Scott Russell Sanders. Copyright © 1989 by *Harper's Magazine.* All rights reserved. Reproduced from the November issue by special permission. The essay also appears in the author's book *Secrets of the Universe: Scenes from the Journey Home,* copyright © 1991 by Scott Russell Sanders.

"Hyde Park" by Robert B. Stepto. First published in *Callaloo,* Winter 1997. Copyright © 1997 by Robert B. Stepto. The essay also appears in the author's book *Blue as the Lake,* copyright © 1998 by Robert B. Stepto. Reprinted by permission of the author and Beacon Press.

"Embalming Father" by Thomas Lynch. First published in the *London Review of Books,* July 20, 1995. Copyright © 1995 by Thomas Lynch. The essay also apears under the title "Gladstone" in the author's book *The Undertaking: Life Studies from the Dismal Trade,* copyright © 1997 by Thomas Lynch. Used by permission of W. W. Norton & Company, Inc.

"Playing Hardball" by Henry Louis Gates, Jr. This essay appears as chapter 7 in the author's book *Colored People: A Memoir.*

Copyright © 1994 by Henry Louis Gates, Jr. Reprinted by permission of Alfred A. Knopf, a Division of Random House, Inc.

"Picking Plums" by Bernard Cooper. First published in *Harper's Magazine*, August 1992. Copyright © 1992 by Bernard Cooper. The essay also appears in the author's book *Truth Serum: Memoirs,* copyright © 1996 by Bernard Cooper. Reprinted by permission of Houghton Mifflin Company. All rights reserved.

"What a Father Leaves" by Roland Merullo. First published in the Fall 1998 "American Families" special issue of *Witness.* Copyright © 1998 by Roland Merullo. Reprinted by permission of the author.

"In the Kingdom of the Jalberts" by Greg Jalbert. First published in *Yankee,* October 1990. Copyright © 1996 by Greg Jalbert. Reprinted by permission of the author.

"Blue Sky, California" by David Beers. First published in the *New York Times Magazine,* May 12, 1996. Copyright © 1996 by David Beers. Reprinted by permission of the author.

"My Father's Fashion Tips" by Tom Junod. First published in *GQ,* December 1996. Copyright © 1996 by Tom Junod. Reprinted by permission of the author.